Il faut cultiver notre jardin.
VOLTAIRE, *Candide*

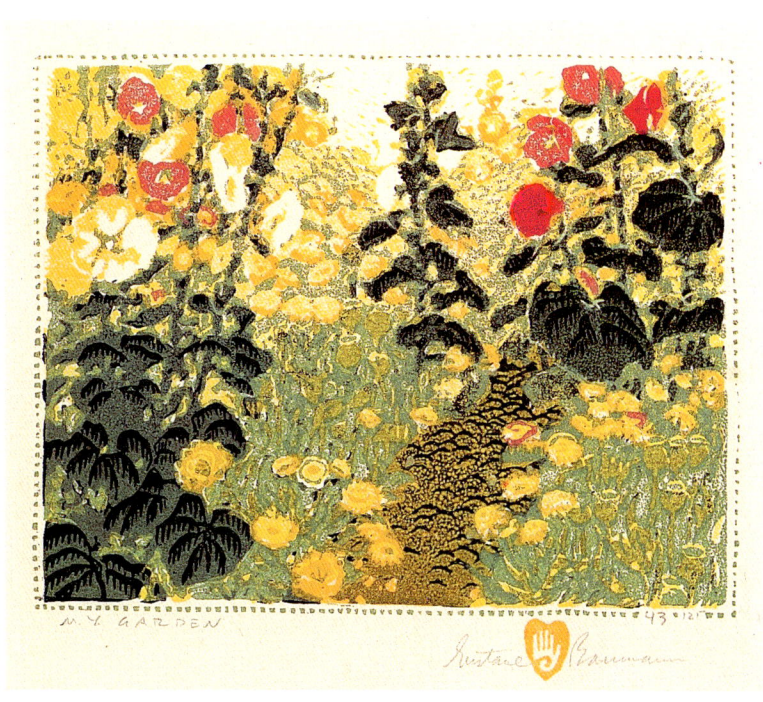

1. MY GARDEN, 1924

Color woodcut, 6 × 7 ½ in.

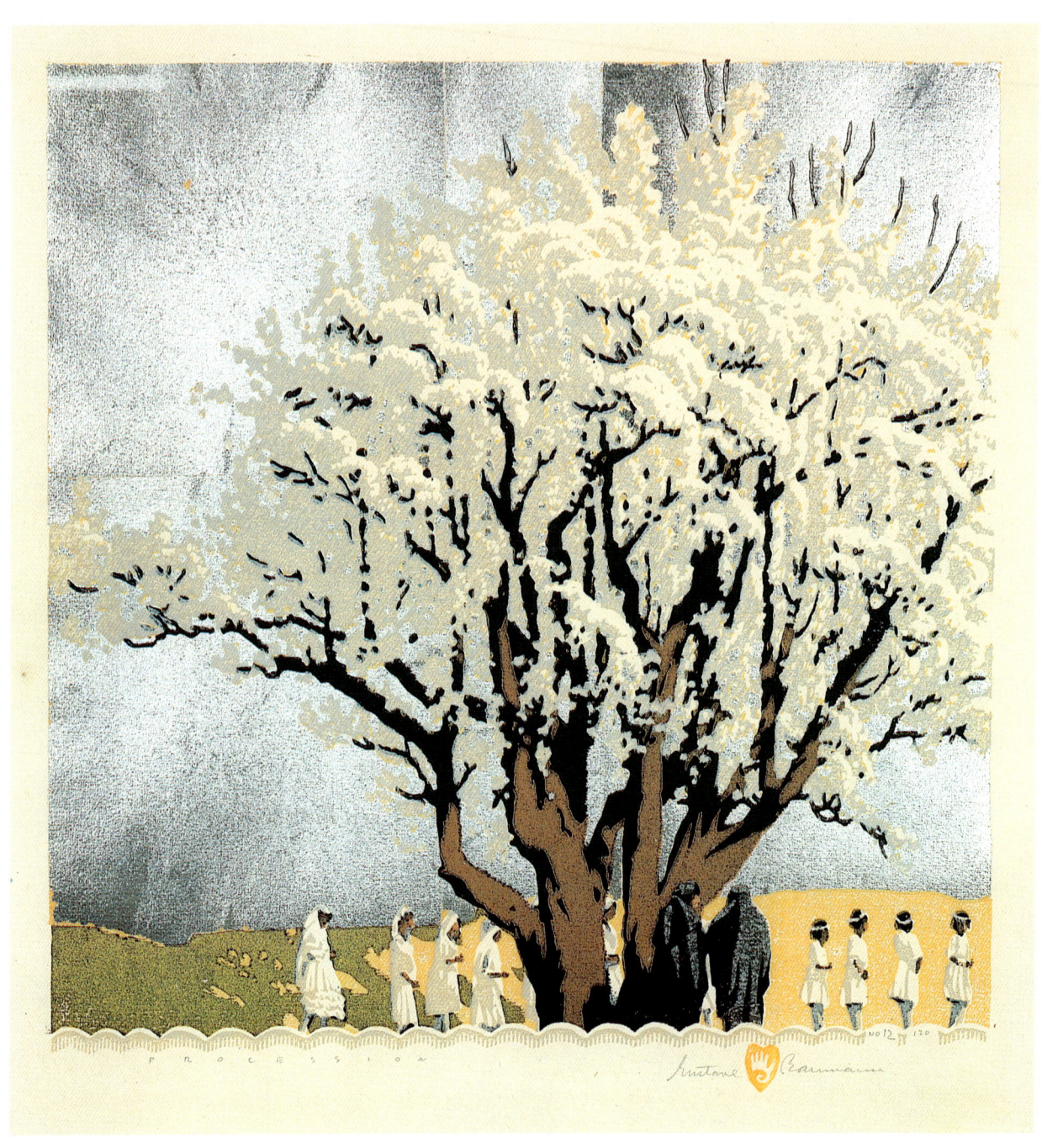

2. PROCESSION, 1930

Color woodcut, 13 × 12¾ in.

GUSTAVE BAUMANN
NEARER TO ART

Martin F. Krause

Madeline Carol Yurtseven

David Acton

Museum of New Mexico Press ❧ Santa Fe

Museum of New Mexico Press is a division
of New Mexico Department of Cultural Affairs.

Manufactured in Korea
Project Editor: Mary Wachs
Designer: Eleanor Morris Caponigro
Compositor: Wilsted & Taylor
Photographer: Blair Clark

Library of Congress Catalog Card Number 92-84066
ISBN: 978-0-89013-251-7 (CB), 978-0-89013-252-4 (PB)

MUSEUM OF NEW MEXICO PRESS
Post Office Box 2087
Santa Fe, New Mexico 87504
mnmpress.org

10 9 8 7 6 5 4 3 2 1

CONTENTS

PREFACE

Of all the artists who have called Santa Fe, New Mexico, their home, Gustave Baumann (1881–1971) is unquestionably one of the town's most beloved and respected. He arrived in 1918 as the small, active art community was just developing into a cultural center for influential and creative people from around the country.

Like other immigrant artists of his generation, German-born Baumann understood the importance of simultaneously establishing a commitment to the local community while keeping professional contacts current around the world. As his reputation as a master printmaker grew internationally, Baumann only strengthened his ties to the Santa Fe art community that was his home for more than fifty years.

The Museum of Fine Arts in Santa Fe is in a unique position to organize the exhibition that is the basis for this publication by having the world's largest collection of works by Gustave Baumann. The collection includes every period of Baumann's artistic career, beginning with his student work in Munich in 1905; his Chicago period of 1906–1909; his 1910–1916 years in Brown County, Indiana; his 1917 works done in New York City, the upstate New York town of Wyoming, and in Provincetown; his work in Arizona and California in the 1920s; and the vibrant and brightly colored woodcuts of New Mexico (1918–1971), the place which provided the artist with the greatest number of subjects.

In addition to cataloging nearly every color woodcut executed in New Mexico, the Baumann collection at the Museum of Fine Arts also includes numerous sketchbooks; preliminary sketches in pastel, pencil, crayon, watercolor; fifty-three gouache paintings that directly relate to the finished woodcut prints; oil paintings; a progressive series of woodcut prints with the blocks; advertising and illustrative material; woodcuts for family and friends' birthdays, anni-

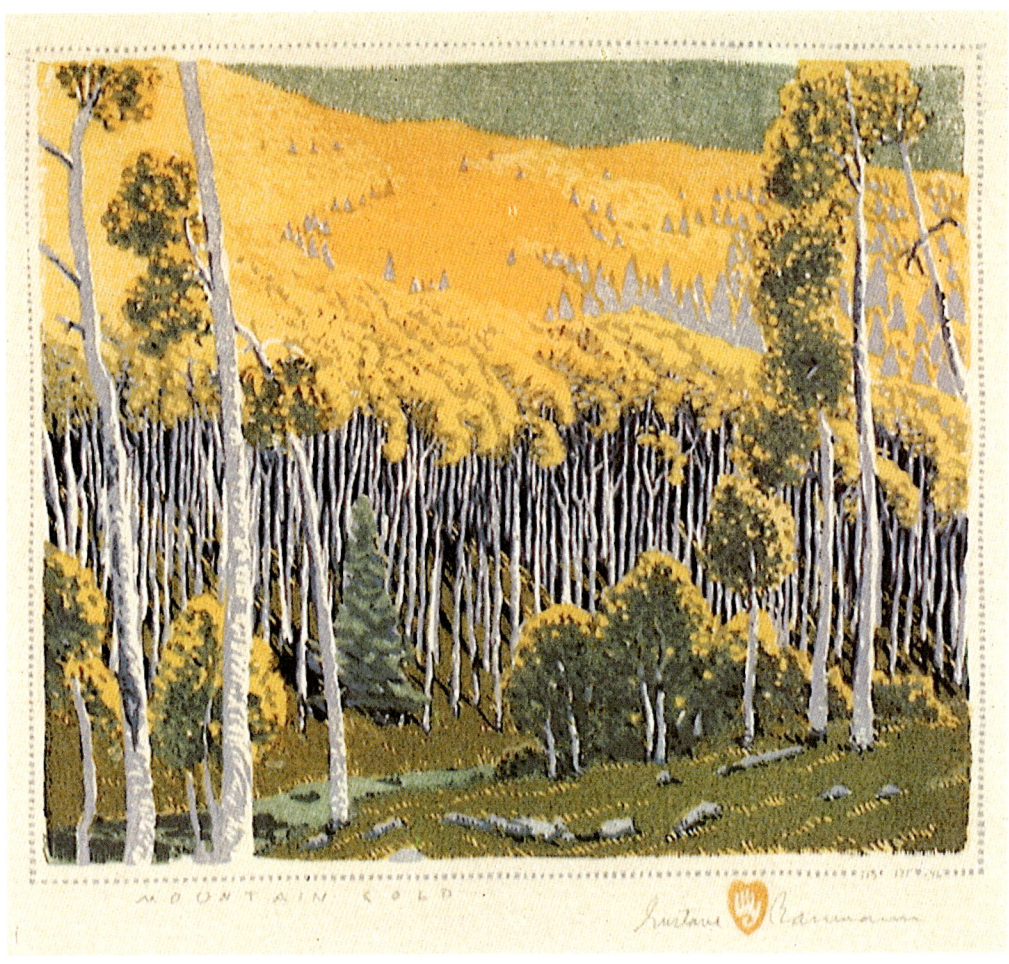

3 . MOUNTAIN GOLD, 1926
Color woodcut, 9¼ × 11 in.

versaries, Christmas, and other holidays; memorabilia comprised of designs, photographs, post-cards, and treasure-filled scrapbooks; and virtually the entire hand-carved marionette collection with over sixty marionettes, set designs, original scripts, stage, and props.

In 1952–1953, a significant number of color woodcuts were purchased through funds raised by the School of American Research. Beginning in 1978 and over a three-year period, the museum received as a gift over five hundred works from Mrs. Jane H. Baumann, the late widow of Gustave Baumann. With funds generously donated in 1989–1991 by Ann Baumann, Gustave and Jane Baumann's daughter, over 1,220 objects were cataloged, organized, documented, photographed, conserved, and matted or encapsulated by the Museum of New Mexico's conservation department, thus making the collection more accessible to future interpretation and research.

In addition, the Laboratory of Anthropology received in 1976 from Mrs. Jane H. Baumann Baumann's personal collection of 131 carved kachinas and seventy-nine American Indian pots.

This unique and extensive collection demonstrates the breadth and depth of Baumann's interests, his creative process, and his outstanding mastery of the color-woodcut medium in which he chose primarily to work. His love and sense of place are reflected in all his work. After seeing Baumann's color woodcuts of New Mexico, one sees "Baumanns" everywhere—his delicate, white blooming apple trees; his electrifying and colorful landscapes; his golden aspens juxtaposed against a cobalt blue sky; and dozens of other examples of his heartfelt response to the environment. Baumann's vision is unique, his color sense extraordinary, his craft exemplary. The museum is indeed fortunate to have this precious collection.

The Museum of Fine Arts and the Museum of New Mexico Press would like to take this opportunity to acknowledge the group of generous people who have offered their steadfast support of the Baumann collection, the exhibition, and publication project, most especially the late Mrs. Jane H. Baumann, for her donation of Baumann's work, and Ann Baumann, for her support and for the funding of the collection's conservation work. Additional thanks are owed to the Conservation Department of the Museum of New Mexico, especially Claire Munzenrider, Patricia Morris, and Paul Smutko. Authors Martin Krause and David Acton gave guidance and invaluable documentation. The book *Gustave Baumann: Nearer to Art* was designed by Eleanor Caponigro; Mary Wachs acted as project editor. Thanks to Museum of New Mexico Exhibitions Department and Judy Shaw, exhibition volunteer; museum volunteers Lyle Crawford, Jim Stevens, and Charles Lamb, who worked with the preservation and cataloging of Baumann's marionettes; TREX, the Traveling Exhibition Department at the Museum of New Mexico, which circulated the exhibition *Gustave Baumann: Hand of a Craftsman, Heart of an Artist*; and the unfailing work by the staff of the Museum of Fine Arts, including Joan Tafoya, Registrar; Charles Sloan, Preparator; Phyllis Cohen, Librarian; Lorraine Cook, Administrative Secretary; and Theresa Garcia, Secretary.

Major funding for the project has been provided by the National Endowment for the Arts.

This book and exhibition are dedicated to the affable spirit of Gustave Baumann, which brought so many community members and artists together to enjoy the arts.

SANDRA D'EMILIO
Curator of Art, 1900–1945,
Museum of Fine Arts

DAVID TURNER
Director,
Museum of Fine Arts

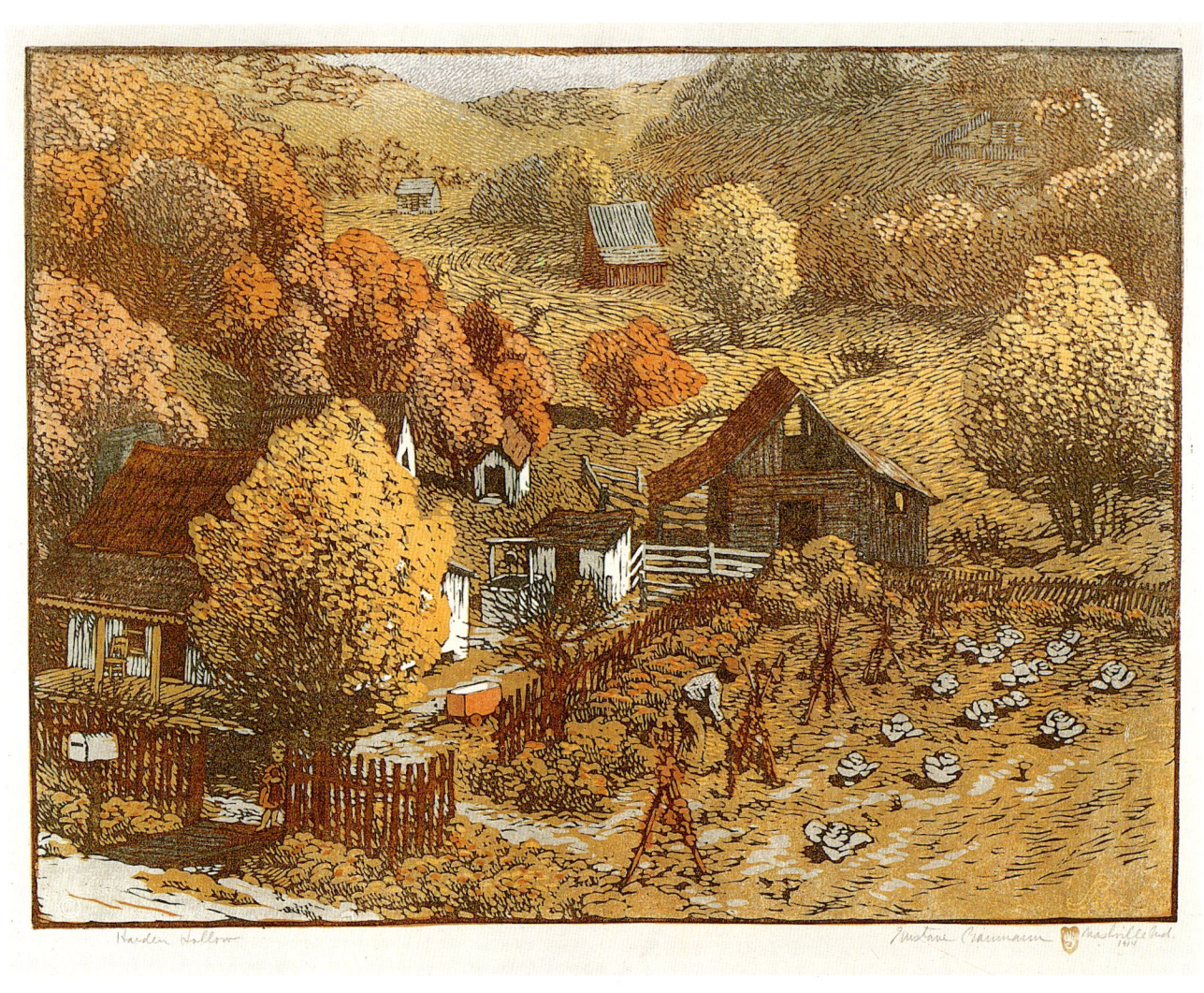

4. HARDEN HOLLOW, 1926

Color woodcut, 9¼ × 11⅛ in.

HAND OF A CRAFTSMAN, HEART OF AN ARTIST

Martin F. Krause
Madeline Carol Yurtseven

In 1915, nine years after a devastating earthquake, San Francisco hosted The Panama-Pacific International Exposition. The world's fair, as was customary, featured an immense art exhibit. In the fine-print category of the American section alone some 2,214 works by 221 artists were catalogued. When the awards of the jury were presented and published in midsummer, the top nine medals went to eight well-known artists and to one unknown – Gustave Baumann.

The Grand Prize, essentially a lifetime achievement award, honored Henry Wolf (1852–1916) who, with Timothy Cole and W. J. Linton, represented the great triumvirate of wood engravers who had prospered in the era before the perfection of photoreproduction. Wolf would barely outlive this honor, and reproductive wood engraving would fail to outlive him. The Medals of Honor went to Daniel A. Wehrschmidt (1861–1932), one of the dying breed of mezzotint engravers who produced reproductions on copper of portraits on canvas, and to Charles H. White (1878–1918), a painter-etcher in the tradition of J.A.M. Whistler, who had been his teacher. Five of the six Gold Medals were awarded to the foremost of America's etchers, proof that etching was primary among the graphic arts in America as in Europe. Allen Lewis (1873–1957), Donald Shaw MacLaughlan (1876–1938), Herman A. Webster (1878–1970), Cadwallader Washburn (1866–1965), and J. André Smith (1880–1959) were all familiar names from recent articles in the influential *Print Collector's Quarterly* and from selective mention in *The Year Book of American Etching* for 1914. Gustave Baumann (1881–1971), the sixth gold medalist, went in all ways against this grain.

Unlike his co-recipients, Baumann had not as yet received mention in art books or notice in national periodicals. While they were represented by New York galleries, his work had not been exhibited beyond the Midwest, and there only in limited fashion. Nor was he inclined, like them, to pursue the accepted repertoire of European picturesqueness. Instead, he was represented in San Francisco by works embodying plain American images drawn from a most sequestered corner of the country: Brown County, Indiana. These prints had not been executed with the flair of the etcher's needle on copperplate, but patiently crafted by knifing and gouging into the plank side of basswood. As Baumann liked to explain with characteristic economy: "Draw directly on the block whatever you want then cut away whatever you don't want and print what is left."[1]

As Baumann could never bring himself to subcontract any of his labor, from the first design to the final printing, his work was bound to be original and personal. The recognition of 1915 was the reward for the individual path he had carefully pursued since his youth in Magdeburg, Germany.

From his father he could claim but two legacies, his given name and a love of woodworking. In 1891, Gustave Sr. moved the family from Germany to Chicago, whereupon he abandoned them to their own devices. His namesake, ten years old and the oldest of four children, began then to assume responsibility, leaving school by sixteen to contribute to the family's support. Having an artistic bent, young Gustave found employment in an engraving house, where he did little more than run errands. To get a little nearer to art, as he later put it, he attended The Art Institute of Chicago, not the regular day classes, which in those years were largely filled by the daughters of the leisure class, but the evening drawing class set up to accommodate students, like Baumann, whose daytime hours were committed to working in the commercial-arts trades.

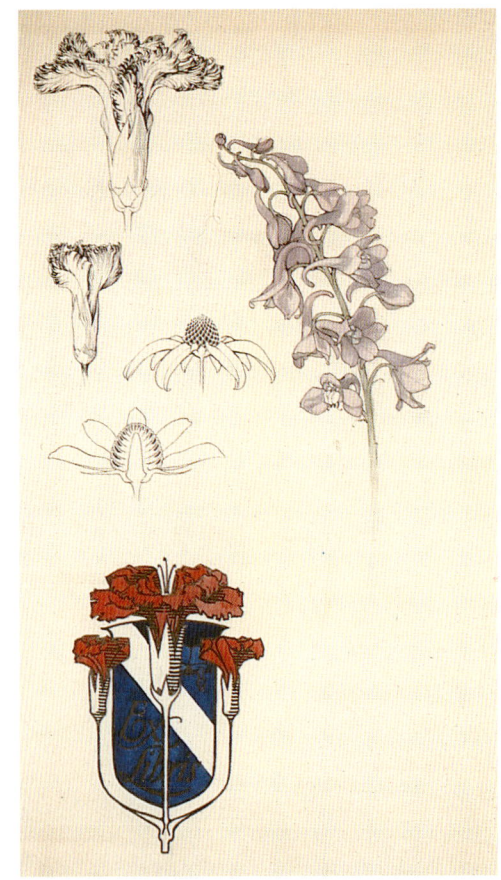

5. UNTITLED
(FLOWER STUDIES), N.D.
Mixed media on paper, 15¾ × 8¾ in.

By 1900 Baumann was employed in the studio of Curtis Gandy, and three years later he was independently listed in the Chicago city directory as an advertising agent with his own studio on Quincy Street. Such on-the-job training in art, albeit art of the marketplace, was invaluable to his development in the fundamentals; it was all Baumann would know until 1905 in Munich.

Although in later years Baumann tended to gloss over this difficult early period in his life, he was unusually reflective in an account of the Baumann family history written in 1970, the year before his death, for his two sisters who had been too young to remember:

Growing up as we did, we were left to shift for ourselves at an early age, there being no choice but to find education where we could and make the most of it within our limitations. . . . The nearest I could come to [art] was by going through the commercial art mill. Somehow I managed to save one thousand dollars. So I gave mother one half and I went to Munich on the rest and stayed a year while mother took her brood for a visit to her Nagel relatives in St. Louis with what was left of her five-hundred dollars.[2]

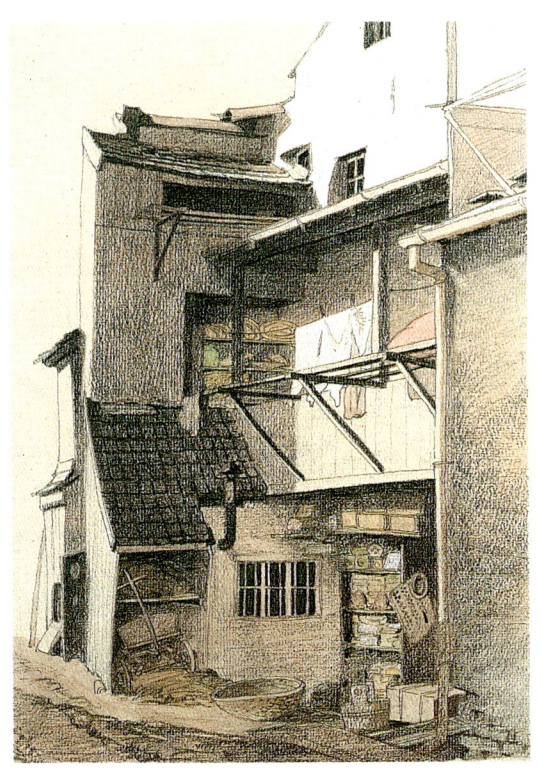

6. LANDSBERG, 1905

Pencil on wash paper, 14 × 10 in.

While most foreign art students in Munich were drawn to the prestigious Royal Academy of Painting, Baumann's immediate interest lay in drawing. With a practical eye toward future employability, he entered the Arts and Crafts School – the *Kunstgewerbeschule*. In so doing he anticipated the direction the twentieth century would take, both in Europe and America, in embracing the marriage of form and function.[3] Art as manifested in architecture, interior decoration, book design, furniture manufacture, advertising, and toymaking enhanced everyday life. Baumann subscribed to this view, eventually employing himself in all of these applied arts.

"If a man tried to harp on one string he'd go flat,"[4] was Baumann's attitude toward his own versatility. His color wood-block prints, which he began making in Munich and for which he would win most renown, were in keeping with his simple, or simply stated, ideal of an art that was within his reach and accessible to everyone:

A fellow ought not try to be an artist unless he has a lot of genius or some useful idea that will give folk something they need. . . . Well maybe I'm wrong, and you never know whether you are doing anything or not until other folk find out for you, but my idea is to produce good pictures at low cost. Each print you see is an original work. . . . Many people think Americans judge art by the price they pay for it and that they will not buy pictures if pictures are cheap. I would not work for folk like that anyway.[5]

And he never did.

In retrospect, Baumann's choice of school was most fortuitous. His professor at the Kunstgewerbeschule was Maximilian Dasio (1865–1954), who specialized in color linocuts. Munich, after 1900, was no less than the center of German block printing in color: "Munich stands absolutely under the sign of color – color in broad, flat areas placed next to one another," wrote a reviewer of a national print exhibition in Leipzig. "The prevailing technique is the woodcut."[6]

Bold, flat areas of color placed adjacent to one another without the interruption of a black outline constituted the Munich manner typified in the woodcuts of Dasio and Hans Neumann and recognizable in the lithographic posters of Ludwig Hohlwein that developed from this woodcut tradition. It became Baumann's style as well. It was different from the Japanese manner in which colors were brushed onto blocks in watercolor fashion and delicately rubbed in the transfer to paper. While the masterful images of Hiroshige and Hokusai were the direct inspiration for the color-woodcut vogue beginning almost simultaneously throughout Europe and America in the last decade of the nineteenth century, the hardiness of the German style reflected its own origins in the sixteenth century and the chiaroscuro woodcuts of Dürer and Cranach.

Baumann, once steeped in the German tradition, remained faithful to it throughout his long career. His approach was evident from his first linocut, executed for Dasio in May 1905 – the elegant *Munich Residence* printed in four colors, one block cut for each. Dissatisfied with the color[7] he simplified his palette for his second effort, *Old Munich* (plate 7), done in July. The design of this view of an ancient timbered house in the old Munich quarter known as the Au is predominantly carried in the black block. The mid-tones are handled by a block for gray and another for brown, with the whites supplied by the white of the paper. A fourth block was cut apparently for the little flashes of red and blue in the flowers and pots on the balcony.[8] Baumann

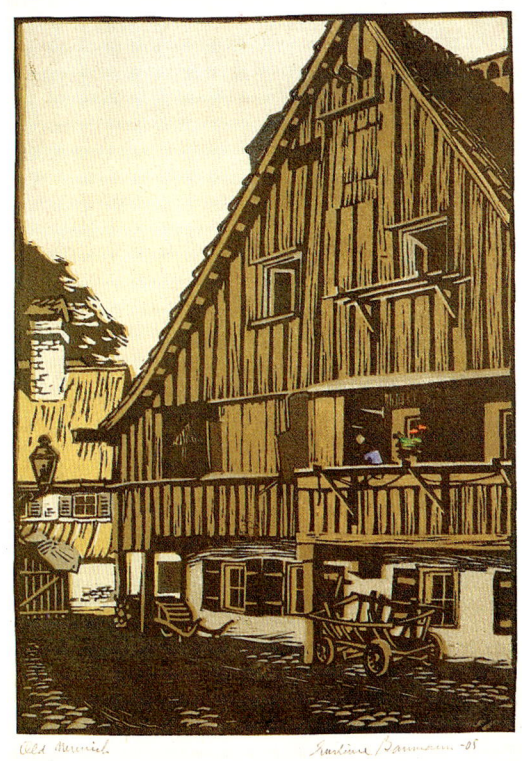

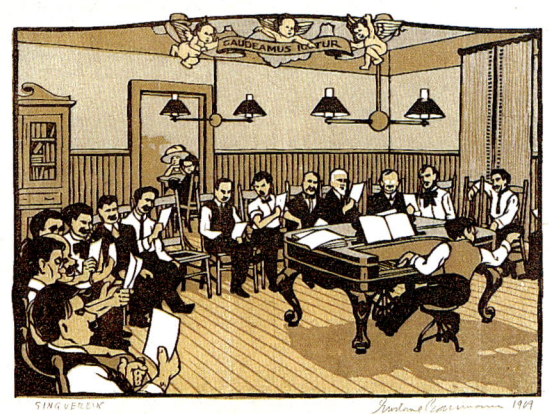

7 . OLD MUNICH, 1905

Color linocut, 11¾×8½ in.

8 . SINGVEREIN

(DIE MEISTERSINGER

VON RAVENSWOOD), 1909

Color woodcut, 7¾×11 in.

found this limited palette, associated with the Munich school of painting, serviceable for his subsequent German prints and for those he would make in America between 1906 and 1912.

Back in Chicago Baumann resumed his work in commercial art, necessitated by the financial plight of his family:

Coming home I found things in a mess and went back into the commercial art mill until we were straightened out. By the time the family was on its feet again, everybody had a job and I felt free to go my own way, which was entirely foreign to family tradition.[9]

This would not become possible for four years, during which the pursuit of his independent art had to be deferred.

Baumann found relief from the daily grind at the Palette & Chisel Club, an organization established in 1895 by the night-school students at the Art Institute (including Baumann's former employer Curtis Gandy) and designed for:

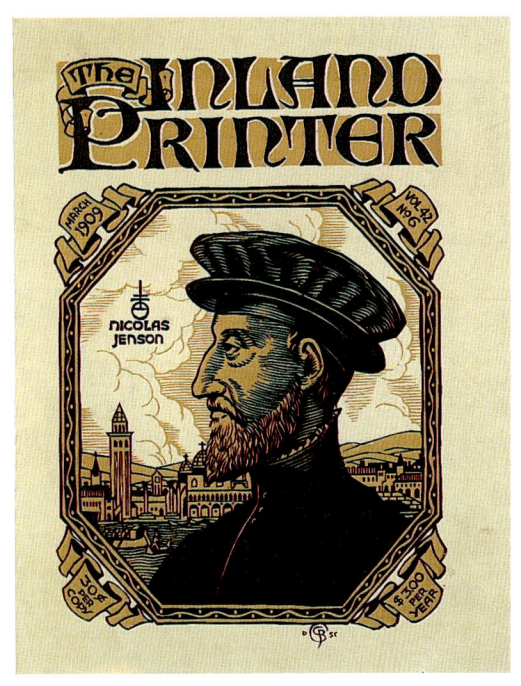

9. THE INLAND PRINTER

(NICOLAS JENSON), MARCH 1909

Color woodcut, 12⅜ × 10 in.

men forced by circumstances to devote all their time to "commercial" art work. The club's object is to keep the interest of its members in "fine arts" alive by devoting their spare time to painting, drawing and modelling, during the winter months in their club room in the Athenaeum Building, and during the summer in the open, near the club's summer camp on the Fox River.[10]

Baumann's name first appears in the club scrapbook in the summer of 1907.[11]

For Baumann the Palette & Chisel Club not only provided a regular escape from his bread-and-butter advertising work, but its membership formed the core of his society for the rest of his life. It included Louis Oscar Griffith (1875–1956), Harry L. Engle (1870– after 1940), Adam Emory Albright (1862–1957), Adolph Shulz (1869–1963), Angus MacDonall (1876–1927), Wilson H. Irvine (1869–1936), Lawrence Mazzanovich (1871/72–1959), Victor Higgins (1884–1949), Walter Ufer (1876–1936), and E. Martin Hennings (1886–1956), all of whose careers began where Baumann's began, in Chicago's commercial art world. They also shared recognition, later in their careers, as among Chicago's most accomplished painters, recognition collectively bestowed in 1916 when the club's twenty-first annual exhibition was mounted not, as usual, in the club's rooms in the Athenaeum, but around the corner and a world away in the halls of The Art Institute of Chicago. To this exhibition and to others later held there, Griffith, Engle, Albright, and Shulz sent pictures from the art colony of Brown County, Indiana; MacDonall, Irvine, and Mazzanovich from Westport, Connecticut; and Higgins, Ufer, and Hennings from Taos, New Mexico. Baumann's life would intertwine with these men in each of these places.

Brown County, Indiana, where Baumann first vacationed in 1910, was about as far removed from the reach of the twentieth century as one could commute to from Chicago. Although only 230

miles south of Chicago and a mere fifty from Indianapolis, Brown County was locked in by timbered hills and impassable roads until 1905 when the railroad tardily reached its borders, then nipping only its northwest corner with a station at Helmsburg. Commerce, when Baumann arrived, was still conducted by horse and wagon along dirt roads. There would be no electricity service for another decade in the county seat at Nashville, nestled in the center of the county in what was appropriately known as "the Peaceful Valley."[12] Brown County was not only rural, it was rustic. Log-cabin living bred an insulated population of self-reliant, hard-scrabble farmers, woodsmen, and craftsmen who settled in places whose names evoked pioneer days – Gnawbone, Stone Head, Bear Wallow, Bean Blossom, and Weed Patch Nob. The primitive aspects of life there attracted the "cliff-dwelling" artists of Chicago and Indianapolis whose journeys were facilitated by the new railroad.

The first to arrive was Theodore Clement Steele (1847–1926), the dean of Indiana painters who, with the other four members of The Hoosier Group, would make nationally known through their art the quietude of the Indiana landscape. In 1907 he bought a hilltop about ten miles west of Nashville, where he built a studio he christened "The House of the Singing Winds." There he sequestered himself to paint scenes of the surrounding woods. Will Vawter (1871–1941) and his wife arrived in Nashville in 1908. He was preeminent among those illustrators who had provided the plates for James Whitcomb Riley's immensely popular poems. Vawter found in Brown County models who embodied the qualities that Riley was conjuring up from his boyhood memories of rural Indiana a half-century before. In 1907 the Palette & Chisel Club also arrived.

Club members Griffith, Irvine, and Engle arrived in March of 1907. They came to Brown County to paint winter scenery but found instead a springtime landscape of dogwood, redbud, and apple orchards in full flower.[13] They returned to Chicago with dazzling reports of the area's natural beauty. Adolph Shulz hiked through the county in June. The following summer these artists returned, accompanied by Albright, MacDonall, and a dozen or more Chicagoans. The contingent of seasonal painters then numbered twenty-five.[14]

In the summer of 1910, Baumann arrived in Brown County in pursuit of a much-needed respite from city life and the commercial-art grind.[15] He came by night train from Chicago, crossing the platform at Indianapolis early the next morning to the waiting Indianapolis Southern and the last leg of the trip. Alighting at Helmsburg, he forewent the stage to Nashville, a journey which Engle had described as "much like an imagined jaunt down the Capitol stone steps in Washington,"[16] and instead walked the six miles to town. The amble prepared him for the county's leisurely pace:

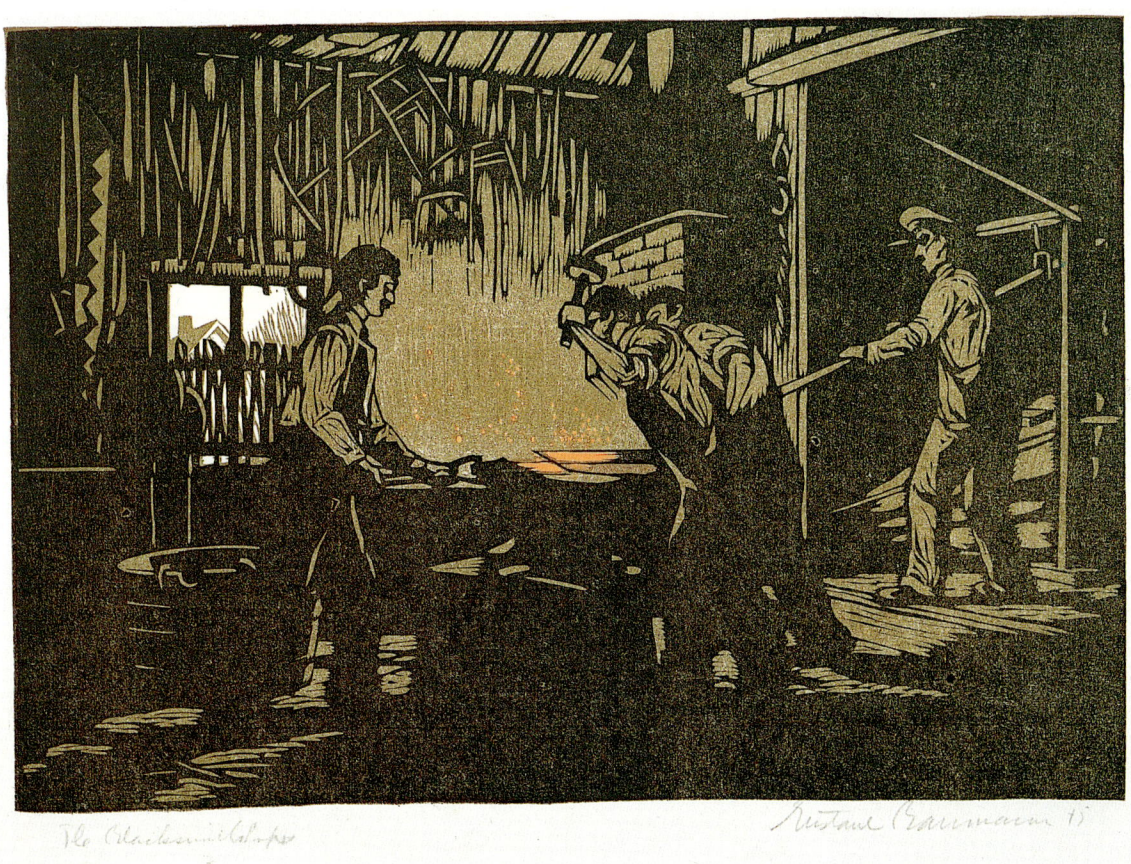

10. THE BLACKSMITH SHOP, 1910

Color woodcut, 9 × 13⅛ in.

The farther I walked, the more enthusiastic I became and before reaching Nashville I was quite ready to buy a 180-acre farm simply because it was for sale and boasted of a fine log house with ideal surroundings for an artist . . . ; you have visions of painting innumerable pictures but that is a delusion. No one in Brown County ever overworks. In a day or so you may begin stretching a canvas, and again you may not, for unexpected paths trail over the hills and tempt you as you walk miles and miles in search of those elusive motives we have all seen but never have been able to grasp.[17]

Although Baumann had not come to Brown County to work, he found it unavoidable.

He rented two rooms above Maurice Miller's drugstore across Main Street from the log jail and brick county courthouse, and there he pursued his art from six each morning until ten each night.[18] Long after the summer had ended and the seasonal artists had filtered back to their Chicago studios, Baumann continued to work.

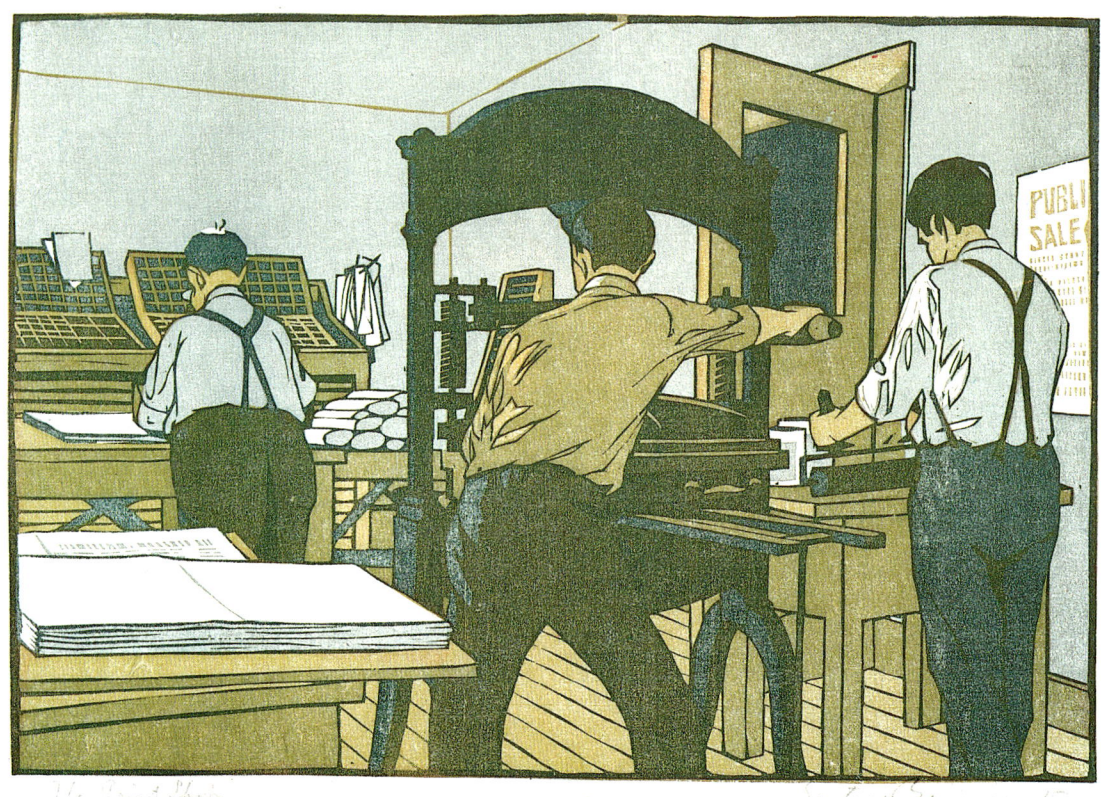

11. THE PRINT SHOP, 1910

Color woodcut, 9 × 13¼ in.

By Thanksgiving,[19] Baumann had cut the blocks (four for each) for the twelve 9-by-13-inch scenes that were to comprise the portfolio he entitled *In the Hills o' Brown*. He need wander no further than the five-block-by-five-block town limits of Nashville to find suitable inspiration. There was the blacksmith shop (plate 10) with its forge glowing red; and the wagon shop and the rug weaver, all of which found their way into the portfolio. Also included was the print shop (plate 11) with Alonzo Allison and sons setting type and working the old-style Franklin press that printed the *Brown County Democrat* and that Baumann used in hand-printing the portfolio that first December.[20] The scenes were rendered in the simplified vocabulary of the woodcut medium, reflecting character types rather than penetrating human portraits. But Baumann instinctively avoided the sort of caricatured depictions so typical of patronizing city artists. For Baumann, these men and women were craftsmen like himself. While most artists had studios, he had a "work shop,"[21] and it was said then, and it would always be true, that "here he claims the hearty friendship of members of the community, who do not always welcome 'them artist fellers' who summer in their midst."[22]

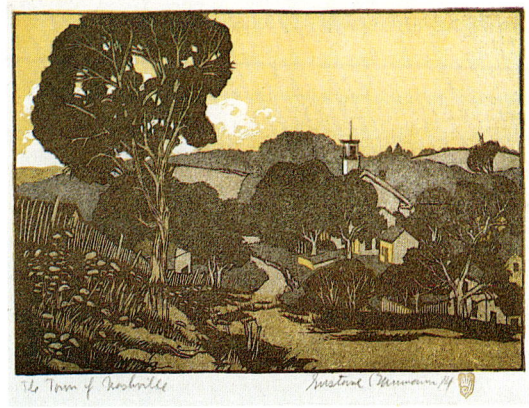

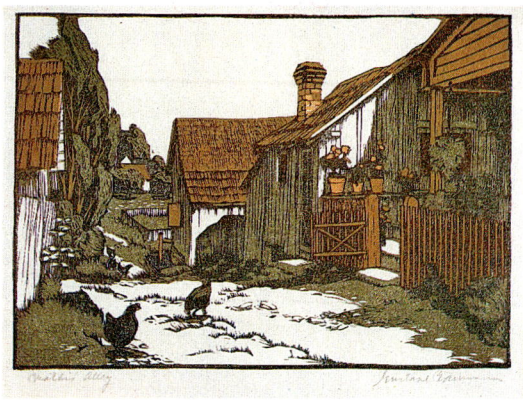

12. THE TOWN OF NASHVILLE, 1910
Color woodcut, 9⅛ × 13⅛ in.

13. MATHIS ALLEY, *ca.* 1910
Color woodcut, 10¼ × 13¾ in.

The portfolio also included views of the town: a prospect of the belfried courthouse from the overlook north of town; the little handmade swinging bridge across the town swimming hole on Salt Creek; and glimpses down alleys or through dooryards. Only the opening plate, *In the Hills of Brown,* can be considered a pure landscape and it is the least accomplished scene of the portfolio. Baumann was not yet a landscape artist.

The portfolio was shown in group exhibitions in the museums of Indianapolis and Chicago in the first months of 1911 and generously reviewed in both cities. This attention generated modest sales at five dollars a print, enough to encourage Baumann to stay on in Nashville for the better part of the next six years, with brief returns to Chicago as business warranted.

Life was simple and the work sustaining. Major attention was devoted to creating twelve color-woodcut illustrations for a series of Riley poems on the months of the year, brought out in 1912 by the Indianapolis publisher Bobbs-Merrill Company under the title *All the Year Round* (plates 14, 64).

Brown County offered Baumann its lack of distraction, a vital ingredient in an artist's development. A Chicago writer observed as much in a 1914 appreciation of the work Baumann was then creating:

Now to be a successful wood engraver you have to have soul, imagination, deftness, ideas and knowledge. Also you have to have atmosphere. Imagine anyone patiently engraving on wood in a metropolitan studio! It can't be done with elevated trains screeching and trolley gongs clanging and newsboys urging you to familiarize yourself with the newest murder or divorce. It calls for solitude, for meditation, for the murmur of vagrant breezes through the hush of noon, for the drowsy hum of bees, for old clothes that fit loosely and for the peace of the countryside. So Baumann selected Brown County, Indiana, as his sphere wherein to work.[23]

Baumann's motto, selected from Voltaire's *Candide* and hung in his Nashville workshop, was "*Il faut cultiver nôtre jardin*" (We must cultivate our garden), a saying which aptly describes the modest plot in the art world that Baumann was nurturing in those years.

From June 1911 until early 1913, Baumann was occupied with a series of four five-color woodblock prints that were far more ambitious than anything he had yet attempted, both in size and complexity. There was an enlarged version of *The Rug Weaver*, a view of a springtime farmyard (*Plum and Peach Bloom*; plate 69), and two autumn landscapes, *Harden Hollow* (plate 16) and *Wash Barnes Cabin*, both expansive views over the hills of Brown County.

By the time the series went on exhibition, in January 1913 at the "Artists of Chicago and Vicinity" show at the Art Institute, Baumann had completed and was ready to print an even larger

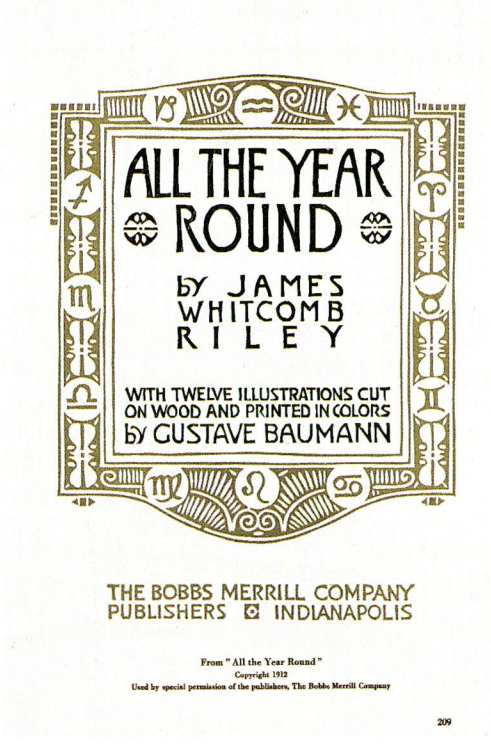

14. ALL THE YEAR ROUND
(TITLE PAGE), 1912
Color woodcut (reproduction), 11 × 8¾ in.

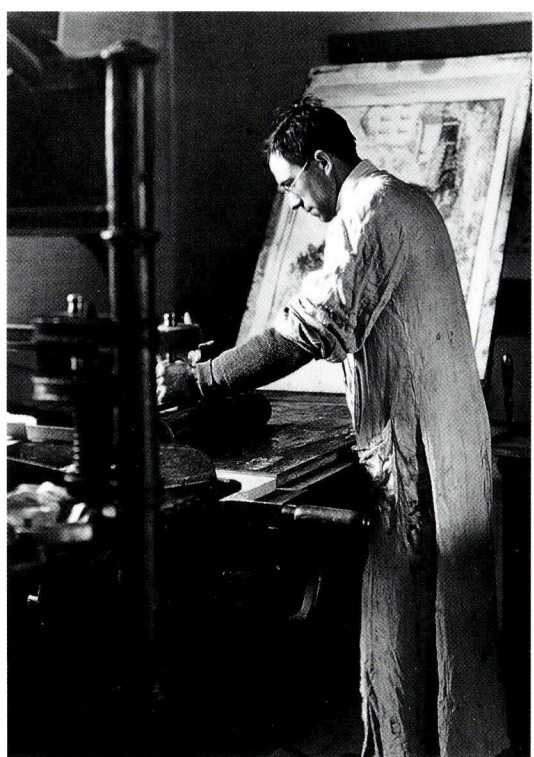

Gustave Baumann in 1913 at his press in Nashville, Indiana, printing The Mill Pond.

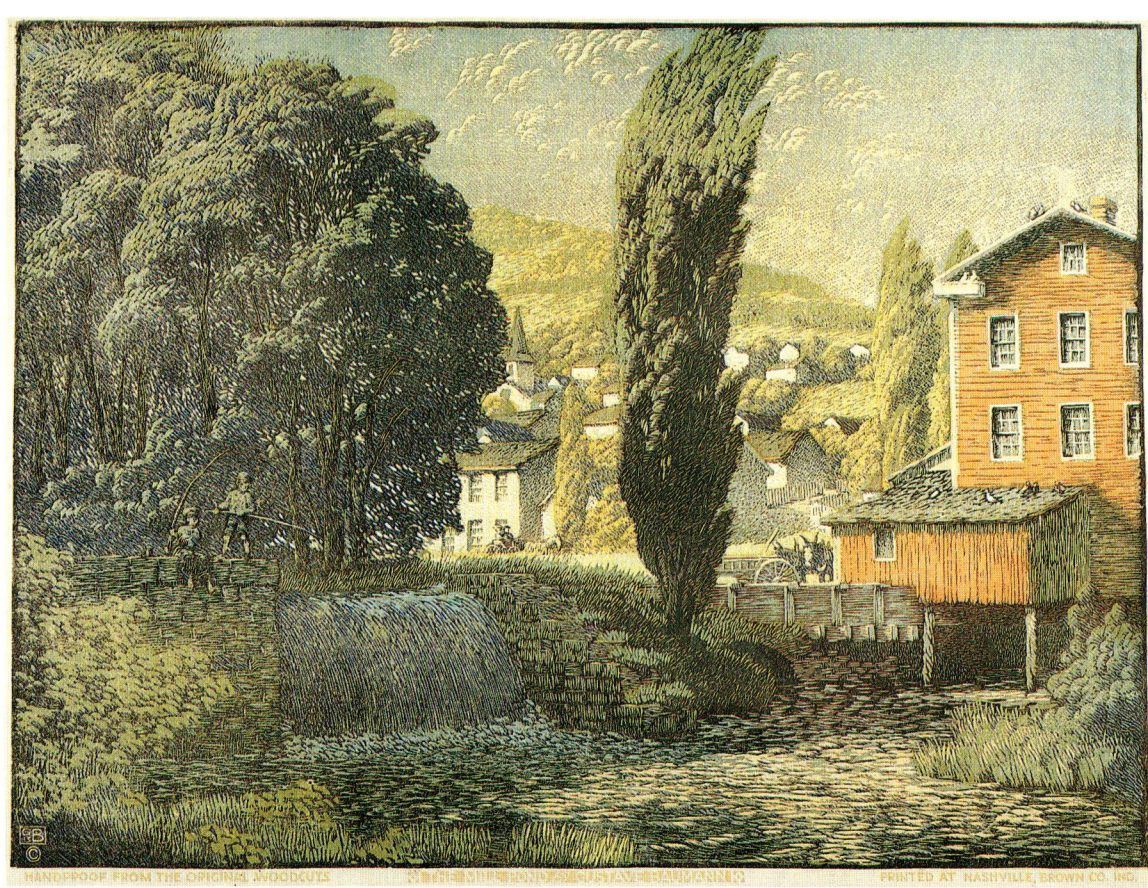

HANDPROOF FROM THE ORIGINAL WOODCUTS · THE SURE AND STEADFAST FRIENDS · PRINTED AT NASHVILLE, BROWN CO. INC.

15. THE MILL POND, 1913

Color woodcut, 25¼×34 in.

(25¼×34 in.) and more colorful (six blocks) woodcut, *The Mill Pond* (plate 15). He now had his own antique Washington (Franklin) handpress and a roomy ground-floor studio at Odd Fellows Hall on the Nashville village green, a space which accommodated his large equipment.

Baumann had envisioned these picture-sized prints hanging in schools where original art was scarce. He waited for a response that never came and conceded that a smaller format was more in keeping with the homey charm of the county.[24] He was also disappointed by the lukewarm reception of *All the Year Round*. He had not only cut the illustrations but also the letterpress and the border designs. It looked like a Baumann book with Riley text. "Consequently," Baumann wrote, "it was a dismal flop."[25]

While he sorted out these problems he would make no new woodcuts for two years. In spite of his conviction that there already were too many painters, he began to paint seriously. In those two years he exhibited only watercolors, gouaches, and paintings in tempera at venues that had previously seen only his woodcuts.[26]

In Baumann's first year in Brown County, he piled his studio with watercolors, although he did not consider himself a painter. When in 1911 a reviewer for the *Indianapolis News* admired the work, Baumann dismissed them with casual humility: "The woods are full of stuff like that. . . . I never finish them but I have to have the practice in getting color and light. You see I don't believe in so many artists trying to do what some other fellow has done successfully. That is what causes such a dearth [*sic*] of poor pictures."[27] Within the next year his attitude would change.

The most remarkable new feature of his color-woodcut *Plum and Peach Bloom*, exhibited in Baumann's first one-man show in Indianapolis in February 1913, was its combination of sculptural structure – inherent in prints made from carved blocks of wood – and a painterly effect antithetical to prints crafted from wood. Said one reviewer, "Exquisite in coloring and astonishing in its technique, for be it said that with the knife in cutting the picture on the block he finds as great a possibility for dash and style as other artists do with brush or pencil."[28] It was painterly because, for the first known time, its genesis and model had been a painting, one which was made to scale and perfectly exhibitable in its own right.[29]

Brown County tended to make landscape painters of artists who typically worked in other media. This was as true of Baumann during his time there, as it was the case for etchers L. O. Griffith and Charles Dahlgreen and the illustrator Will Vawter, all better remembered in Indiana as landscape painters.

Baumann's friendships with Vawter, Griffith, T. C. Steele, and Adolph Shulz influenced the art he created in southern Indiana. He adopted their practice, stemming from their primary concern for the theme of landscape, of sketching in nature. Like others whose residency was year-round, Baumann sketched throughout the year and at different times of the day. He was inspired by his painter-friends, but to different ends. While they sought to evoke the natural poetry of nature, its diffuse light and opalescent atmosphere, Baumann was concerned with the decorative aspects found in the landscape. Instead of emulating their impressionism, he painted like the block printmaker he was.

However distinct their artistic aims, the year-round resident artists of Nashville were few, and a natural camaraderie developed among full-timers Steele, Vawter, and Baumann.[30]

The paintings of 1913 and 1914, left to the Brown County Art Gallery Association in Nashville by Baumann's widow, anticipate the woodblock prints he would create in the years immediately following the San Francisco exposition. In this period, Baumann shows an increasing confidence

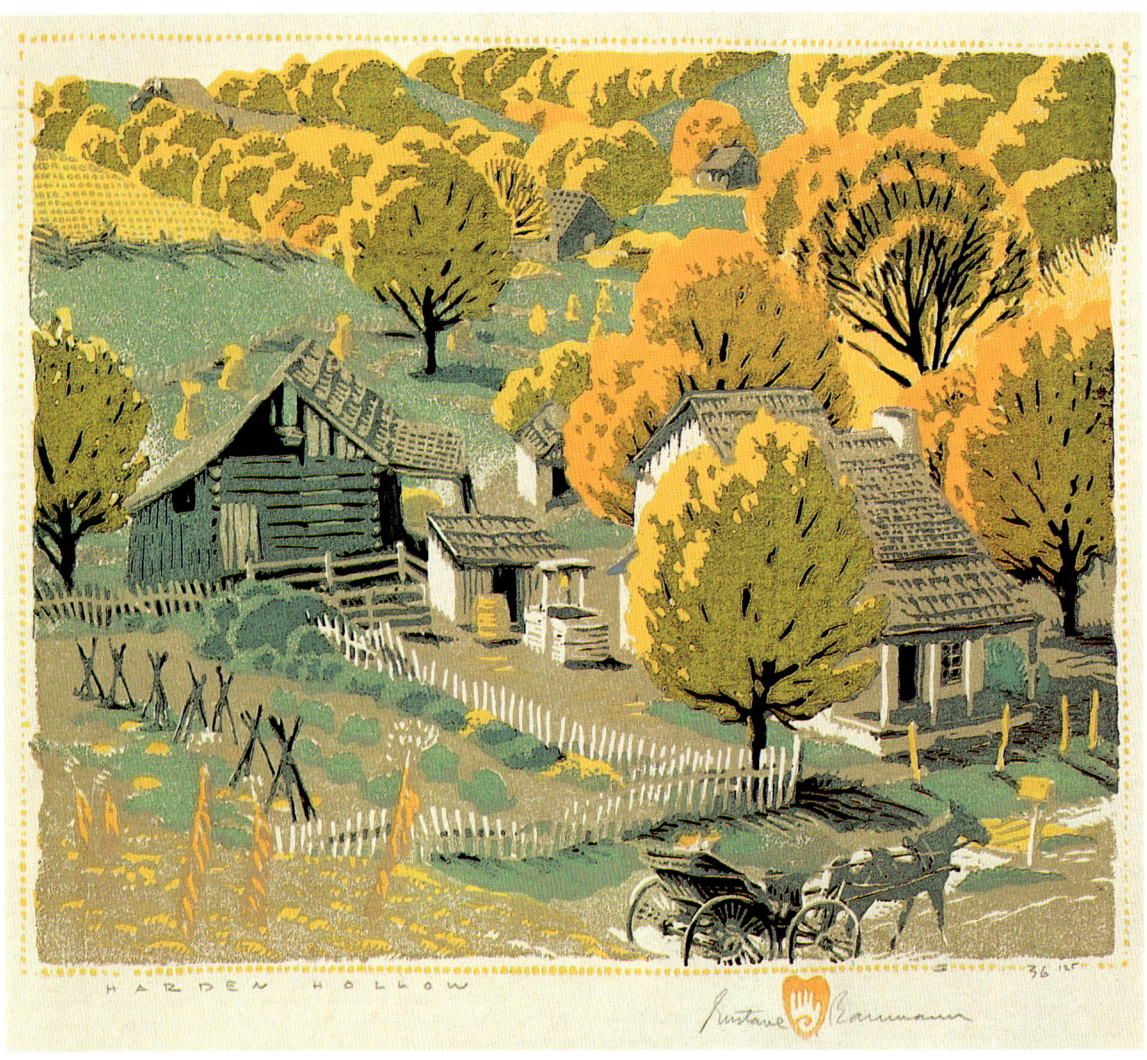

16. HARDEN HOLLOW, 1911–1913

Color woodcut, 19¾ × 26½ in.

in his ability to produce pictorial effects without the illustrative means refined in his Chicago years. The gouaches depict seasonal landscapes of the Nashville area, with a preference for expansive views of gently rolling hills. An occasional cabin or barn is tucked into clusters of trees down rutted, meandering roads, but the human element, central to the woodcuts of the "Hills o' Brown" portfolio and *All the Year Round*, is wholly absent.

Baumann now rarely employed black to create form and define space. He abandoned his muted palette for colors higher in key. There is a distinctive effort to enhance color and contrast in order to make the decorative element more explicit. Baumann showed the work unto itself, but the gouaches, with their sculpted areas of color, could also be transferred directly to wood

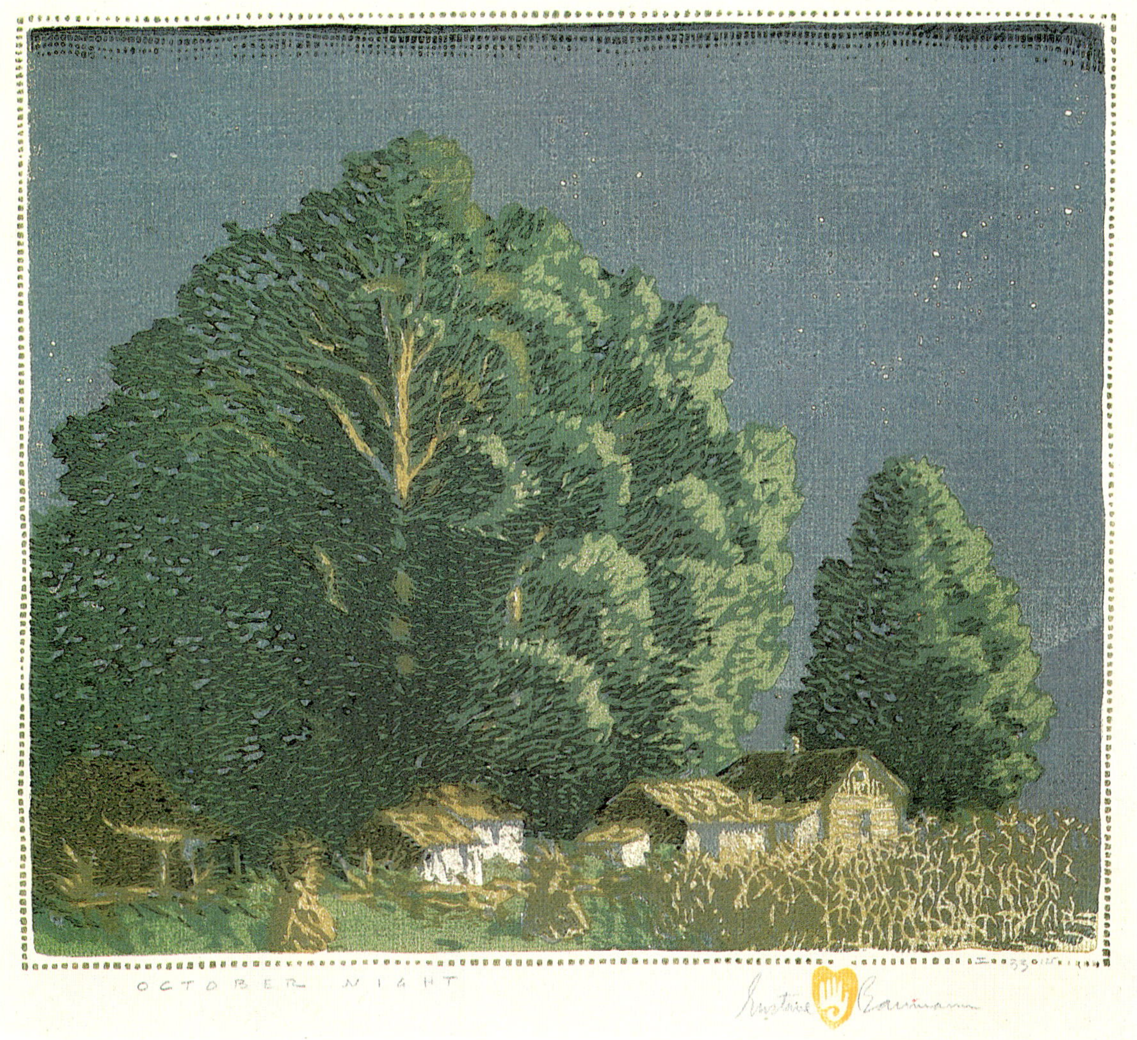

17. OCTOBER NIGHT, 1916

Color woodcut, 9½ × 11⅛ in.

and cut. Indeed some of them would be, but not until the 1915 Panama-Pacific Exposition revived general interest in wood-block printmaking.

Baumann was not the only wood-block printmaker to be recognized by the 1915 awards in San Francisco. While woodcuts represented a scant five percent of the exhibited prints, their printmakers garnered fifteen percent of the awards. In addition to Baumann's gold medal, Edna Boies Hopkins (1872–1937), Bertha Lum (1869–1954), and B. J. O. Nordfeldt (1878–1955) won silvers; Elizabeth Colwell (1881–1954/56), Arthur Wesley Dow (1857–1922), and Helen Hyde (1868–

1919) were awarded bronzes; and Margaret Jordan Patterson (1867–1950) received honorable mention. All belonged to the so-called "modern" group of block printmakers that was distinguished from the class of professional, reproductive wood-engravers to which Henry Wolf belonged.[31] Beyond that they had little in common. Among their number were the frank Orientalists Helen Hyde and Bertha Lum, who drew deep inspiration from nineteenth-century Japanese woodcuts. Both had studied in Japan with surviving masters of the tradition and had settled there for many years. Hyde and Lum produced Japanese subjects in the Japanese manner, employing master cutters, inkers, and printers in accordance with the traditional Japanese division of labor.

Other printmakers had studied Japanese techniques abroad, but then applied them to American subjects according to methods less foreign. Arthur Wesley Dow was the dean of this group and the pioneer of modern American color wood-block printmaking. It was his contention that only those prints that were created entirely by the individual artist, from first design to final printing, could be called original. Dow underscored this principle in the title of his first exhibition of color prints at Boston's Museum of Fine Arts in 1895: "Designed, Engraved and Printed by Arthur Wesley Dow."

His method was transmitted to the scores of teachers-in-training who attended his classes at Pratt Institute and at Columbia University, Edna Boies Hopkins among them. Nordfeldt subscribed to similar notions, though gleaned from Frank Morley Fletcher in England in 1900. In turn he passed them on to Elizabeth Colwell, his student at Chicago's Academy of Fine Arts before 1907. In San Francisco, Nordfeldt showed eight woodcuts done in the Japanese method, all made in 1906 but representing his most current efforts in the medium.

Baumann also showed eight prints, all from three to five years earlier and representing his newest work. He constituted yet a third strain – printmakers trained in the German tradition, but whose work was adapted to American subjects. And there were Americans such as Margaret Jordan Patterson, who learned the European method and produced most of their work abroad.

Such was the state of the American color-woodcut *impulse* (for it was not a movement) in January 1915 when entries were called for in San Francisco.[32] Only one year later the situation would be radically different.

In the months following the awards presentation, Baumann took the lead. He organized an exhibition for The Art Institute of Chicago, "American Block Prints and Wood Engravings," which opened on February 2, 1916, for two weeks. It was the first exhibition of its kind, with 147 prints, most of them in color, by twenty artists (twelve women and eight men), nearly all the serious workers in the field. The eight medal winners from San Francisco were invited, along with three who had not been honored: Michael C. Carr of San Francisco and Ada Gilmore and Mildred McMillen, both of Provincetown. Also included were nine new names in block print-making:[33] Dean Babcock of Colorado; Gordon Ertz of Chicago; Eliza Draper Gardiner of Providence; Rudolph Ruzicka and Florence Wyman Ivins of New York City; and an enlarged contingent from Provincetown: Ethel Mars, Mary Bacon Jones, Tod Lindenmuth, and Juliette S. Nichols.

The phenomenal swelling of the ranks of modern block printers working in America between the call for entries in San Francisco and Baumann's exhibition a year later was due in large part to the outbreak of World War I in Europe and the repatriation of American wood-block artists who had been perfecting their art in Paris and Brittany.

Ethel Mars, born in Illinois and trained in Cincinnati, and her companion Maud Hunt Squire had studied in Munich in 1904 and since 1907 lived in Paris, associating with Gertrude Stein and her circle.[34] Mars specialized in color woodcuts and Squire in color etchings of the *Intimiste* sort. They freely offered training to other American artists visiting Paris. By 1911 Margaret Jordan Patterson had produced her first woodcuts under Mars' tutelage, as did Ada Gilmore and Mildred McMillen, arriving from Chicago in 1913. Then came the war.

Mars and Squire were listed among the artists returning to New York on *La Touraine* in mid-September 1914.[35] Gilmore and McMillen may have been with them. Nordfeldt interrupted what he had hoped to be a lengthy French sojourn and was back in New York in October.[36] Edna Boies Hopkins returned to Cincinnati from Paris, her residence since 1905. Even Helen Hyde, after fifteen years in Japan, returned to the United States in 1914.

Concurrent with the opening of the Panama-Pacific, in spring of 1915, Mars, Squire, McMillen, and Gilmore settled in Provincetown, a location as reminiscent of their beloved Brittany as could be found in the United States. Nordfeldt joined them early in the summer, as did Juliette Nichols, also returned from France. Ada Gilmore later described that summer:

The six artists decided to do nothing but wood-block prints for that season and a very interesting community art life began. Until then few painters had remained in Provincetown through the winter. They all worked steadily that first season and a great many good prints were produced. Each artist's work developed individually, except as a group they expressed a new modern note in design and color.[37]

These six were soon joined by Mary Bacon Jones and Tod Lindenmuth.

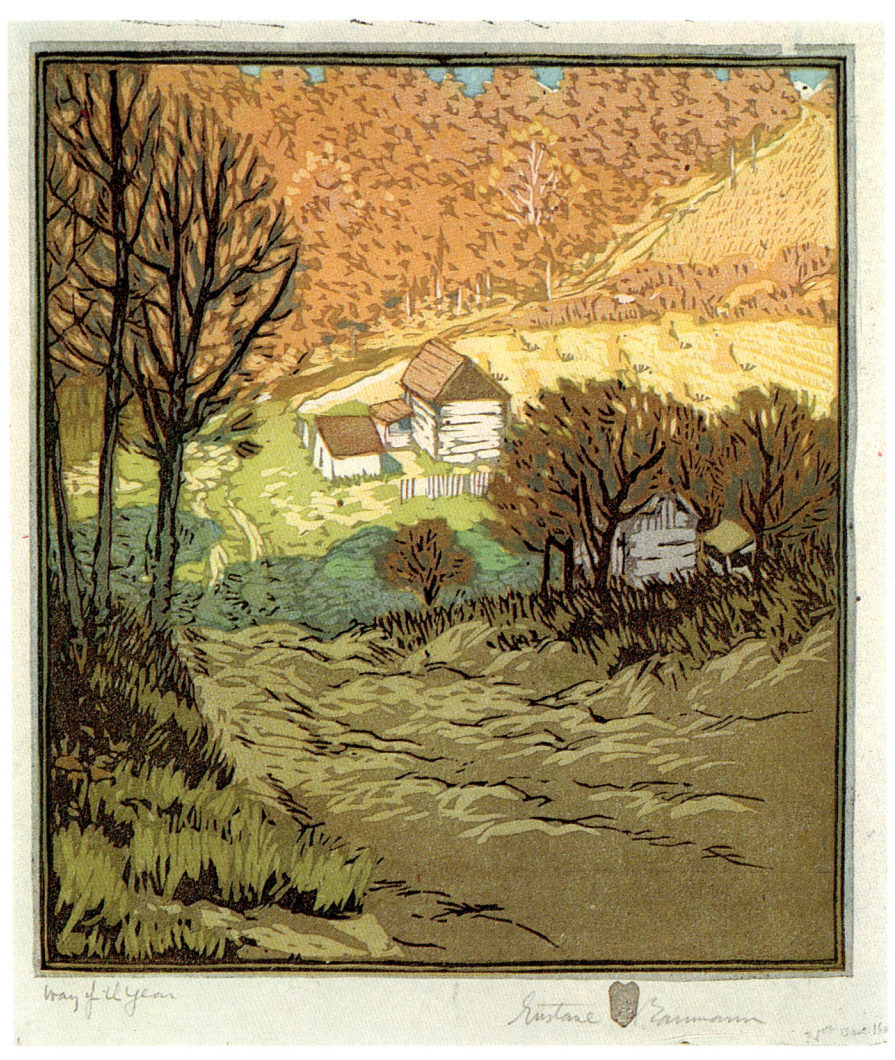

18. WAY OF THE YEAR, 1916

Color woodcut, 11 × 9⅞ in.

Nordfeldt, who had not made a new wood-block print in nine years, having attended in the meantime to his painting and etching, took the lead in innovation. Bridling at the chore of carving a separate block of wood for each color in the print, he devised a shortcut by carving a groove around each element in the design and selectively brushing his inks onto each area; the single block could then be printed in one pass. The effect was bold, modern in its primitivity, and yet still decorous. The method was soon adopted by others and became synonymous with the art colony. It became known as "the Provincetown Print."

Nordfeldt's six new Provincetown prints received their first public airing at Baumann's Art Institute show the following February (1916).[38] The Provincetown prints were not the only in-

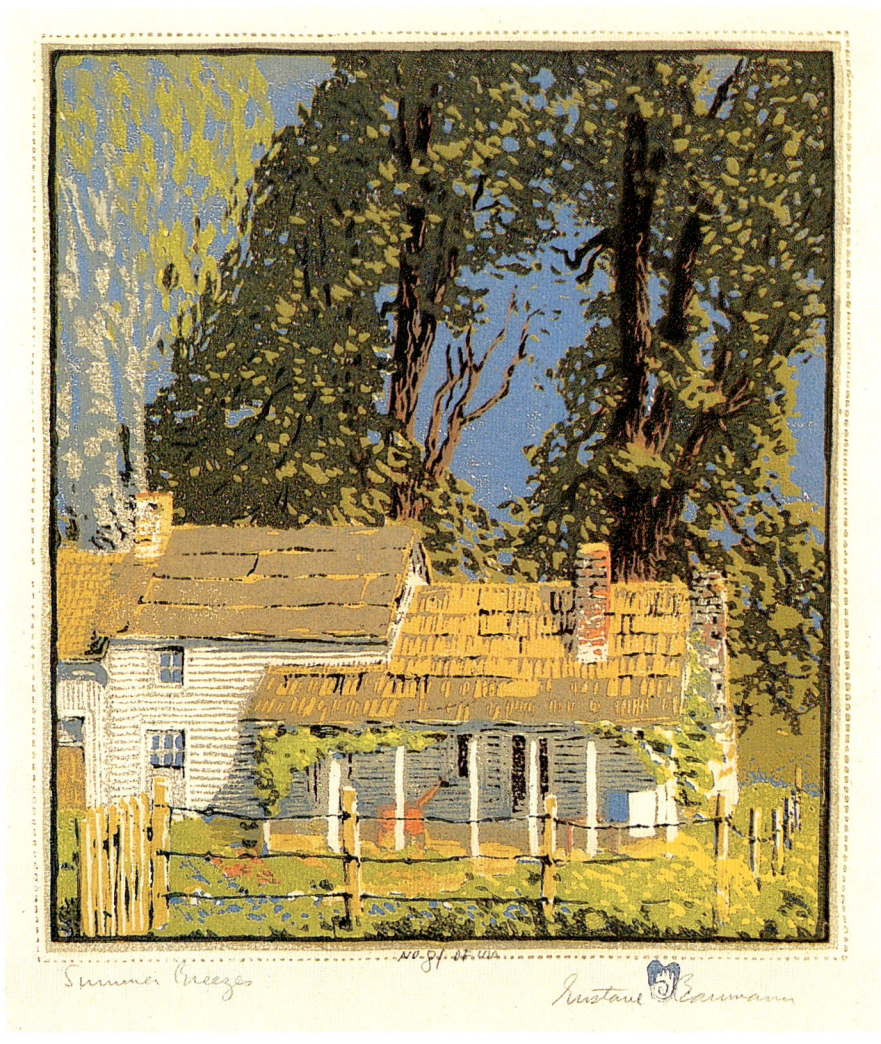

19. SUMMER BREEZES, 1916

Color woodcut, 11 × 10 in.

novations on view in Chicago. Baumann's eight wood-block prints were unlike anything he had done before.

His new landscape work – *The Landmark* (plate 71), *Summer Breezes* (plate 19), and *Way of the Year* (plate 18) – was in all ways more sophisticated than what had come before. While the forms remained solid, the images now were built up from six and seven blocks, with intermediate colors achieved by the overprinting of translucent inks. With these new prints, Baumann abandoned smooth Japanese papers in favor of the German Gladbach, a stock that had more tooth, allowing the white of the paper to break up flat areas of color with an impressionistic effect. These advances Baumann had already explored in field studies in tempera on brown paper.

Years later he described his method:

I usually work from a color sketch in four or five colors made with a brush stroke as sharp and direct as the gouge will cut. Whichever color carries most of the drawing is cut first, after it has been traced through the sketch onto the block. A proof from this block is then transferred to all the other blocks. . . . But problems not inherent in sketching become very exacting in the cuttings; these sometimes lead one to cut away the right color in one block and leave the wrong one in another. To get essential intermediate tones, colors are superimposed.[39]

Baumann almost immediately recognized in these new Brown County prints his own mature manner.[40] While in subsequent years he would suit his colors and styles to the subjects at hand, the technique remained unaltered. Now wanderlust struck him and he decided to move on.

His intention, in the spring of 1916, was to go west with his friends E. Martin Hennings and Victor Higgins,[41] the latter of whom already had established himself as a resident of Taos. Instead, the summer found Baumann back in his studio in Brown County, working to fulfill obligations.[42] There were woodcut illustrations to complete for Kendall Banning's book *Pirates* and a commission from Packard for a woodblock print calendar for 1917. By the year's end these were completed, and after sending out Christmas cards from Nashville, Baumann packed up his studio and left Indiana with no intention of returning.

Instead of going west, he went east. By May 1917 he was establishing his studio in the art colony of Westport, Connecticut, on Long Island Sound within easy commuting distance of Manhattan. There he found himself in the company of a congregation of well-known il-

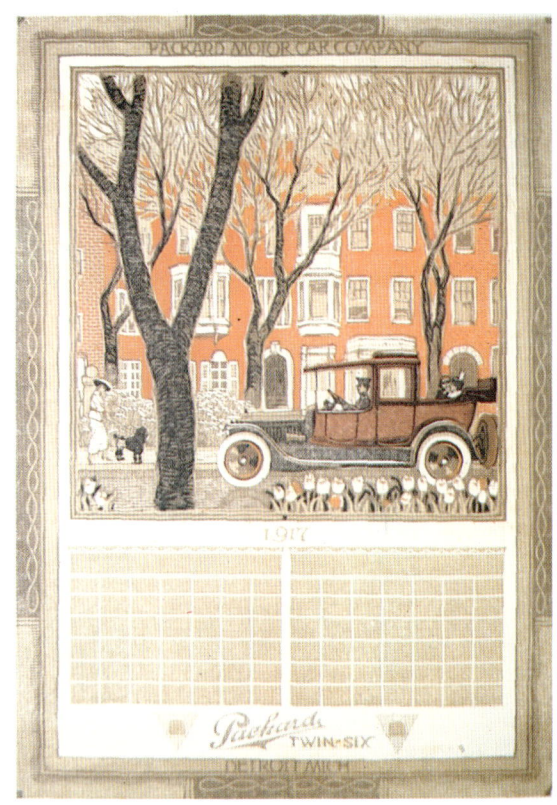

20. THE PACKARD CALENDAR, 1917

Color woodcut (reproduction), 11 × 8¾ in.

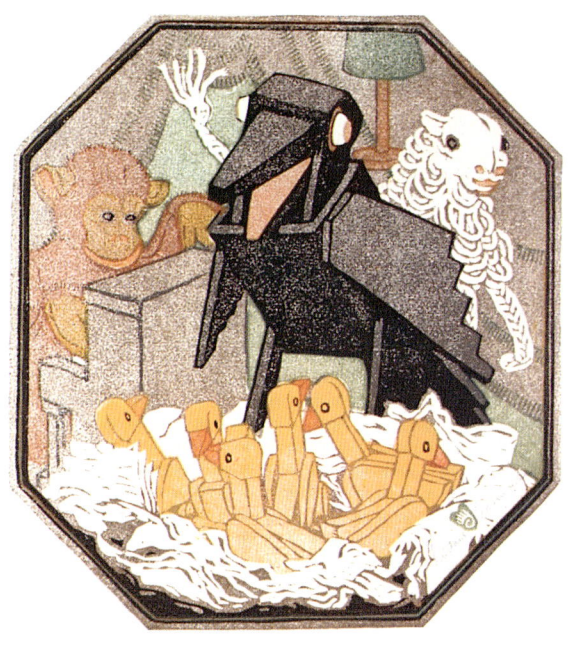

21. PLAYROOM SYMPOSIUM, 1916

Color woodcut, 11 × 10 in.

lustrators that included his old comrades Angus MacDonall and Lawrence Mazzanovich. He did not stay long. He summered in the hill country of western New York State, a guest of Lydia Coonley Ward, a Chicago-based philanthropist whose summer home was perched in the hills above the village of Wyoming. Each year at "Hillside" she organized a summer school for villagers of all ages, importing specialists in the sciences, education, and the arts. That summer, Baumann taught manual training and toymaking. Afterward, he detoured to Provincetown to join Nordfeldt and the rest of the regulars who were there as usual that year.[43] By December he was noticed in his New York studio.[44]

He had not neglected his own work in these unanchored months. Prints representative of his stays in New York City, Wyoming, and Provincetown were ready by December 3 for their first showing at the second annual exhibition of the Painter-Gravers of America, an organization established in New York the previous March principally by well-known painters who wished also to be known for their printmaking. Childe Hassam, J. Alden Weir, John Sloan, George Bellows, Frank Benson, Nordfeldt, and Baumann were among the founding members.

Baumann had completed sixteen new woodcuts in 1917 – eight in Wyoming, five in Provincetown, and three in New York City. While the new work is consistent with the direction Baumann had been forging, each grouping represents something distinctive. The Wyoming series is most reminiscent of the Brown County Baumann had left behind with its verdant country views of Mrs. Coonley Ward's legendary orchard, the porch at "Hillside" (*Summer Shadows*, plate 72), and the view from the porch down the valley into Wyoming (*Road to Town*, plates 22, 23).

The New York City prints are comparatively glaring with the stark whiteness of the skyscrapers silhouetted against brilliantly blue skies and, in *Fifth Avenue* (plate 73), enlivened by an equally brilliant display of American flags signaling America's entry into World War I. The same brilliance can be seen in Baumann's studies for these prints, for the first time executed with

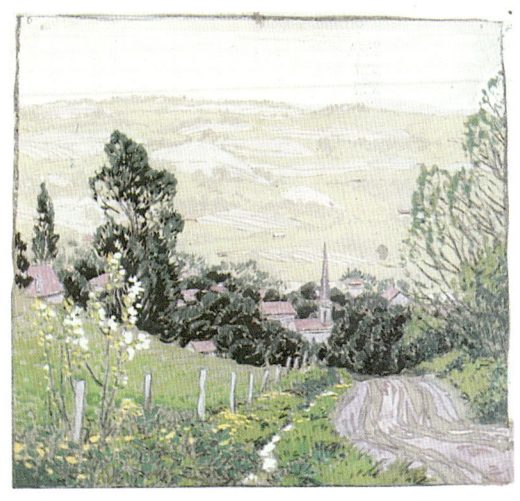

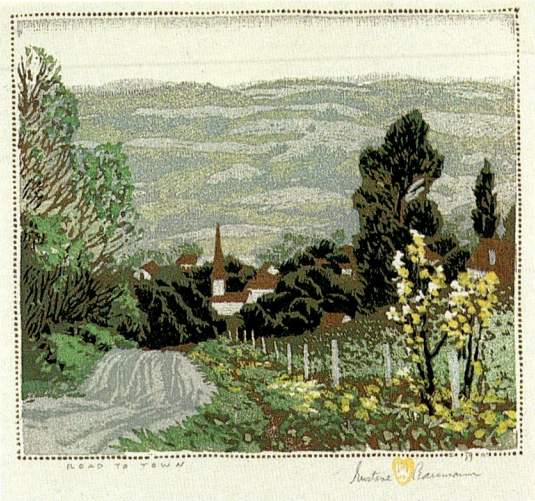

2 2 . R O A D T O T O W N
(W Y O M I N G , N E W Y O R K) , *ca.* 1 9 1 7
Gouache, 10⅝ × 11¼ in.

2 3 . R O A D T O T O W N , 1 9 1 7
Color woodcut, 9½ × 11½ in.

transparent watercolor on white paper rather than his usual rich opaque tempera on brown paper.

The palette in the Provincetown prints is appropriately subdued, reflecting the fall-gray tones of the weathered clapboard houses (*Tom A Hunting*, plate 28) and the blue-gray seas of *Idle Fleet* (plate 74).

In the spring of 1918, Baumann prepared his first major touring exhibition. It consisted of twenty-four highlights of his past two years' work and a new educational offering: the tempera sketch for the woodcut *Summer Breezes* (plate 19), its seven blocks, seven proofs showing each color printed separately, and another seven demonstrating the progressive building of the image to completion. The exhibition opened at Milwaukee Art Institute in June, traveled to The Cleveland Museum of Art in July, and ended its tour in Chicago at The Art Institute in December. Two months earlier it had caught up with Baumann at the new Museum of Fine Arts in Santa Fe. Baumann had finally taken Walter Ufer's suggestion, made in Chicago a couple of years before, and gone to Taos.[45]

Riding the Santa Fe Railroad into New Mexico on the second day out from Chicago, Baumann saw the dawn break on a landscape that could not fail to impress a flatlander from the Midwest.

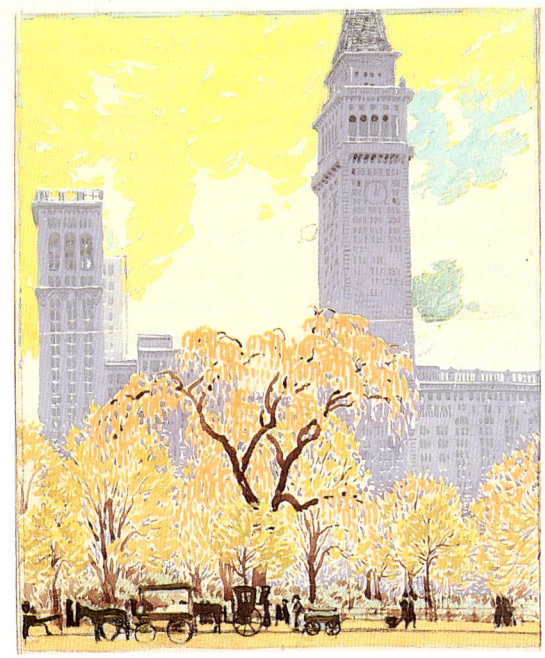 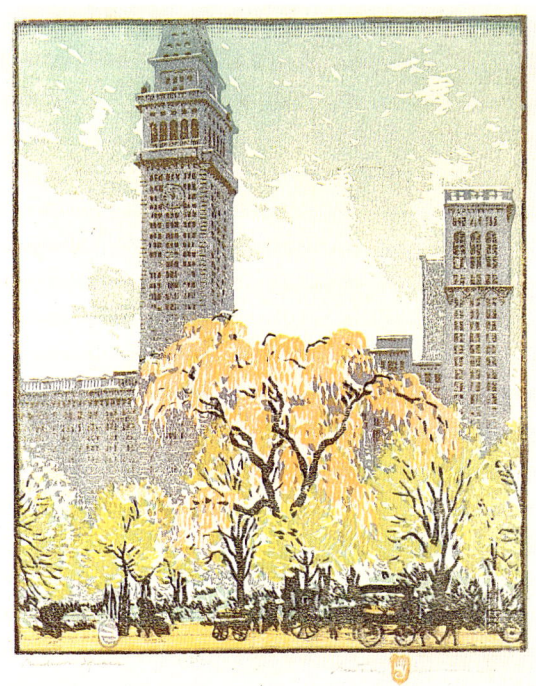

24. MADISON SQUARE, 1917

Gouache, 13⅜ × 11¼ in.

25. MADISON SQUARE, 1917

Color woodcut, 13¼ × 11 in.

Instead of the familiar well-ordered farms and green woods of that region, New Mexico offered a sweeping dun-colored earth punctuated by juniper and piñon and out of which adobe houses emerged as if having been grown. Hills and mesas seemed just to occur, and the distant mountains were all around. Fifty years later Baumann still remembered his introduction to the Southwest:

There is no mountain so tall as when you see it from level prairie ground: There it is, bathed in inscrutable blue. The train engine gives a whistle as if the engineer saw it too. While it is an old story to him, the passengers feel as if they are getting somewhere different from where they've been and read the railway folder for perhaps the tenth time. They reset their watches from Standard to Mountain time and glue their noses to the windows.[46]

Baumann landed in Taos ahead of Ufer's summer arrival and by early July was made note of in the local papers.[47] The art community was in full tilt. Some were familiar faces from Chicago: Higgins was there, as were Harriet Blackstone, Ethel Coe, and Henry Balink.[48] Old-timers in residence included Oscar Berninghaus, Joseph Henry Sharp, E. Irving Couse, and Ernest Blumenschein and Bert Phillips who together had discovered Taos for outside artists twenty years before. There were newer arrivals fleeing the war in Europe: the Julius Rolshovens and the Burt Harwoods; and those of a more modernist sensibility such as Leo Stein, Leon Gaspard, Paul Burlin, and Marsden Hartley. Baumann recorded his first impressions of the group in a letter to a friend back in Indianapolis: "You probably will be surprised at my sudden jump but here I am, after deciding that no matter how many people liked the East, I did not. It is a little too hot to do much work, but wonderful material and an interesting bunch of folks working. . . ."[49] But, as he concluded his letter, "the world is so beautiful it is difficult to restrain the gypsy instinct and I will probably move again."

By the end of the summer he was tiring of "interesting folk" and the atmosphere of the Taos art colony, just as he probably had tired of the colonies of Brown County and Provincetown. As he remembered the situation, "I found [Taos] a wonderful place to work but difficult to live in. A concentration of high-powered artists brings its subtle problems."[50] For this reason, and finding himself financially strapped, Baumann left Taos in October 1918 and stopped in Santa Fe to open his Museum of Fine Arts exhibition. He had every intention of moving on after a few days, for Chicago and New York.[51] A timely loan of five hundred dollars arranged by Paul Walter, curator at the museum, made it possible for him to stay on. In the work space provided in the museum basement, he carved into wood the sketches he had made in Taos. Early in the following year he sent east for his presses.[52]

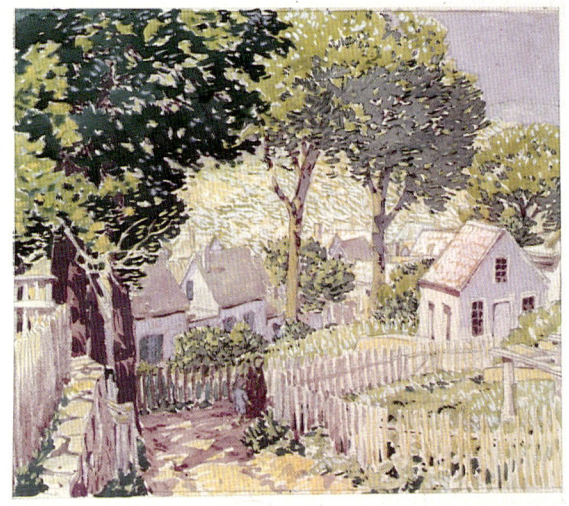 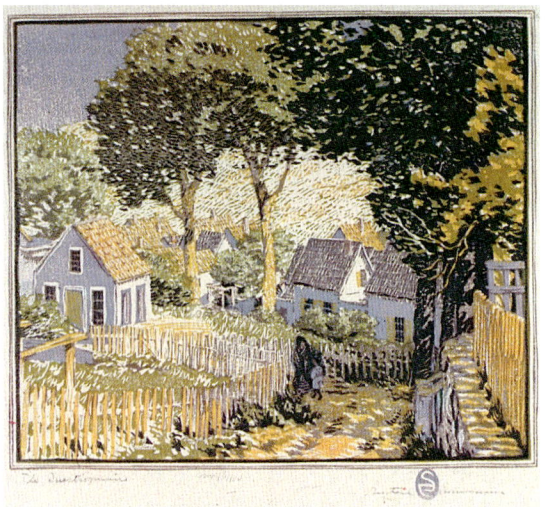

26. THE QUESTIONNAIRE, *ca.* 1917

Gouache, 14 × 18 in.

27. THE QUESTIONNAIRE, 1917

Color woodcut, 9½ × 11 in.

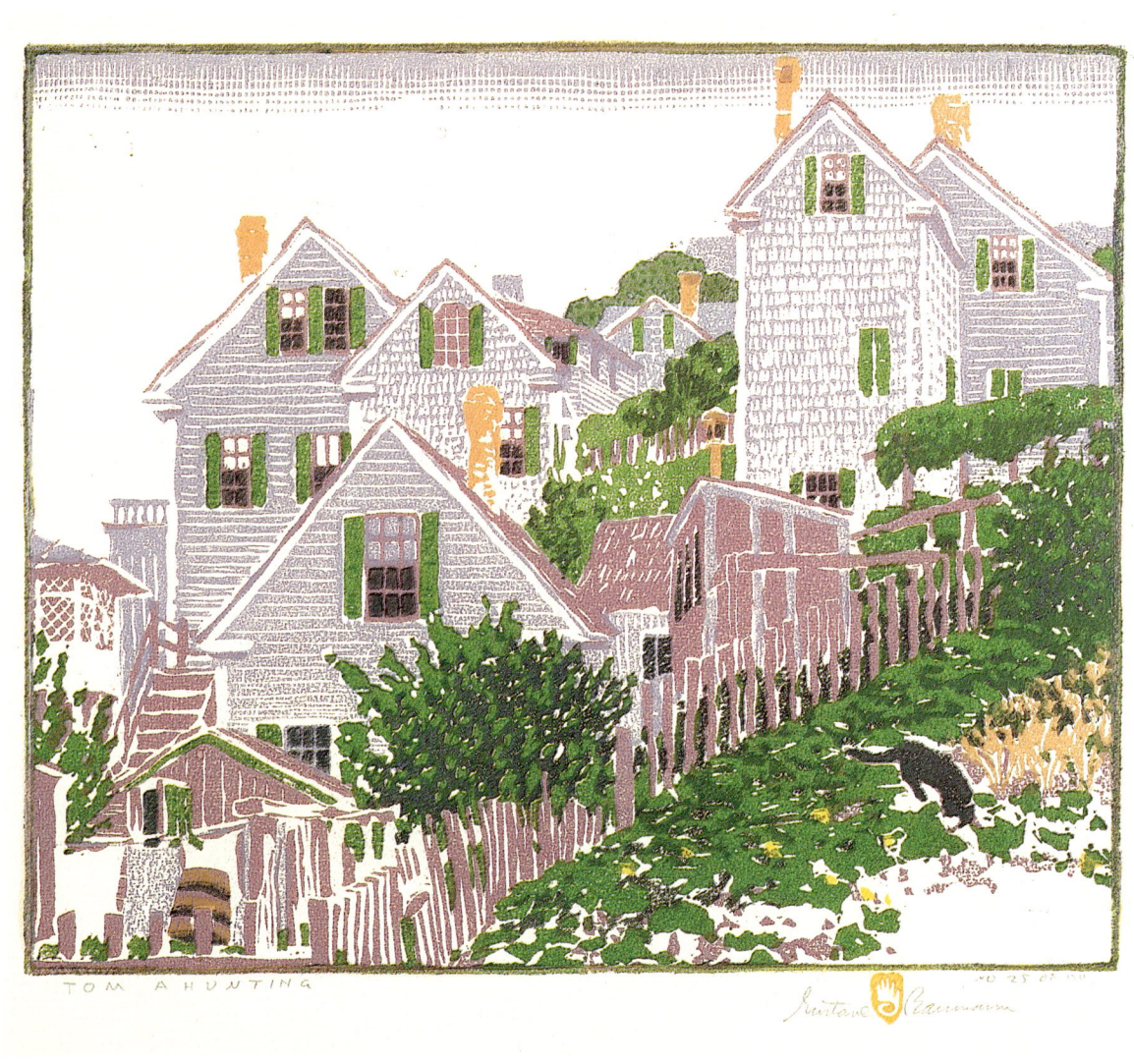

TOM A HUNTING

28. TOM A HUNTING, 1917

Color woodcut, 11 × 13¼ in.

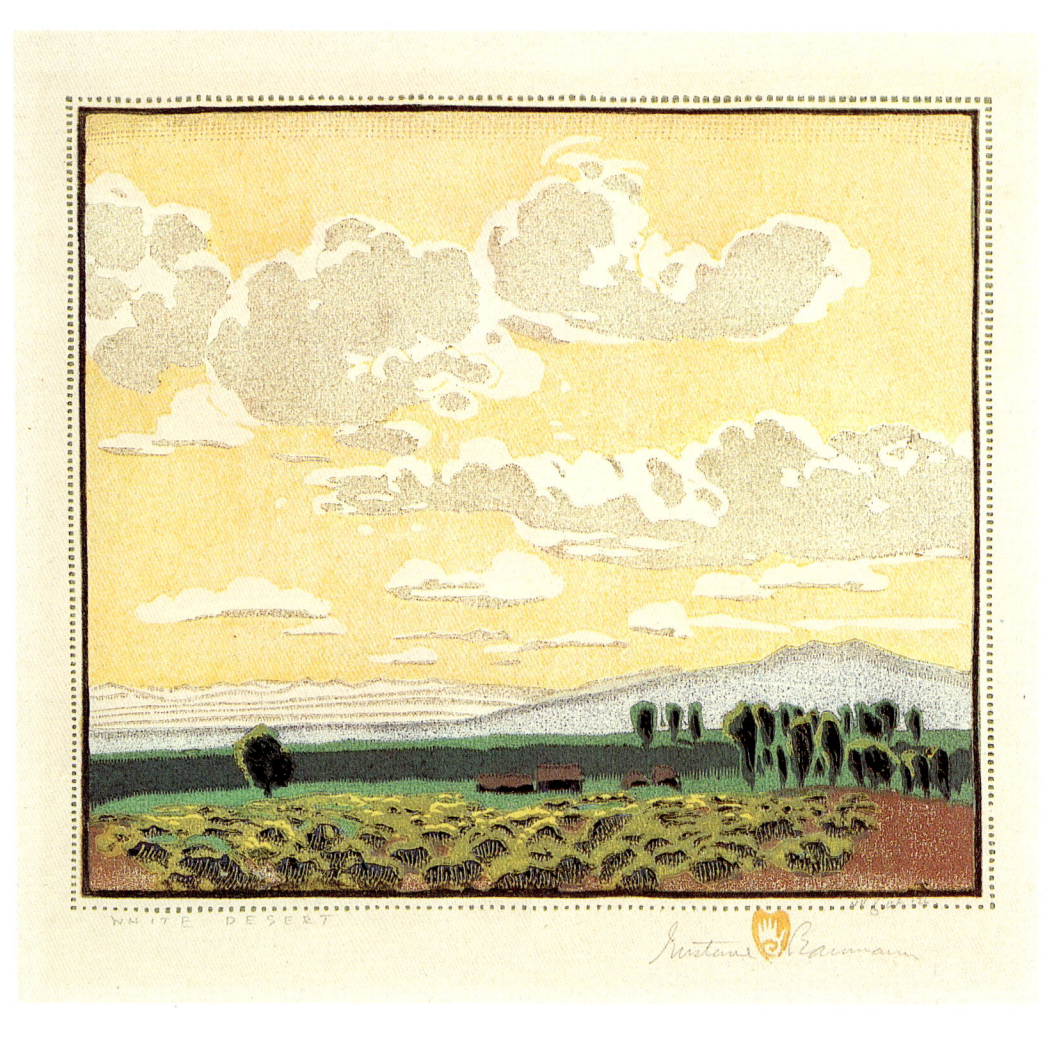

WHITE DESERT

29. WHITE DESERT, 1930

Color woodcut, 9½×11⅛ in.

GUSTAVE BAUMANN
IN THE WEST

David Acton

"Given a free choice in the matter," Gustave Baumann once wrote, "I would have selected the Southwest as the place to be born. I would then have learned Spanish, along with riding a horse and predicting the weather."[1] In fact, the artist lived and worked in New Mexico for more than fifty years, and views of the West provided subjects for the majority of his prints and the basis of his enduring reputation as an artist in America. The landscape of the West and the culture and art of its native peoples influenced and molded his style as a printmaker.

Before his arrival in New Mexico, Baumann was a professional graphic designer and printmaker, trained and practicing in the European tradition. His art education in Chicago and Germany was quite conventional, and he was little influenced by the newest avant-garde styles. Rather, it was the customs and techniques of Old World craftsmanship, and especially the traditions of accessible German folk art, that moved him. Baumann cherished his privacy and preferred to live simply, close to nature. Thus he found Brown County, Indiana, and its artists' colony at Nashville, to be an ideal place to pursue his art. His contentment there was reflected in adept, straightforward prints that depict a wholesome, rural American life-style. Meant to appeal to a wide audience, these woodcuts are imbued both with the rugged fertility of the Midwest and the artist's abundant sympathy for the region. During more than six years' activity in Indiana, Baumann strove to transform his devotion to printmaking into a career, and enduring elements of his style and working methods developed at this time. He experimented with etchings and aquatints printed in color, the technique most favored by the local Brown County printmakers, but felt that he had "no feel for metal or the sensitive line of an etching. . . ."[2] He refined his block carving and printing techniques, especially concentrating on multicolored prints. Yet his woodcuts of this period have a distinctly European look, more closely resembling the prints of German artists like Switbert Lobisser, Frido Witte, or Karl Hennemann than those of contemporary American printmakers who specialized in country subjects.[3] While such American artists as Asa Cheffetz and Thomas W. Nason also produced bucolic rural landscapes, their more precise, miniaturist manner was inherited from American wood engravers of the nineteenth century.[4] Baumann admitted that he lacked the "delicate but rigid touch necessary [for] engraving on box wood."[5]

His early woodcuts generally were narrative vignettes in heavy, stylized decorative frames; they often incorporated typography. By the 1910s these prints began to lose their illustrative bookishness as characteristics of the Arts and Crafts movement gradually appeared and Baumann's images became more picturesque than anecdotal. These Indiana woodcuts reflected their making in the patterning made by regular gouge marks in the wood. They displayed stylized, dotted, or decorative white-line cross-hatching, along with multiple and dashed-border lines that the printmaker would continue to use throughout his oeuvre. The palette of Baumann's Midwest prints was cool and subdued, reflecting not only the muted hues of the region but also the soft pastels favored by the Brown County etchers. The artist developed a habit of highlighting and enlivening the compositions of his color prints with touches of bright local color. He also adapted the flowing contour lines that circumscribed forms into component cells in colleague Louis O. Griffith's color aquatints.

It was during his years in Indiana that Baumann developed his personal seal, representing the image of a human hand opened over the heart, a gesture meant to imply a heartfelt pledge or the symbol of giving. This was an appropriate emblem for a devoted craftsman who found ultimate fulfillment in working with his hands.[6] From this time on the symbol nearly always appeared with the artist's signature in the lower-right margin of his prints. Usually colored cadmium orange, the seal was often printed from a separate stamp.[7] When he reprinted woodcuts from blocks made before its development, the artist even substituted the heart-and-hand mark for his earlier monograms.

From 1912 through 1916, Baumann periodically returned to Chicago for commercial artwork that helped to financially sustain his Nashville printmaking workshop. It was during this period that he began to think seriously about New Mexico. He had first heard of the area years earlier during his employment with the design firm of Curtis Gandy, among whose clients was the Santa Fe Railroad, requiring Gandy to live in Albuquerque for a period. From there he reported his New Mexico adventures in letters sent back to Baumann at the home office. These missives contained detailed accounts of Indian life in Hopi country and the Rio Grande pueblos. When he returned, Gandy brought with him a collection of Indian crafts and artifacts, and for months afterward the unreceptive Baumann was subjected to his colleague's memories of New Mexico. Several years later, during one of his necessary Chicago stints, Baumann encountered Walter Ufer, a painter and designer of his acquaintance who had studied in Dresden and Munich. Despite his sophistication, this artist was incurably charmed by New Mexico and could talk of nothing but his plans to return there.[8] Baumann decided that he had to see the Southwest for himself, and he made plans to meet Ufer and Victor Higgins in Taos in the summer of 1916. It wasn't until spring of 1918 that his plans coalesced.

Traveling on the Santa Fe Railroad, enjoying the amenities of Harvey House hotels along the way, it took Baumann thirty-six hours on the rails from Chicago to Lamy. There he boarded a narrow-gauge train connecting to Taos junction. The magnificent landscape mesmerized and exhilarated him, for it seemed so strange, exotic, and ancient. "I recall seeing Taos from the Ranchos side [west] in the evening light as a thin line of houses that seemed to be of one piece," he wrote. "It looked like something out of biblical history that had been preserved all these years."[9] Overwhelmed by the country's natural beauty, the artist frantically filled his sketchbooks. He found that nearly every village alleyway provided an engaging image, and he felt free to give personal interpretation to his landscapes. Baumann also was captivated by the seclusion of Taos, and felt in harmony with nature and the native peoples there. He discovered a solitude and artistic inspiration that he had long been seeking, similar to that which he had known in Indiana.

The influence of New Mexico on Baumann's woodcuts was gradual. *La Loma, Taos* was among his first prints executed in the West (plate 32). While the painted gouache model for this print seems naturalistic and evocative, the woodcut is quite similar to the prints that the artist had made in Provincetown, Massa-

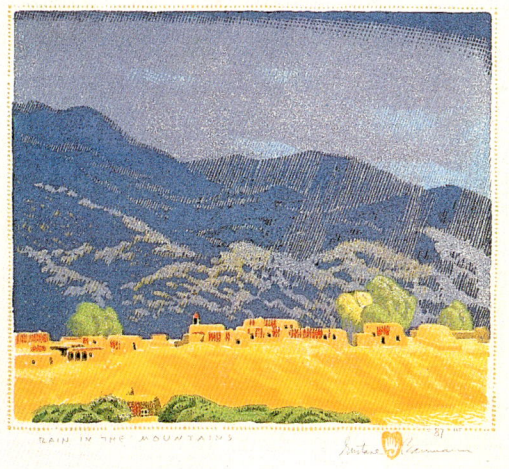

30. RAIN IN THE MOUNTAINS, 1926

Color woodcut, 9×11 in.

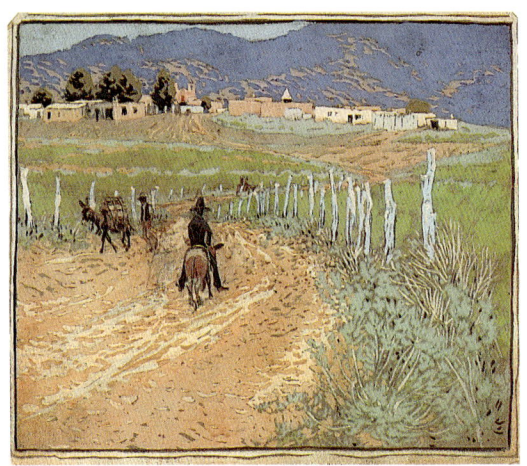

31. UNTITLED
(LA LOMA, TAOS), 1919
Gouache, 9½ × 10¼ in.

chusetts, in the summer of 1917. The horizon is set high in the composition, and the viewer overlooks the scene as if standing on a hilltop. In the woodcut Baumann altered the central figures of his painting, a burro and rider ambling up the road. The dominant pastel earth tones are little different from those of his Provincetown prints, which were suggested by the washlike watercolors favored by the woodcut artists of Cape Cod. Baumann also cut his blocks to allow the color of the paper to show through, creating foreground highlights where cells of printed color are separated by white lines. This device is similar to the look and method of the single-block color woodcuts of Provincetown.[10]

After several weeks of working in Taos, Baumann made an arduous car trip south to explore Santa Fe. This town seemed a little quieter, and its artists' community less self-consciously bombastic. "The town as a whole gave one the feeling of a fairly well-adjusted mixture of Spanish and Anglo culture," he wrote, "with the Indians as an uninterrupted civilization still pervading it all, making for a unique situation not likely to be found anywhere else."[11] Baumann was delighted by the new Santa Fe fine arts museum, where he found paintings by many of his Taos friends, some of which he had seen in progress. He was welcomed by the museum's director, Dr. Edgar Lee Hewett, and its curator Paul Walter. Like Baumann, Walter was a German émigré, and friendship between the two men was immediate.

"I became painfully aware that the summer was drawing to a close," Baumann remembered. "I had investigated the mountain and desert and all the fascinating corners of Taos, but learned too late that a palette and theories regarding color East of the Mississippi should all be tossed in the river as you cross the bridge. My summer's work looked very sad indeed. I felt I wanted another try at this obstreperous material."[12] He decided to settle in Santa Fe permanently and planned a return to Chicago, where he could earn enough in commercial design to finance the move and his first uncertain months in New Mexico. However, Walter convinced him that this postponement was unnecessary; the curator provided some financial support and arranged a work space in the museum basement. The Santa Fe Bank agreed that an investment in this ob-

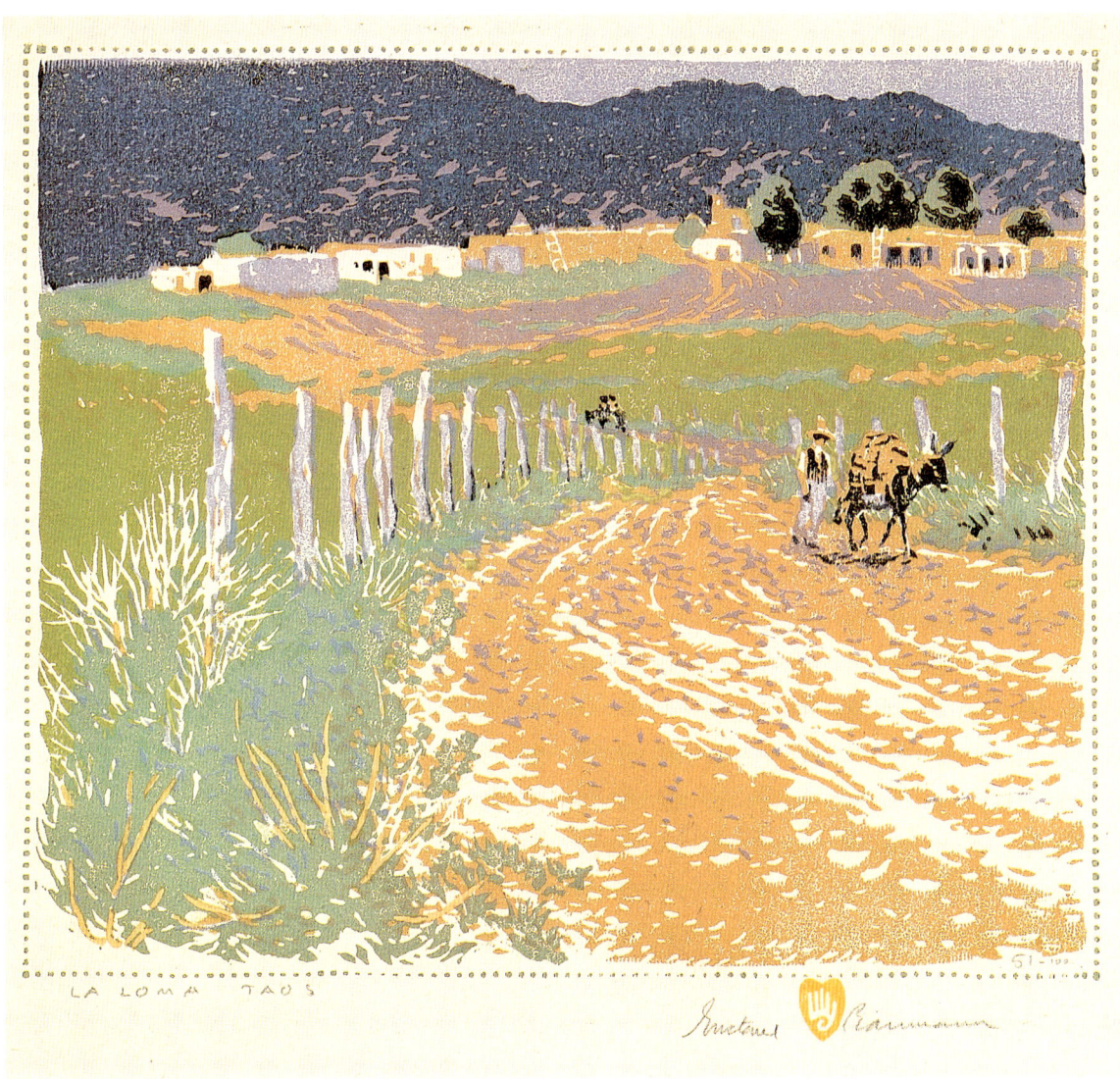

32. LA LOMA, TAOS, 1919

Color woodcut, 9½ × 11¼ in.

viously talented young artist was a safe one, and Baumann was soon settled comfortably.[13]

At first, the artist rented a little house on the old Canyon Road at the corner of Garcia Street. The cottage had a garden full of zinnias and marigolds enclosed by a white picket fence, which made their way into Baumann's prints. Several gregarious artists lived in the neighborhood. Some were established figures, like John Sloan and Julius Rolshoven, who had come to New Mexico in search of peace and quiet and the inspiration of nature's grandeur.[14] Others, like Bau-

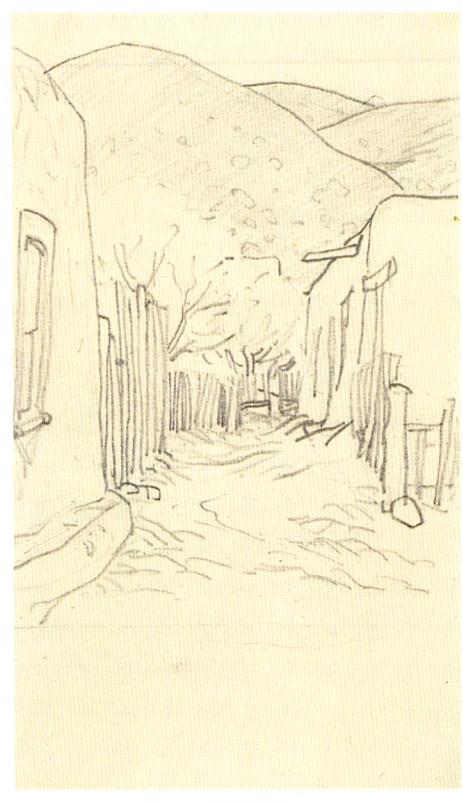

33. UNTITLED (PUEBLO SCENES,
DETAIL), N.D.
·
Pencil, 14 × 20 in.

mann, were young and ardent and seeking an affordable place where they could work in a supportive community. Their exotic new surroundings prompted several of these artists to affect the habits and trappings of cowboys and Indians, and they were always gathering for a party of some sort. Baumann became a popular and ubiquitous member of the artists' colony, joining in on every prank hatched by this mischievous fraternity. He was one of the group who helped establish Mary Austin's Community Theatre, and served as the designer, set builder, and stage manager for its inaugural production in 1919.[15]

After settling in his new home, Baumann worked to capture in his prints the spirit and atmosphere of New Mexico. He frequented nearby Bandelier National Monument in the Jémez Mountains west of Santa Fe, drawn by its magnificent natural beauty and fascinating archaeological sites where ancestors of the modern Pueblo people had lived for centuries beginning in the late 1100s. In Frijoles Canyon, the ruins of houses built from bricks of volcanic rock could be explored, along with cave dwellings excavated into the canyon walls. The site was still rich with artifacts. Enchanted, Baumann returned to these canyons regularly through the years and interpreted their mysteries in many paintings and prints. For the color woodcuts made at this time, the artist selected landscapes that were unmistakably southwestern and used peculiar points of view to emphasize their vast scale.[16] One of these prints, *Ceremonial Cave* (plate 34), shows how Baumann strove to break from the mood and style of his earlier woodcuts. The scene looks out from the cool, shaded cave entrance into glaring sunlight. An overhanging stone arch sweeps across the top of the composition and spirals away from the viewer, leading the eye into depth and giving a sensation of the enormity of the natural structure. Beyond, adobe and tufa brick dwellings cling to the cliff wall, buttressed there by repellent-looking yucca spikes. A deep vista at the print's edge

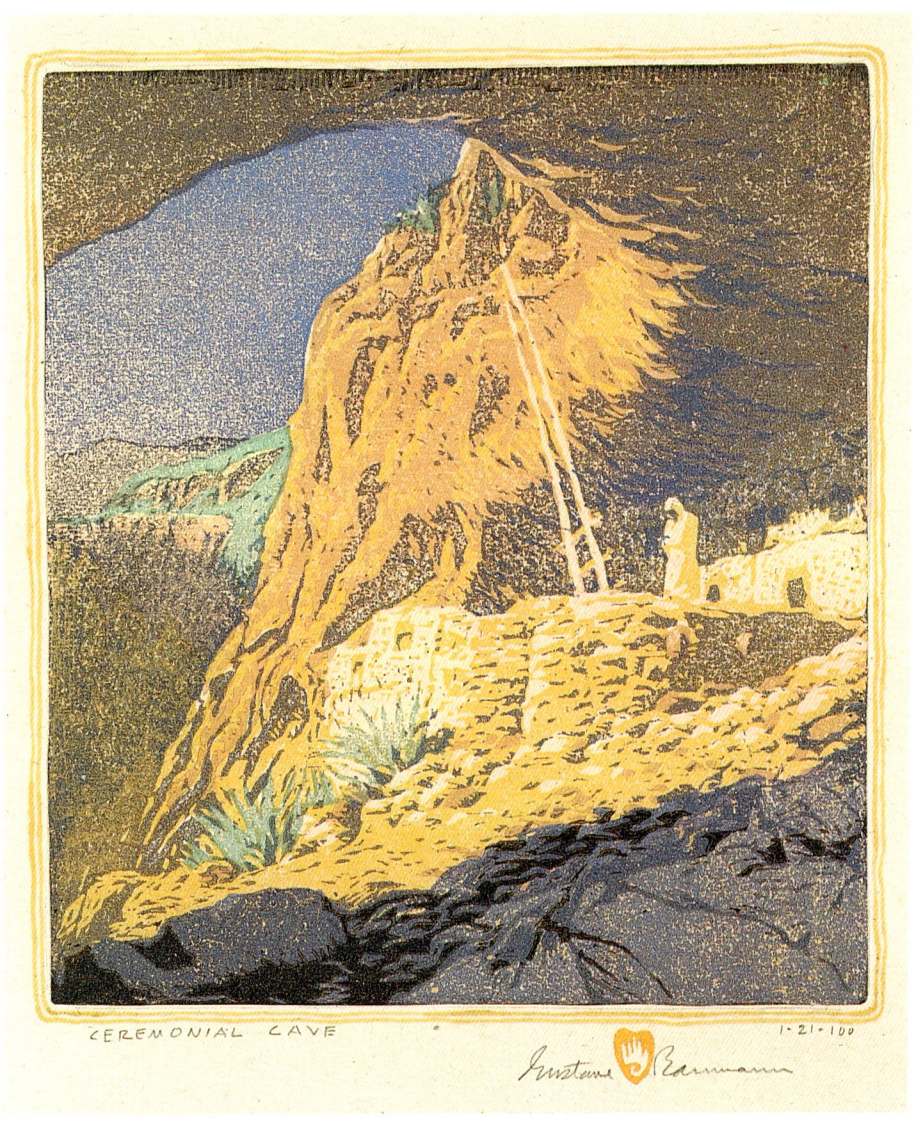

CEREMONIAL CAVE   1-21-100

Gustave Baumann

34. CEREMONIAL CAVE, 1919

Color woodcut, 10¾ × 9¾ in.

gives a glimpse of blue sky and the sheer walls of a distant canyon. Silent and enigmatic, a lone draped figure looks over the precipice, heightening the mystery of this image. Although this figure subtly implies that this is a sacred cave, it is a small unobtrusive detail that seems almost incidental. The artist employed a favorite device of dramatic shifts of light and color to enhance a sense of space, yet his palette remains fairly dim. Its softness even gives the sensation of blurred color that one experiences in the blindingly bright sunshine, when the pupils close down tightly.

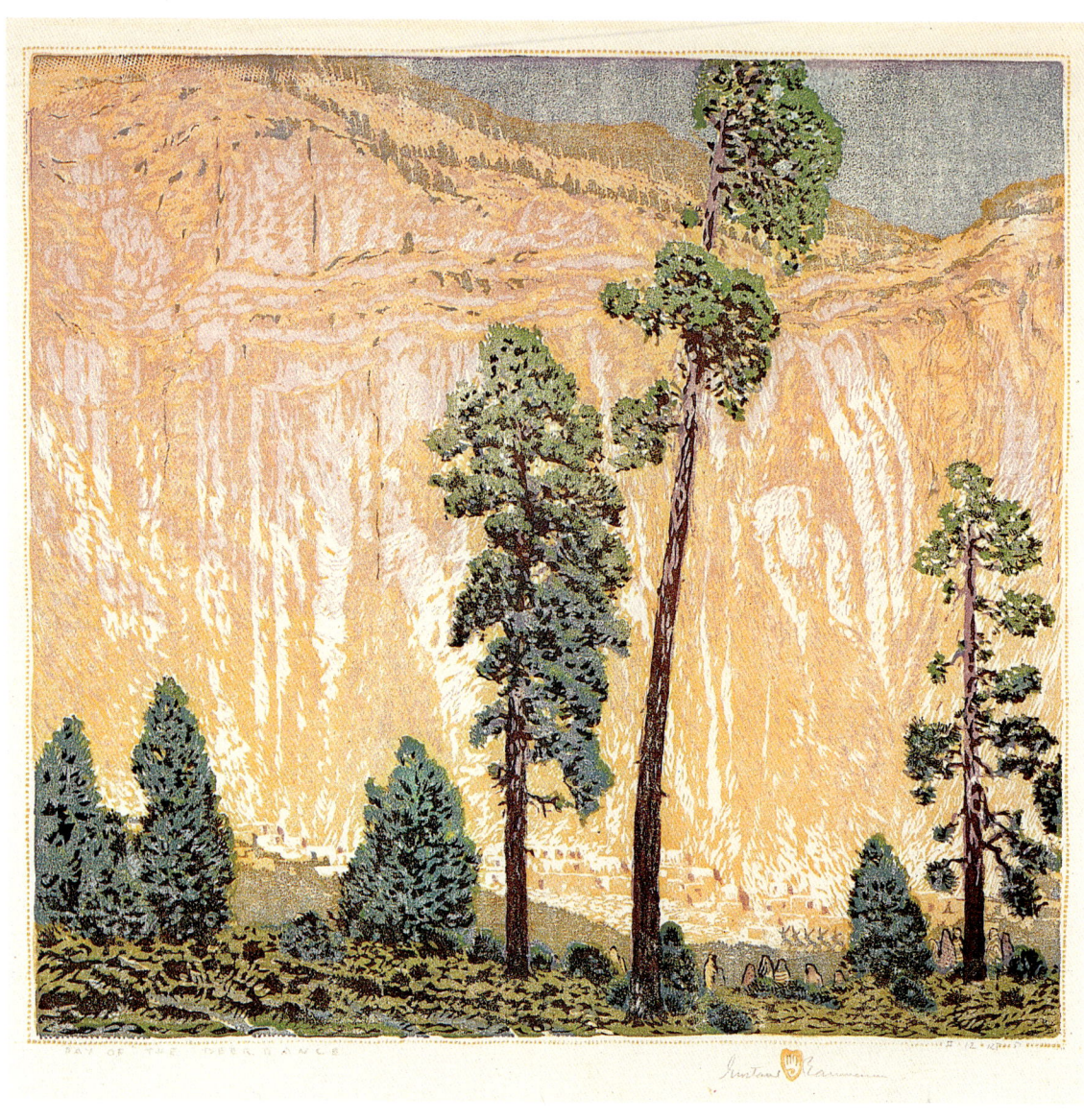

35 · DAY OF THE DEER DANCE, 1918–1919

Color woodcut, 19¼×21½ in.

It was during this time, in the spring of 1919, that Baumann also made his first prints of the Indian pictographs at Frijoles Canyon, recording in sketches and rubbings the ancient drawings and carvings found inside the cave dwellings (plate 47). The primal images he chose to translate into woodcut represent a ritual dance and preparations for the hunt, as well as the stalking and shooting of deer with bows and arrows on the mesa above the canyon. The artist was stirred by their economy and emotional impact and discovered in their formal vocabulary a strong par-

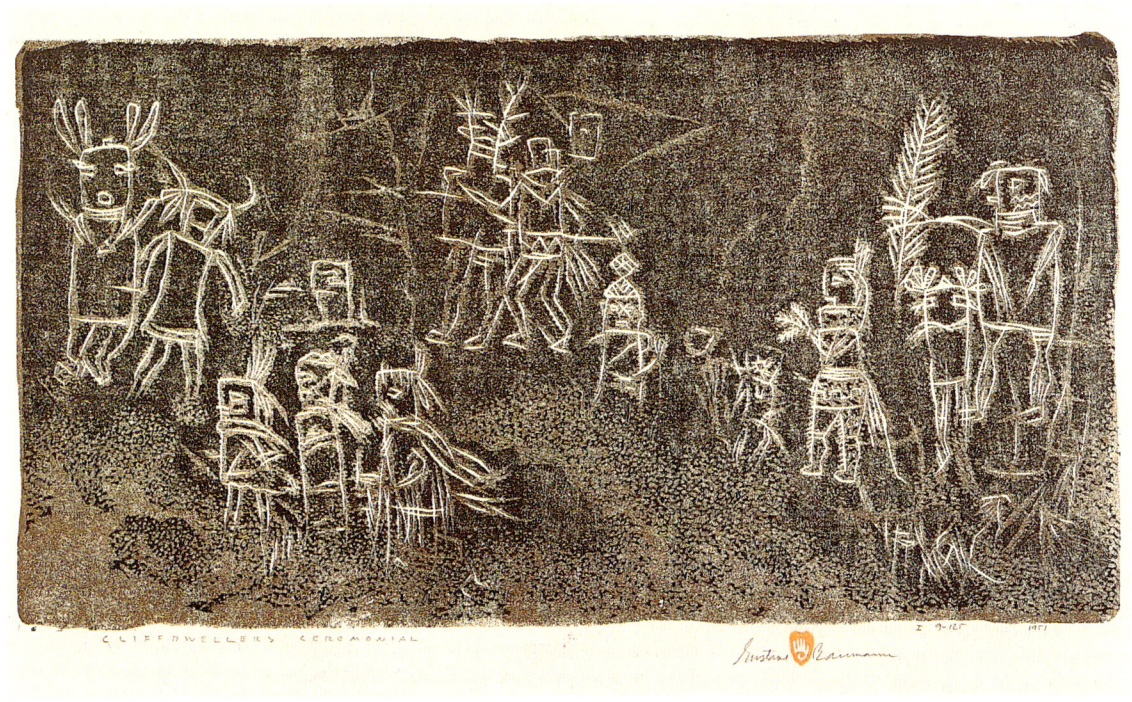

36. CLIFFDWELLERS CEREMONIAL, 1951

Color woodcut, 10⅝ × 20⅝ in.

allel with modern art.[17] In April 1919, soon after they were made, several of these prints were exhibited at The Art Institute of Chicago; in the following year they were shown in that city at the Cliff Dwellers Club.[18] These expansive, mysterious woodcuts marked a certain change from Baumann's snug Indiana views exhibited in Chicago in previous years.

In 1919 the artist saw the Grand Canyon for the first time. Like every visitor to this spectacle he was awestruck by its scale, its dramatic effects of atmosphere and light, and by its preternatural color. In the months following his return to Santa Fe, Baumann made five vivid color woodcuts that reflect the impact of this experience.[19] In the attempt to express its intensity, Baumann amplified his colors, mixing pure, brilliant hues, frequently placing them immediately alongside their complements, and overprinting in layers to enhance their saturation. These venturesome prints were remarkably successful in capturing the effects of thin, clear atmosphere and keen, crystalline light.

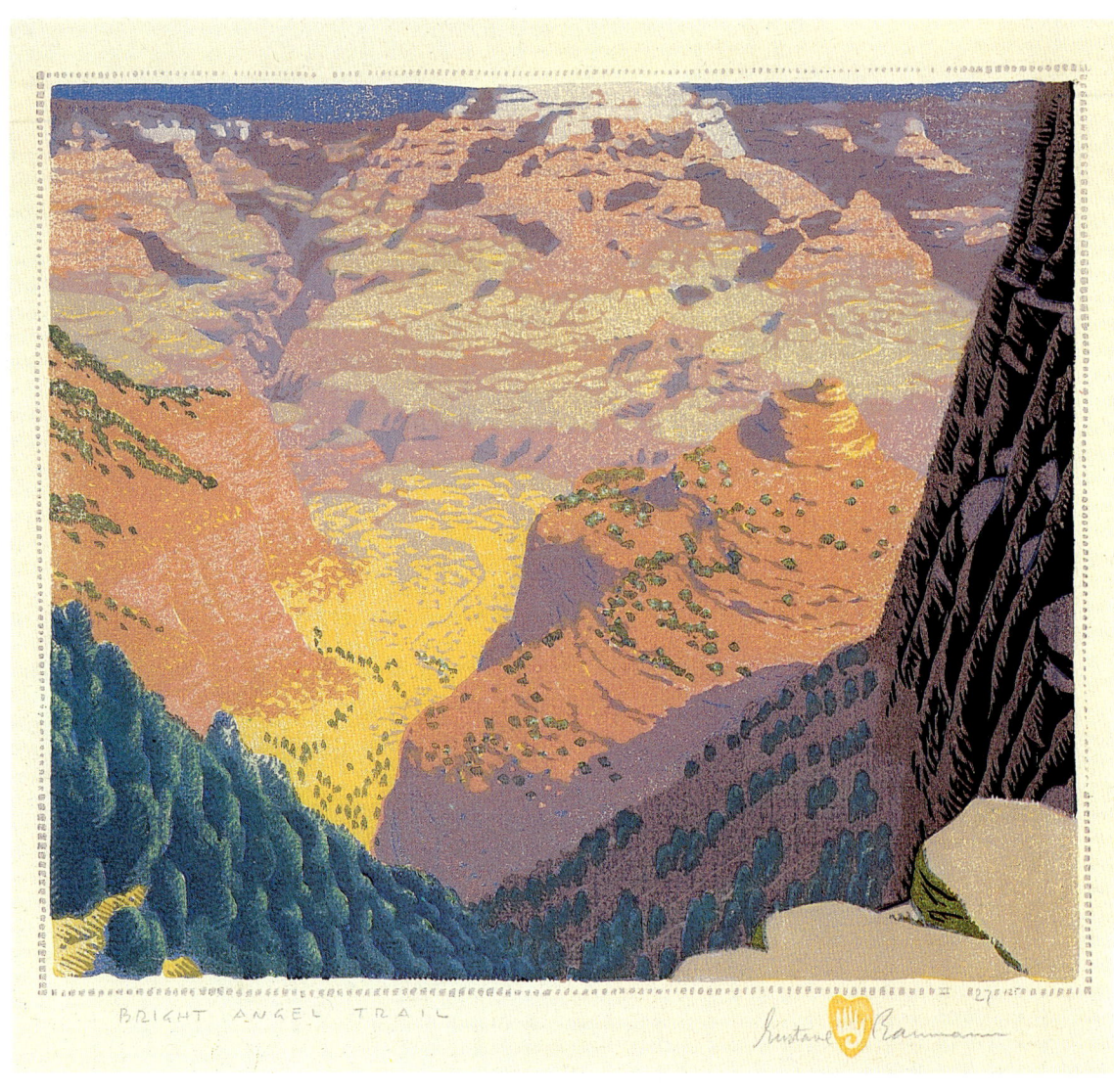

37. BRIGHT ANGEL TRAIL, 1921

Color woodcut, 9½ × 11⅛ in.

For example, Baumann's Grand Canyon view entitled *Bright Angel Trail* (plate 37) contrasts a range of purple, mauve, and buff pinks with highlights of rich lemon yellow. Glimmers of the same acid yellow on the butte in the middle ground show that this color was meant to represent alpenglow, the evening reillumination of cliff walls and summits observed after the chasms have passed into shadow. These hues seem fantastic to anyone who has never witnessed the magnificence of a Grand Canyon sunset. Baumann's daring composition looks over the edge of the south rim, down into the mile-deep gorge to where the serpentine trail winds down the abyss to the Colorado River and along Bright Angel Creek. The artist set his horizon at the top of the

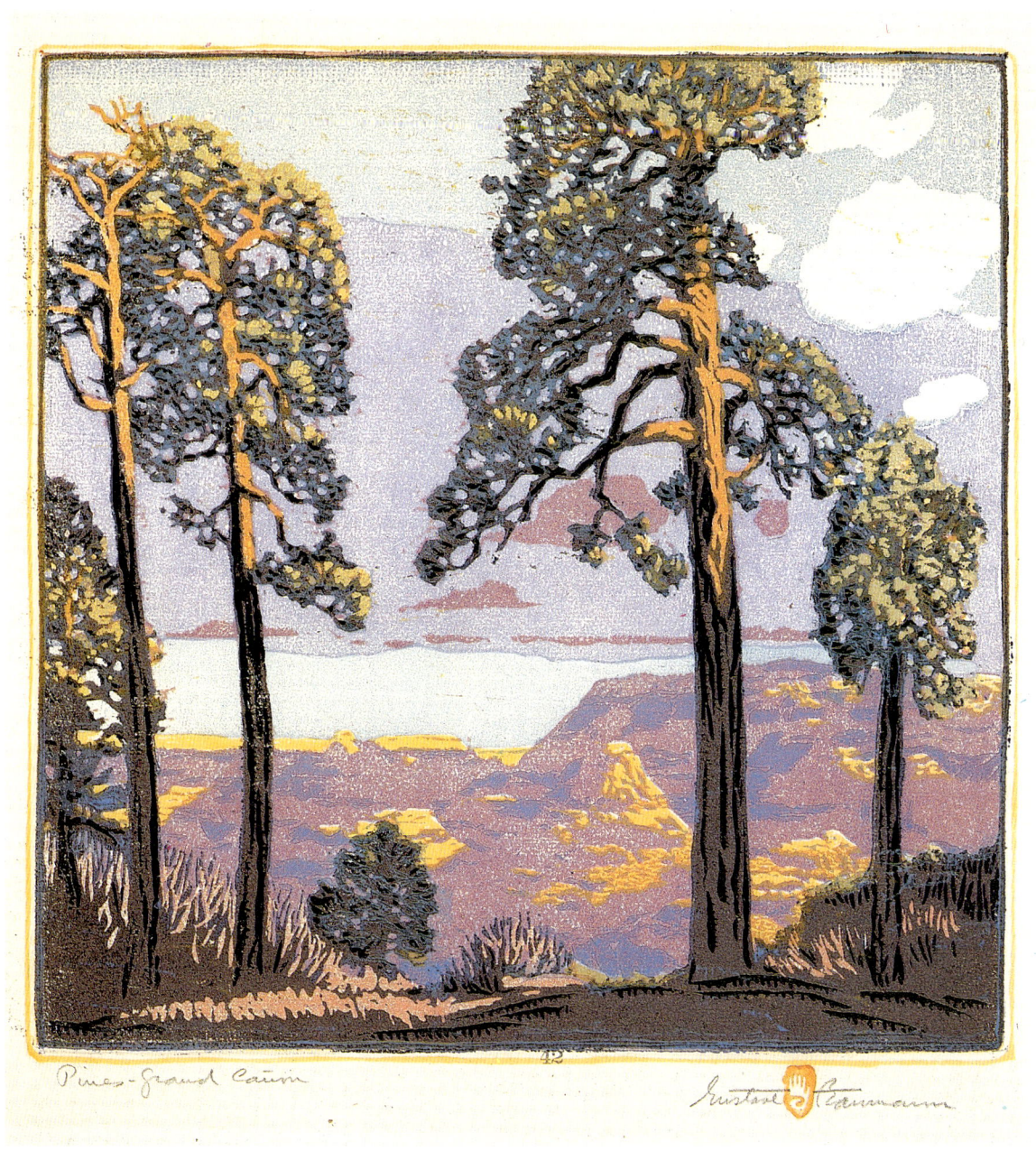

38. PINES – GRAND CAÑON, 1921

Color woodcut, 12⅞ × 12⅞ in.

composition, and the entire image is given to a nearly vertical view into the canyon. As the rocky forms begin to lose substance, eclipsed by the impact of their shifting, unnatural colors, Baumann's image approaches abstraction. In this sense it is reminiscent of the work of Arthur Wesley Dow. This prominent East Coast aesthetic theorist, art educator, and woodcut artist was enchanted by the Grand Canyon – as were his students Alvin Langdon Coburn and Georgia O'Keeffe – and he experimented with picturesque views that straddled the borders of non-objective abstraction.[20]

In the other Grand Canyon prints of the period, Baumann focused on foreground trees, ancient and windswept, with vast and vivid chasms falling away behind them. Such is the case in another sunset view, *Pines – Grand Cañon* (plate 38), where the landscape's scale is implied by the towering trees, highlighted at their tops with their bases in shadow. Purple and gold in the distance and the illuminated clouds contribute to the eerie drama of this image. In his succeeding prints the artist began to routinely use this bright new palette, suggestive of the clarity and saturation imparted by the intense southwestern sunlight and arid atmosphere. Baumann integrated major forms so that they appear inextricably bound together. He often implied details rather than painstakingly depicting them, and rhythmic, flowing lines and repetitive patterns often stylized his compositions. Yet the artist's goal was unchanged, for he sought above all to evoke natural ambiance and to depict the mercurial, sensuous effects of nature. Thus, ironically, the Grand Canyon, where colors seem unearthly and the effects of light exaggerated, spurred Baumann to a new, successfully evocative mode in his woodcuts.

The artist conscientiously worked at building a national reputation, regularly submitting his prints to exhibitions across the country. He sent seven color woodcuts of New Mexico subjects to the "Exhibition of Etchings and Block Prints" at The Art Institute of Chicago in spring of 1919.[21] A solo exhibition of Baumann's woodcuts was mounted at The Museum of History, Science and Art in Los Angeles in December 1919. Thirty-six prints were included, among them views from Indiana, Cape Cod, and New Mexico.[22] The landmark exhibition of American color woodcuts at the Detroit Institute of Arts was dominated by Baumann's prints; he even loaned a set of blocks to this show, along with a preparatory drawing and seven progressive proofs.[23] The following year he sent a handful of prints to the "First International Print Makers Exhibition" in Los Angeles, sponsored by the Print Makers Society of California. Over the next sixteen years, he contributed to most of this organization's influential annual exhibitions.[24]

In 1920 Baumann completed twelve prints of similar format and uniform sheet size, which he gathered together in the *New Mexico Portfolio*.[25] Small, immediately striking in their design, and attractive individually or as part of a suite, the woodcuts were conceived and designed primarily for tourists who visited the Southwest. The suite included views similar to those of the Grand Canyon prints, along with pleasing florals such as Baumann had long produced. The bulk of these new woodcuts represented picturesque landscapes of historic sites around Santa Fe,

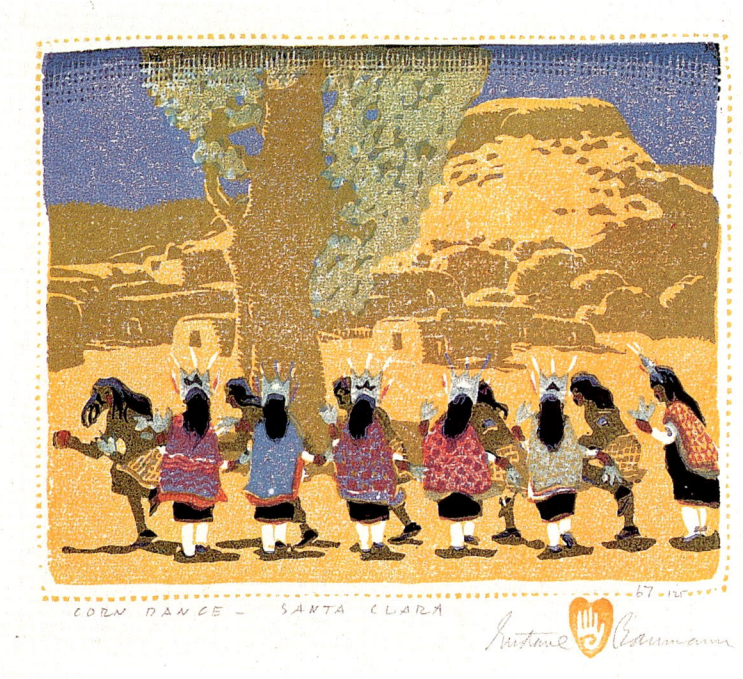

39. CORN DANCE – SANTA CLARA, *ca.* 1920
Color woodcut, 5⅞ × 7½ in.

including the *santuario* at Chimayó, Taos Pueblo during the feast of San Geronimo, and the pueblos of Santo Domingo and Santa Clara. In these prints, for the first time, Baumann methodically applied the saturated palette of his Grand Canyon prints to narrative subjects and figures primarily of a picturesque and decorative nature. Like a miniature stage set, nearly every composition is embellished with visual props typical of the Southwest: a burro grazing on the desert scrub or a bright string of drying red chiles.

Corn Dance – Santa Clara (plate 39), from this portfolio, depicts one of the most spectacular public dances of the Pueblos, performed during the summer for the ripening of the corn and a successful harvest. The position of the two lines of male and female dancers in Baumann's print pinpoints a specific moment in the dance's choreography. The artist silhouettes the frieze of figures before a cottonwood tree, distant adobe houses, and a towering butte. He economically renders this typically southwestern setting with just two tones of golden bronze while emphasizing shadows and the intensity of the sun. Most of the women are turned away from the viewer, with the men behind them screened from our view. Thus, our attention is directed away from individual personalities to the pattern made by the positions of bodies and the colors of costumes.

It was not long before Baumann outgrew his tiny Canyon Road cottage and the sometimes-distracting activity of the neighborhood. In 1921 he moved into a remodeled Methodist church on Santa Fe's lower San Francisco Street. One of the oldest buildings in the historic plaza area, the church stood back from the road, leaving room for a front garden. Tall side windows flooded the spacious nave with north light, making it ideal for a studio; two small classrooms under the choir loft had been converted into bedroom and kitchen. A soothing ambiance was created by a colony of pigeons that roosted in the bell tower and cooed unceasingly. Here Baumann was exposed to life beyond the art colony, as San Francisco Street at the time bordered a rough neighborhood of unsavory characters. During the two years he lived there, Baumann met several "wild-west" eccentrics.[26]

The enduring popularity of his landscapes, combined with his own insatiable wanderlust, induced Baumann to continue his travels in the West, and late in the summer of 1920 he took a sketching trip to northern New Mexico. He made many gouache paintings in the upper Pecos River Valley, from which ten woodcuts were later executed at his Santa Fe studio. These prints approximate a visual diary of the artist's wilderness excursion. It was golden autumn in the high country, while the valley meadows remained green and lush, an elevational range that Baumann unified with his palette. The woodcuts capture the glowing chartreuse hues of the mountains as the deep green of the aspen leaves begin to fade to a yellow made all the more luminous by the autumn sun. Small daubs of color, applied and often overprinted in almost pointillist fashion, convey the look and method of Baumann's gouache preparatory models in a manner appropriate to their subject. The stippled quality of New Mexico's autumn colors and the shimmering effect of aspen leaves quavering in the wind are tellingly conveyed.

Mountain Pool (plate 40) is an outstanding print from this group, one that skillfully evokes a captivating atmosphere with illusive effects of space, light, and color. Surrounded by a ring of aspen trees, a quiet pond stands dappled and reflective in the sunshine. At the same time, long shadows suggest a radiant evening. While the foreground screen of tree trunks is in shadow, those on the opposite bank are bathed in warm, alluring light. Silhouetted branches and their scattered leaves above, along with the shaded jumble of brush on the forest floor, frame this vista, imparting a sense of discovery and enhancing the inviting promise of warmth and tranquility beyond. For this composition, as in all of his Pecos River Valley prints, Baumann em-

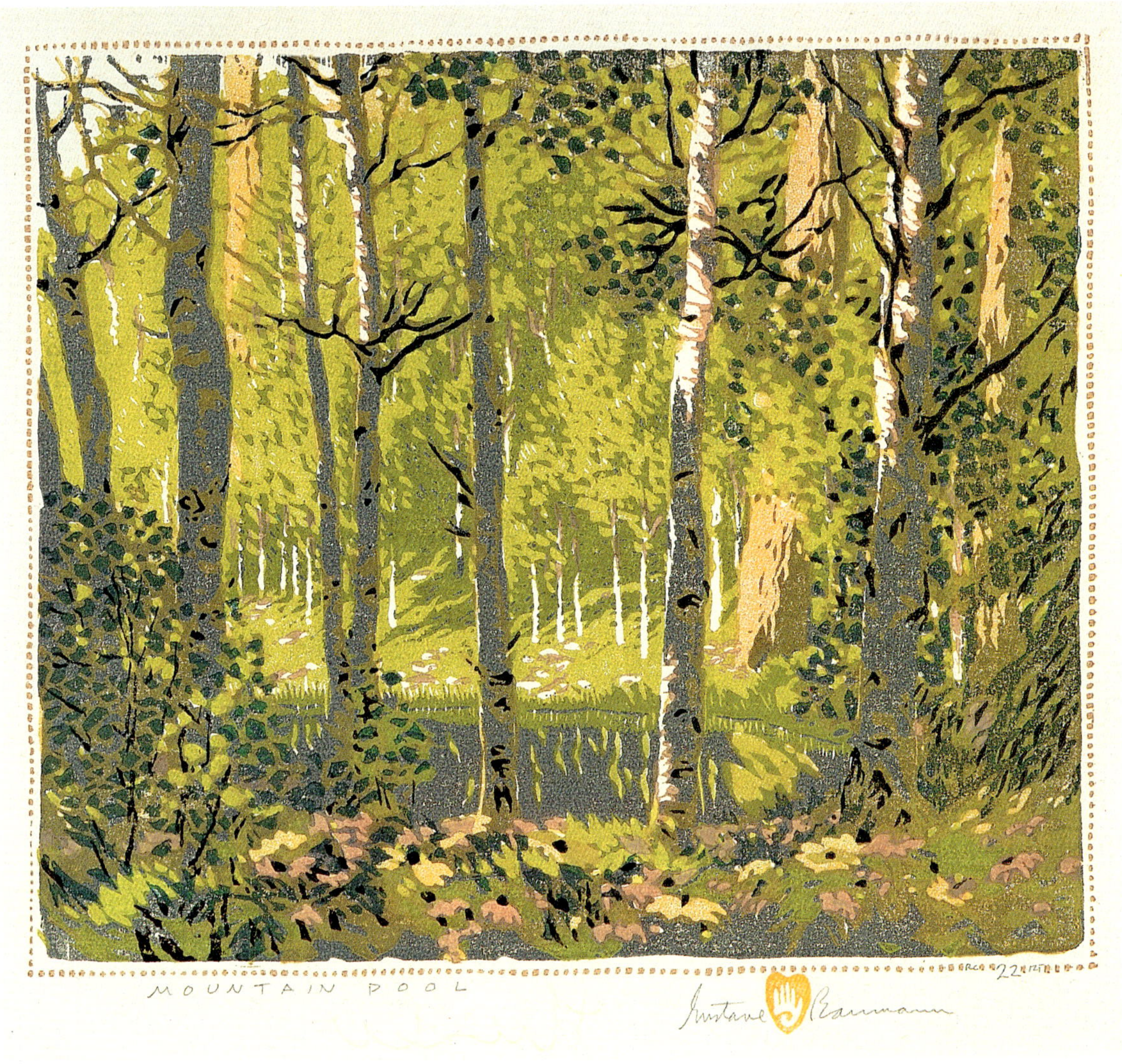

40. MOUNTAIN POOL, 1920

Color woodcut, 9½ × 11⅛ in.

ployed a proven formulaic scheme. In *Mountain Pool*, the dramatically lighted portal configuration is reminiscent of Baumann's *Summer Shadows* (plate 72), made in Wyoming, New York, nearly five years before.

The decade of the 1920s was a golden era for Gustave Baumann's color prints. He worked steadily with great commitment, producing as many as sixty color woodcuts in these years. This work sustained his reputation nationally, while his gregarious enthusiasm assured his continued prom-

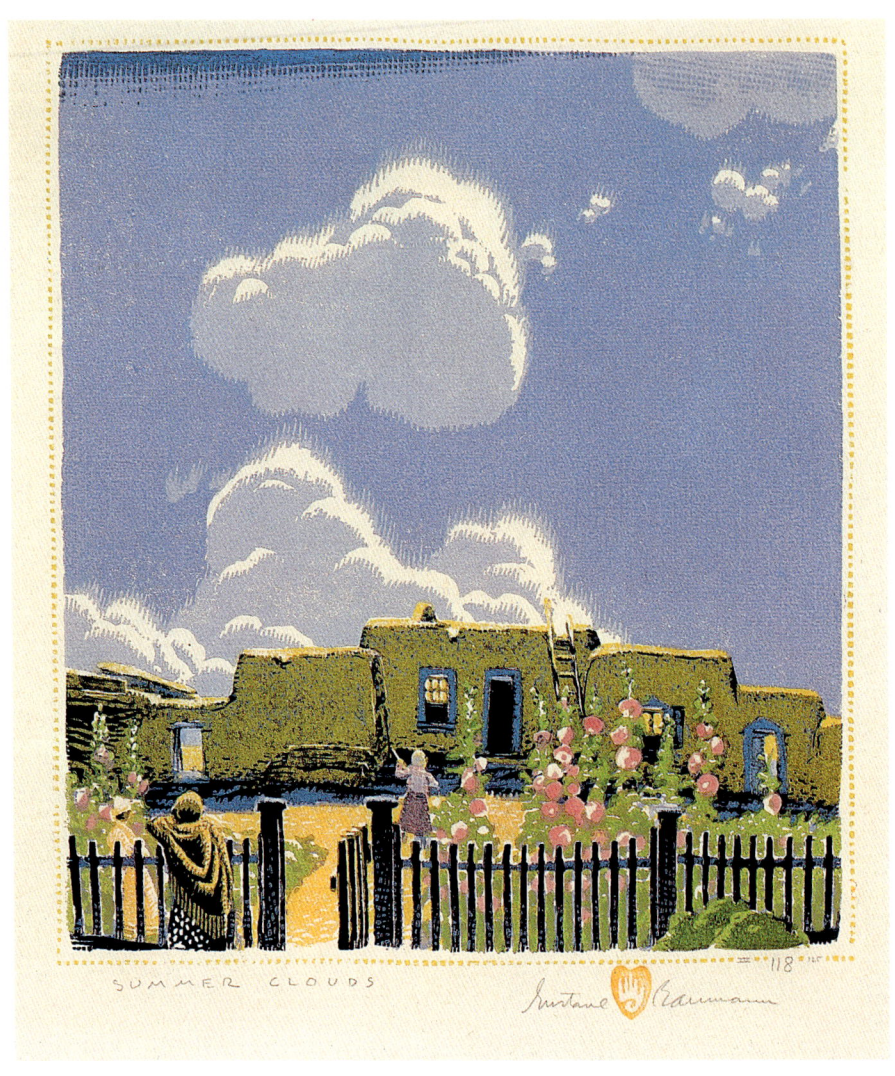

41. SUMMER CLOUDS, *ca.* 1923
Color woodcut, 10¾×9½ in.

inence in the local artistic community. He was among a group of artists who formed the Society of New Mexico Painters in 1922. He also helped organize the Santa Fe Art Club, which, like the Taos Society of Artists, intended to sponsor national group exhibitions of members' paintings.[27] Baumann's prints of this period ranged widely in their imagery but generally were bright, boldly designed, and recognizably western. The woodcut *Summer Clouds* (plate 41), created in Santa Fe about 1923, is typical of this time. The artist leads the viewer in a friendly impromptu visit to the cozy home of a New Mexican neighbor.[28] The adobe's low profile and earthen hues grow naturally from the landscape, yet these colors are almost complementary to the surrounding sky. The juxtaposition seems to push the house forward. In the wingwalls flanking the building, doors stand open to reveal the sky beyond, enhancing the illusion of depth. A picket fence and a screen of hollyhocks impede our approach only momentarily, for the front gate and door stand hospitably open. We identify with the woman who leans on the fence with her back to us, watching or chatting with the homeowner as he sweeps the front path. This uncomplicated, welcoming vision of a simple life-style, which is strongly localized, pleasant, and picturesque, demonstrates why Baumann's prints were so broadly popular.

The traditional southwestern *casita* of *Summer Clouds*, with its adobe and mud plaster walls and fenced front yard full of flowers, is similar to the home that Baumann built for himself in Santa Fe in 1923. That house still stands at 409 Camino de las Animas, near the northeast corner of the Old Santa Fe Trail, and retains much of its individuality. The artist himself designed the functional bachelor's cottage (his bachelorhood would end in 1925), organized around a large studio. Working plans were drafted by the architect T. Charles Gaastra and the house built by the architect's brother, contractor George Gaastra.[29] The front façade is dominated by a slightly projecting entrance block, with a small porch and canopy supported by wooden posts that Baumann carved and decorated. Along the street he constructed a low fence picketed with natural logs and a wooden gate of sawtooth slats that resemble the design of an Indian blanket. In time, Virginia creeper enveloped the fence. On the roof of the house still stands Baumann's wrought iron ornament in the form of a bemused face, designed from the letters of the word *"Koshare."* This clownish but sacred character of traditional Pueblo ceremony captivated the artist and was a source of identification. Occasionally he used this *Koshare* pictogram in place of his signature in oil paintings.[30]

One entered the Baumann house into a long, central space illuminated by a skylight; this served as reception room and gallery. Along the top of the walls here, and in most of the rooms

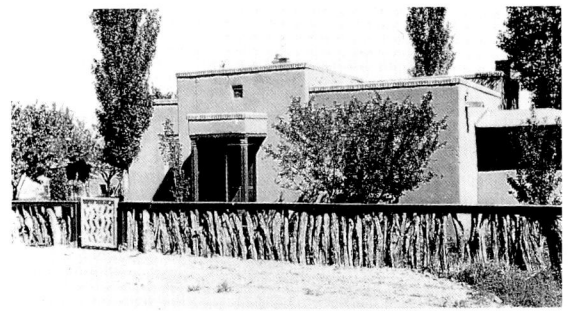

The Baumann residence at
409 Camino de las Animas, ca. 1925.

in the house, the artist painted a colorful ornamental band in patterns derived from Indian design. In two corners of the gallery are radiators, hidden behind wooden screens made of panels and slats from disused printing blocks; their carved surfaces and the absorbed ink colors enhance their decorative effect. Over the fireplace in a rear corner of the gallery was mounted Baumann's long two-panel woodcut

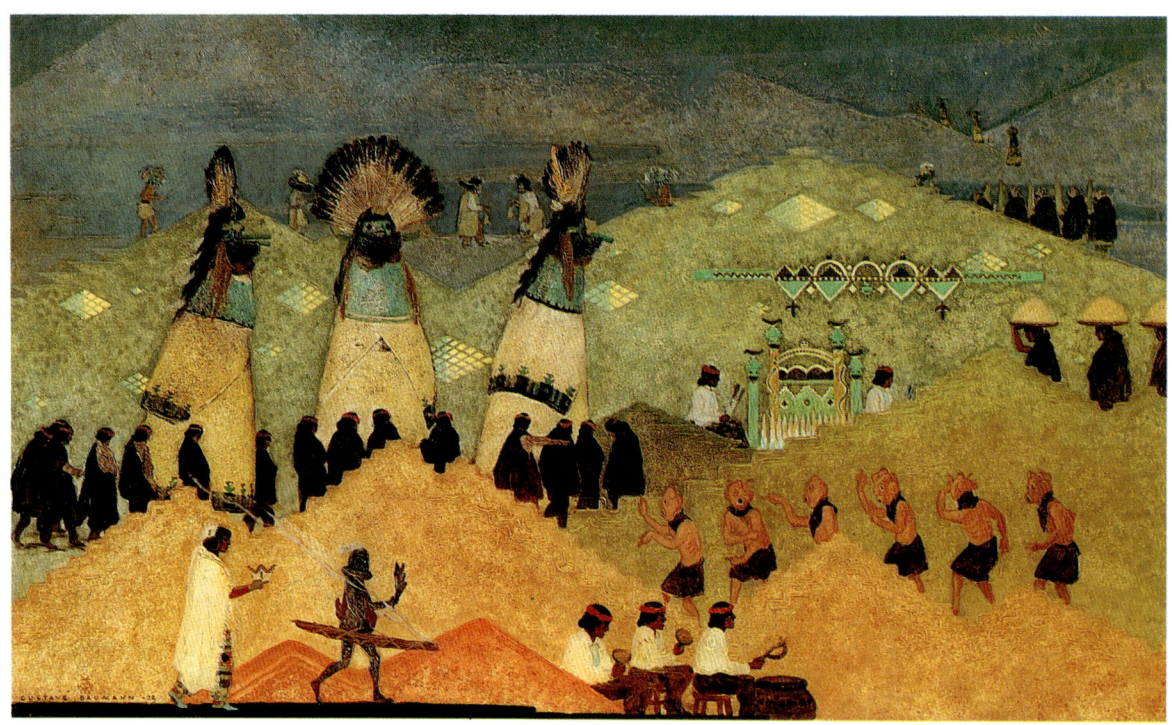

42. THE SHALAKO, 1923

Oil, 35½×60 in.

representing the Frijoles Canyon pictograph of the deer hunt. Other paintings and prints for sale were displayed here, hanging on the walls and propped on the bookcase. Behind the gallery, a windowless concrete room with a steel door served as a fireproof vault for storage of printing blocks, artwork, and important documents. It was entered from a central hall that also accessed the single bedroom, bathroom, and the large north-facing studio at the rear of the house. On high shelves circling the walls of the hall was a portion of Baumann's large collection of Hopi *Kachina* dolls. On the west side of the house, the kitchen and dining room formed a slightly projecting wing. As Baumann's family grew, the little house was progressively expanded. Late in the 1920s an extra bedroom and screened porch were added; some years later a detached studio was built and, later in the decade, enlarged.

At Christmastime in 1923, Baumann attended holiday celebrations at San Felipe Pueblo, where he met old friends from Colorado who had traveled to the festivities along with their local theatrical group, the Denver Atelier. Among the group was Jane Devereux Henderson, a talented actress and classically trained operatic contralto who had studied in New York, London, and Paris. In December 1924 she lived with an Indian family at nearby Santa Clara Pueblo, where she researched Native American music.[31] An attentive courtship began, and in 1925 Gustave Baumann and Jane Henderson were married in the garden of the bride's family home in Denver. After their return to Santa Fe, the couple established their popularity in local artistic and social circles. Mrs. Baumann led the cast in several productions of the Santa Fe Players. Along with the artist Olive Rush, she was among the founding members of the Santa Fe Friends Meeting, the Quaker Church.

In about 1924 Baumann took a trip to Arizona in search of unusual and provocative subjects for his prints. In the arid brilliance of the Sonoran desert he found a distinctive ambiance that he later captured in four woodcuts.[32] Two of these focus on specific desert plants: the blooming *cholla* and towering *saguaro* cacti in one, and in the other the wispy *palo verde* coupled with the spiny *ocotillo* (plates 96, 97).* In addition to an accurate representation

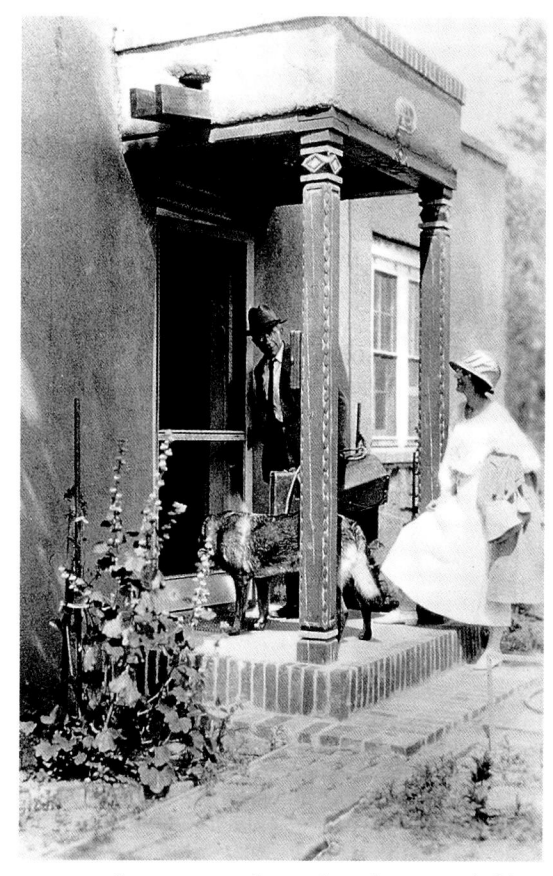

Jane and Gustave, with Punch, at home, probably in 1925, the year they were married.

of these common, exotic-looking plants, Baumann strove to depict their austere native environment, using intense hues and exploiting paper color to suggest the sandy desert soil reflecting the sun's unremitting heat. Shimmering passages of shade are rendered by printing blue over black. Baumann's interest in the geology of the region is reflected in his view of *Wild Horse Mesa* (plate 43). Its vivid colors in startling juxtapositions create the effect of intense light and expansive space similar to that achieved in the artist's Grand Canyon views. Although the colors of this print appear exaggerated, the artist based his palette, as well as his design, on careful observation. Years later he noted that "there are samples of colored sand in my storeroom from the red, the blue, the white and black forests of Arizona. Colors that shimmered with rainbow

*Baumann's unorthodox spellings in titles of works are most apparent in southwestern Hispanic and Native American regionalisms.

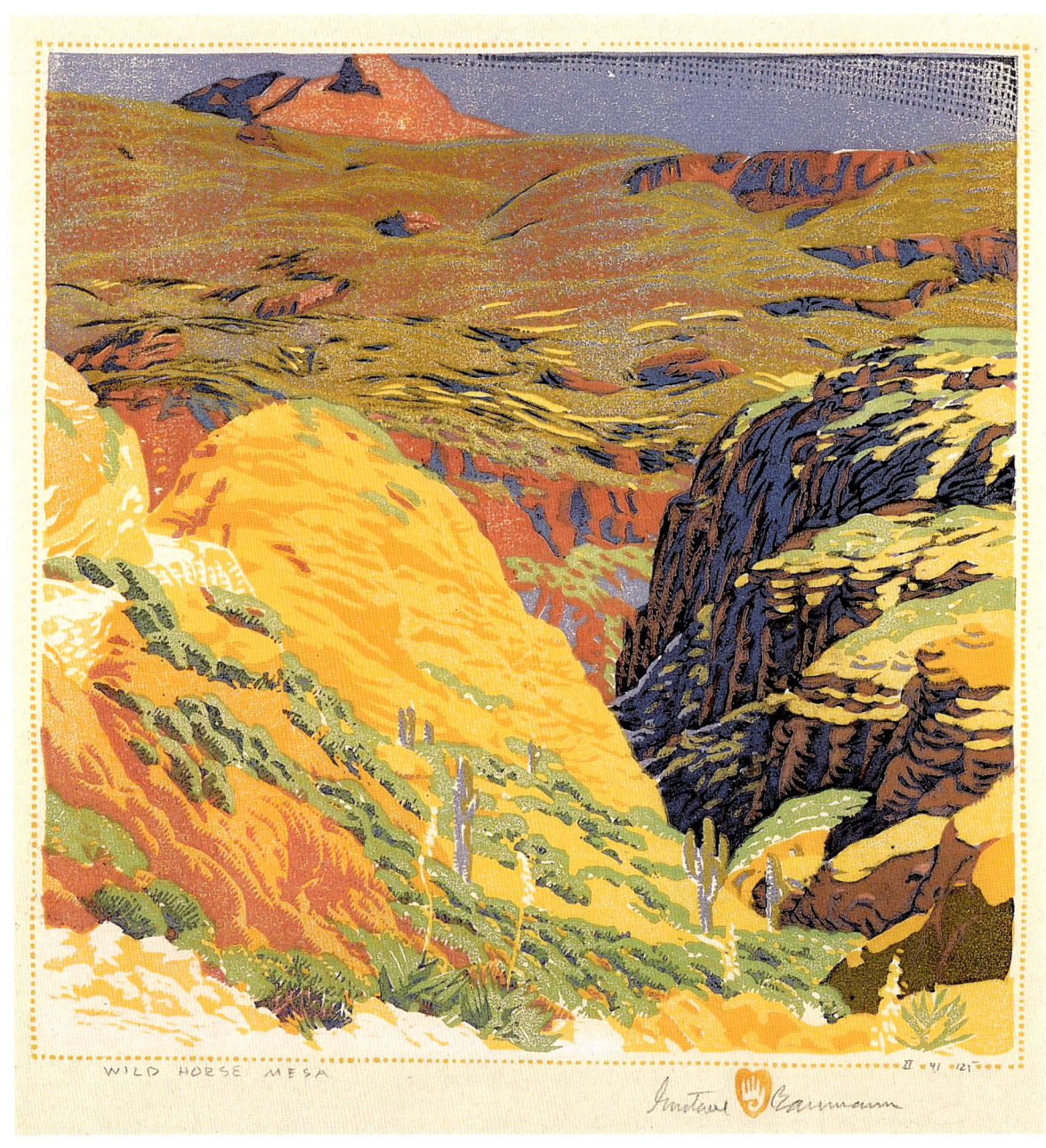

WILD HORSE MESA

43. WILD HORSE MESA, 1924
Color woodcut, 12¾ × 12¾ in.

iridescence until I thought I had discovered a new source of pigment. What I could not bring with them was the atmosphere that made their color."[33]

Also in the mid-1920s Baumann traveled to California. The woodcuts resulting from this trip

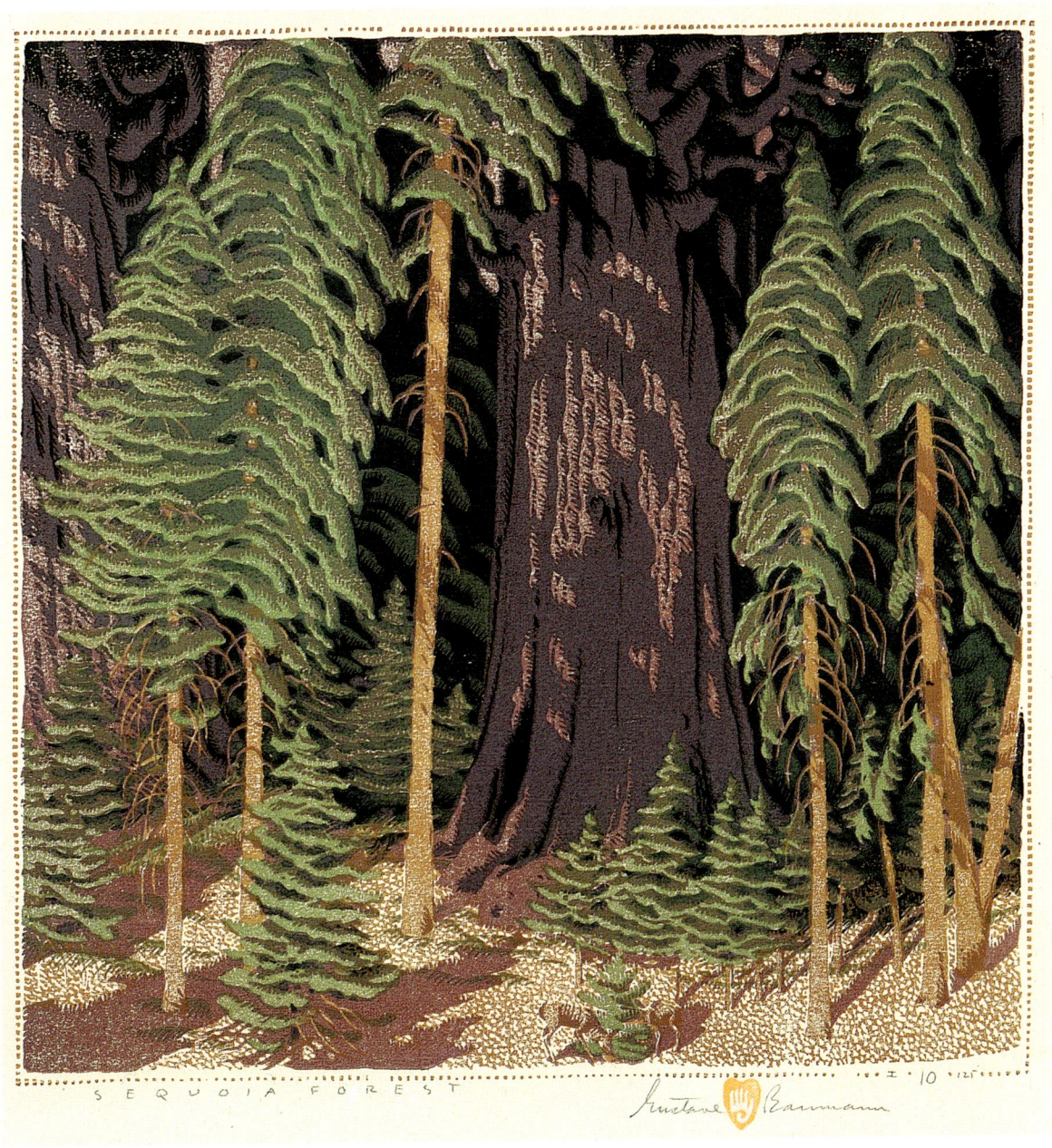

44. SEQUOIA FOREST, 1928
Color woodcut, 12⅞ × 12¾ in.

suggest that he explored the Pacific Coast from Laguna Beach north to San Francisco Bay.[34] Once again, color integrates this group of prints. To capture the sensations of bright light, silvery ocean reflections, and cool coastal breezes, the artist used a soft palette of pale, interstitial colors. With these colors he often employed black to strengthen shadows and emphasize rugged, curvilinear forms. Baumann even turned to silver leaf for some of his prints of the California coast, a technique he had not used in his woodcuts in more than a decade. Although many of these prints depict the ocean shore, most do not focus on the sea itself, but rather on dramatic surfside cliffs and bristly, craggy trees. At Point Lobos and Monterey the artist made drawings of gnarled cypress growing tenaciously from rocky cliffs, resulting in prints that bear a strong similarity to his Southwest subjects. An exception is *Pelican Rookery* (plate 98), which may be characterized as Baumann's only seascape. A rocky outcropping where the seabirds nest emerges from an azure sea, as gentle swells break around it. The artist skillfully captured the movement of the water with interweaving wave forms in blue and purple, punctuated with surface reflections and passages of foamy white. The viewer looks down on this scene, presumably from a high coastal precipice, and upon hovering gulls, which imply an apposite movement to the languid swells, giving this image a palpable sense of motion.

Other California prints represent seaside communities with red-tiled roofs, groves of eucalyptus trees, and vividly colored mountains. Baumann also saw the great Californian sequoia and redwood trees when he visited Sequoia National Park and Muir Woods. In the color woodcut *Sequoia Forest* (plate 44), he attempted to depict this experience with a view of the illuminated edge of a dark, impenetrable wood. The sun plays on the foliage of several dissimilar pines, but the composition is dominated by the trunk of an enormous sequoia, looming like a medieval tower. It is rendered in tones of purple and black, similar to those of Baumann's other California prints. The conical shapes of the little pine trees, and their proportions which seem to grow by degrees, direct the eye upward, subtly suggesting the astounding stature of these giants that soar to heights we can only imagine. A more immediate sense of the scale of this scene is given by the tiny deer that nibble at the shoots of the sapling in the foreground.

Baumann's California prints were the latest of the woodcuts included in his solo exhibition at the Worcester Art Museum in Massachusetts in the spring of 1930. This seems to have been the artist's most extensive show in the East.[35]

Baumann's prints of the 1920s were acquired by serious collectors and museums, but the foundation of his renown and financial success was in sales to middle-class customers who purchased one or two color prints to decorate the walls of their homes. This was an era of widespread and enduring popularity for the Arts and Crafts style in home furnishings, for the slatted Mission furniture of Gustave Stickley and Elbert Hubbard, and for the art pottery produced by Rookwood and Grueby.[36] Baumann's brightly colored, craftsy prints were the perfect pictorial foil in

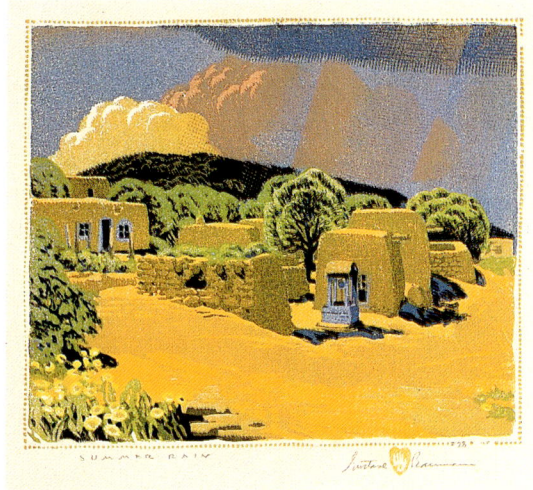

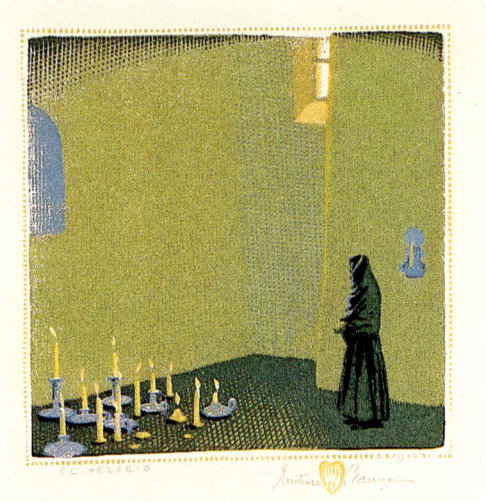

45 . SUMMER RAIN , 1926
Color woodcut, 9 × 11 in.

46 . EL VELORIO , N. D.
Color woodcut, 8 × 8 in.

this severe, muted style of decor. Even in his artistic maturity, Baumann retained the flowing contour lines that first appeared after his youthful exposure to *Jugendstil* and was encouraged by the Art Nouveau–influenced etchers of Brown County. His prints also had a linear decorative component, seen in the systematic patterning of his cross-hatching and in the omnipresent dotted borderline that insistently denied the illusion of Baumann's compositions. Their Arts and Crafts character is demonstrated by the frames that the printmaker sometimes made for his woodcuts. Carved of his favorite soft basswood, these moldings were usually quite wide, and ornamented by one or two simple protruding fillets. Baumann normally finished the frames with an impasto layer of enamel paint, with a mottled surface like adobe. They were usually painted a neutral tan, their color thoughtfully chosen to complement the dun hue of Baumann's favorite oatmeal paper, which fell next to the painted frame when the print was mounted as the artist preferred, without any mat.

Baumann sold prints in galleries across the country, working at one time or another with dealers in Chicago, Denver, Santa Fe, and the venerable Weyhe Gallery in New York. Generally, however, he avoided trading with art dealers, whose commercial expectations made him uncomfortable. A remarkable number of prints were sold directly out of the artist's home, to collectors and customers who wrote or visited. The responsibility for these transactions fell to Mrs. Baumann, who managed the correspondence and accounts and welcomed customers in the little gallery at the house. For the most part, Baumann remained insulated in his studio, emerging only occasionally if visitors were important enough to be invited to stay for afternoon coffee.

The Great Depression had a powerful impact on Santa Fe and its artists, most of whom depended on selling artwork for their livelihood. As tourism waned and the market evaporated, Baumann altered his activity, eventually producing fewer large color prints. President Roosevelt's New Deal programs brought much-needed support for those artists who stayed in New Mexico. The first of these programs was the Public Works of Art Project in 1933, which attempted to organize relief by extending payments for commissioned public projects such as post office murals and easel paintings to decorate the walls of libraries, government office buildings, and schoolrooms. When the Treasury Department, which administered the program, sectioned off the country, the central office for the thirteenth region was established in Santa Fe, with administrative responsibility for Arizona and New Mexico. Having at the time no knowledge of or experience in art, the area director Jesse Nusbaum engaged Baumann as regional coordinator.[37] It was his responsibility to arrange projects, to monitor artists' progress, and sometimes to motivate them to work steadily according to schedule. Baumann found this position most challenging. It went against his nature to lavish meticulous attention on paperwork, and he felt sympathetic to artists more concerned for the integrity of their work than for punctuality. It was particularly difficult to balance the government's changing bureaucratic requirements with divergent attitudes about the purpose of art in Santa Fe's polyglot community, where Native Americans, Hispanics, and émigrés from eastern academies intermingled. Although he was frustrated by these administrative tasks, the artists with whom he worked were grateful to Baumann for his understanding and support.

In his own work, in response to the depression's shrinking market, Baumann undertook works of art that had much broader potential distribution. In 1929 he had already turned his attention to an old challenge, the illustrated book. In that year he published *Chips an' Shavings*, "among which a Hoosier carpenter and his friend the barber, discourse on hair-register and other intricacies of the color wood-cut; with three wood-cuts in the early Indiana manner and a few studio secrets (*cum grano salis*, as they used to say)."[38] As the extended subtitle implies, this book presented some of the principles and practical secrets of the subject that Baumann knew best, color woodcut. These were contained in a Twain-like yarn, well suited to the narrative quality of his Indiana woodcuts, the blocks of which were now more than fifteen years old. The artist hand-printed the three color prints that were bound into this book in an edition of one hundred. It is likely that the modest success of this project encouraged him to undertake his most im-

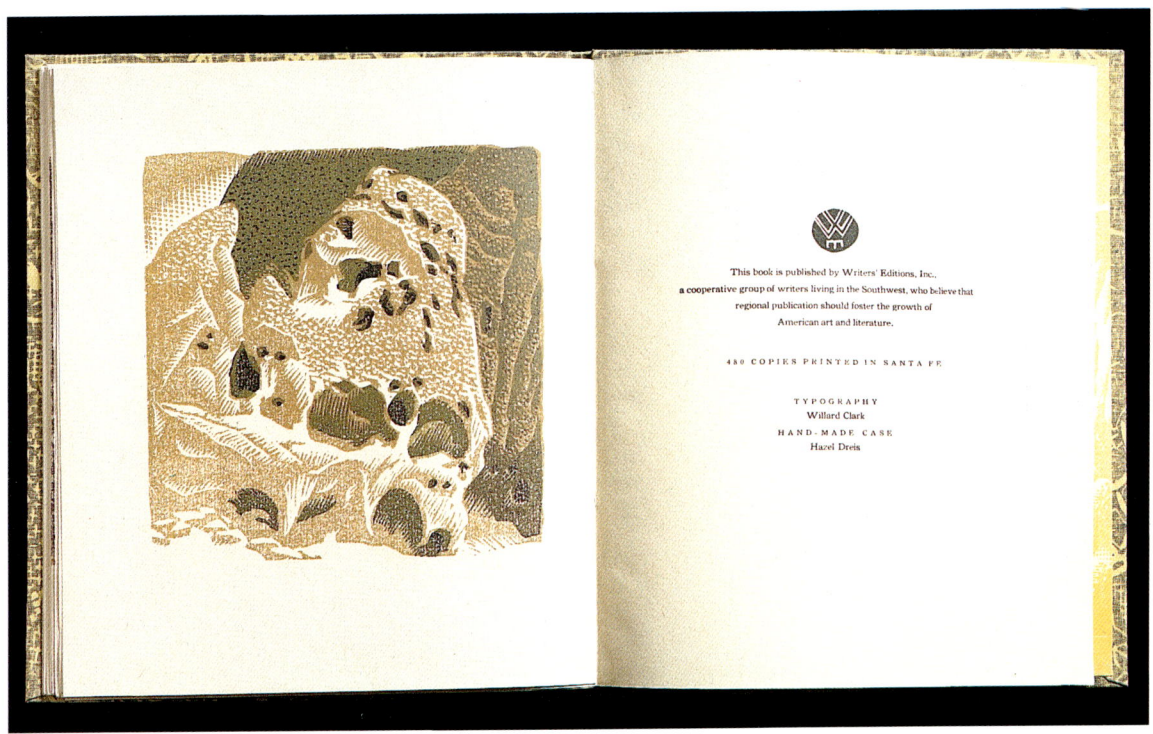

This book is published by Writers' Editions, Inc.,
a cooperative group of writers living in the Southwest, who believe that
regional publication should foster the growth of
American art and literature.

480 COPIES PRINTED IN SANTA FE

TYPOGRAPHY
Willard Clark
HAND-MADE CASE
Hazel Dreis

47 . FRIJOLES CANYON PICTOGRAPHS (COLOPHON) , 1939

Color woodcut

portant illustrated book, the profusely illustrated *Frijoles Canyon Pictographs*, which also arose from earlier work.

Throughout his years in New Mexico, Baumann never lost his fascination with the ruins and cave dwellings of the Pajarito Plateau, and their haunting wall paintings and petroglyphs,[39] first glimpsed even before his arrival in Taos in 1918. From the narrow-gauge train that ran up the Rio Grande Valley, he noticed that "jutting out of the water here and there were black rocks with strange pictographs on them that puzzled me then, but would at a later time have ultra-modern value that no one had even thought of before."[40] Months later his curiosity drew him back to the area, to Puyé, Otowi, and Frijoles Canyon. Exploring the plateau region was an exciting adventure that thoroughly captured Baumann's imagination. "Sitting under tall pines," he wrote, "near the little river which gives the canyon its Spanish name El Rito de los Frijoles, one sees the towering cliffs above, and at the base of these cliffs, evidence of habitation that invites speculation as to just what life must have been here in by-gone days."[41]

Baumann did just that in the *Day of the Deer Dance* (plate 35). This woodcut is quite unusual

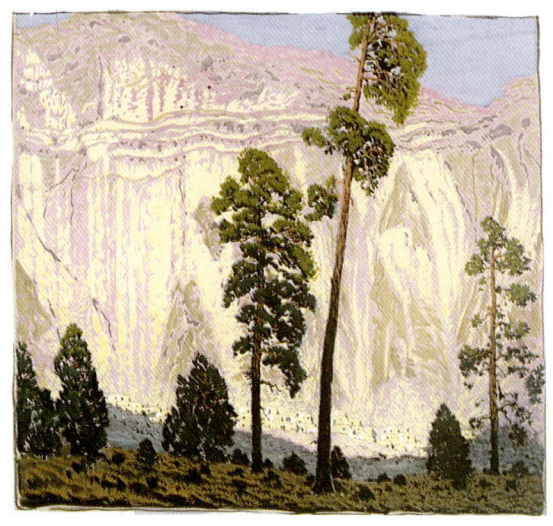

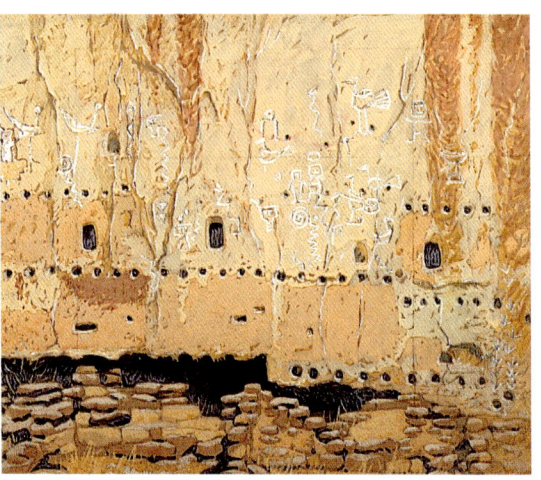

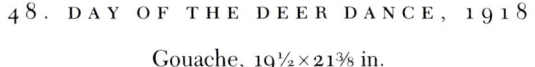

48. DAY OF THE DEER DANCE, 1918

Gouache, 19½ × 21⅜ in.

49. UNTITLED

(PAST HISTORY), 1946

Gouache, 9 × 10⅝ in.

in the printmaker's oeuvre, for it represents events that took place centuries ago, set in a specific, observed location, and with details suggested by the prehistoric dwellers' own images. In the middle distance of this expansive view, hunters dressed in antlers and buckskin perform a ritual dance to ensure the success of their upcoming expedition. We observe this ceremony along with the brightly clad women gathered among the juniper and mesquite along the foreground riverbank. The immensity of the landscape is suggested by leaps of scale between the nearby trees and those far away atop the mesa, and between the diminutive figures in the foreground and their distant dwellings. Visually and practically, these people and their culture blend harmoniously into the natural environment. Although their rituals echo through centuries, their transience – and our own – is implied by their scale within this vast, magnificent landscape.

In the late 1930s, when he realized that several of the original cave paintings had disappeared in the years since he recorded them, Baumann embarked on *Frijoles Canyon Pictographs*, published in 1939 by the Santa Fe publishing cooperative Writers' Editions. Baumann wrote and illustrated the book, printing the woodcuts in his own studio. Block printer Willard Clark set and printed the text. The foreword was written by archaeologist Alfred V. Kidder, who as a Harvard graduate student had assisted Edgar L. Hewett in his excavations at Puyé and Frijoles Canyon in the first decade of the century. Baumann's text offers a brief description of the canyon, its history and artifacts, and an account of his experiences there. This text is punctuated by nineteen freely transcribed woodcuts representing vignettes from the images on cliff and cave

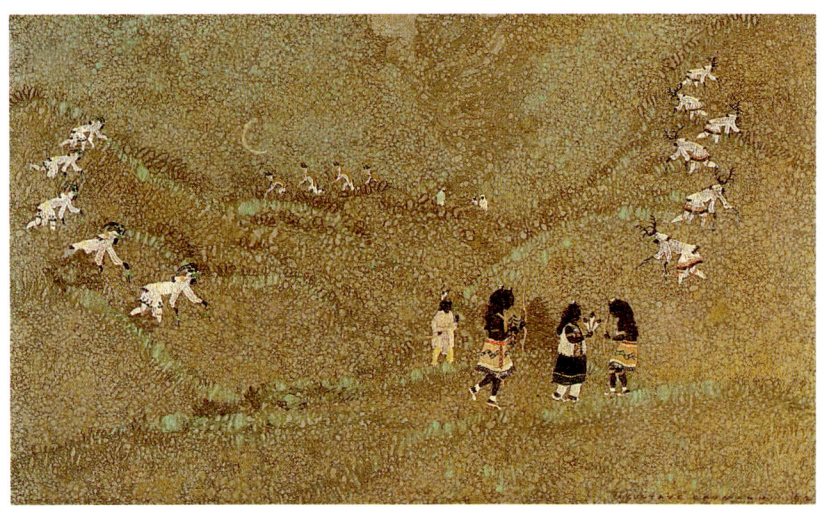

50. WINTER CEREMONY – DEER DANCE, 1922

Oil, 30⁷⁄₁₆ × 52⁹⁄₁₆ in.

walls, printed in a sandy brown color. Several of the pictographs represent wild game; others show divinities and spirits. There are also fragmentary designs of the sort that appear on pottery. Some of the more interesting woodcuts represent horses and riders, veiled women with wide European skirts, and an Indian with a gun, images recorded at the site centuries after its prehistoric abandonment. These may have been executed by transient Pueblo hunters or by European settlers themselves some time after major Spanish settlement of the Rio Grande Valley around 1700. Spaced throughout the book are six color prints representing some of Frijoles Canyon's most elaborate pictographs, as well as both a glimpse inside a cave dwelling and an overall view of the canyon's south wall. In the center of the book are two pages that fold out to reveal *The Deer Hunt* pictograph, reprinted from Baumann's original blocks carved in 1918. On every page, down to the book's endpapers that carry a woodcut aerial panorama of the canyon's south wall, Baumann lavished loving and meticulous care. The book was a notable success.

Some of the most important compositions in *Frijoles Canyon Pictographs* were later reworked into larger, full-color woodcuts. *Past History* (plate 104), created in 1946, is a more detailed version of the frontispiece representing a segment of the canyon wall, pierced by caves and ornamented with pictograms. The craggy irregularity of the rock, the myriad holes that puncture it, and the stacks of tufa bricks before it and their shadows create an engaging flat pattern. These ruins tell an archaeologist's tale of the evolution of the dwellings. The small holes aligned in neat rows held roof beams for the brick structures built into the cliff. Their distinct ranges show that these houses grew progressively to at least three stories. Larger, oval holes are the doors to cave chambers carved deeply into the rock, accessible from the roofs of the second and third floors. To embellish the high exterior wall the builders apparently stood on the rooftops. Another large color woodcut that developed from the book was *Wings of Prophesy* (plate 105), completed in 1955. Here the artist focused on one of the canyon's most striking and accomplished petroglyphs, representing three birds on the wing. The center figure has plumage different from the others and seems to be the surrounded prey of eagles, distinguished by their hooked beaks and large talons. Their elongated bodies and the sweep of their wing feathers suggest swift and agile flight. The lower bird opens its mouth to emit an almost audible cry, evoking the drama of the chase.[42]

From his first years in New Mexico, Baumann was interested in traditional Pueblo and Hopi dolls and figurines, whose craftsmanship and childish delight combined with deep cultural significance in ways the artist found enchanting. He collected them avidly and became knowledgeable about their forms, decorations, and meanings. Among those he collected were the popular Kachina dolls, the representations of deified ancestral spirits (also called Kachinas) the Hopis believe periodically visit and effect our world. In Hopi rituals conceived to summon these spirits and encourage their intercession – particularly for beneficial weather and bountiful hunts and harvests – dancers impersonate the Kachinas with vivid symbolic costumes and by performing specific dance steps. Traditionally during these ceremonies Kachina dolls are presented to the children. Carved from cottonwood roots or branches, the dolls are gaily painted and decorated with buckskin, horsehair, and feathers.

The first woodcut representing Baumann's budding doll collection was *Strangers from Hopi Land* (plate 102), created around 1920. Judging from the number of times he submitted it for exhibition, he was proud of this print. A more ambitious piece, *Hopi Katzinas* (plate 103), suggests how extensive the artist's collection of dolls had become by about 1925, and how the artist delighted in their every detail. The composition is simple and uncluttered, so as not to detract from the dolls' splendid or-

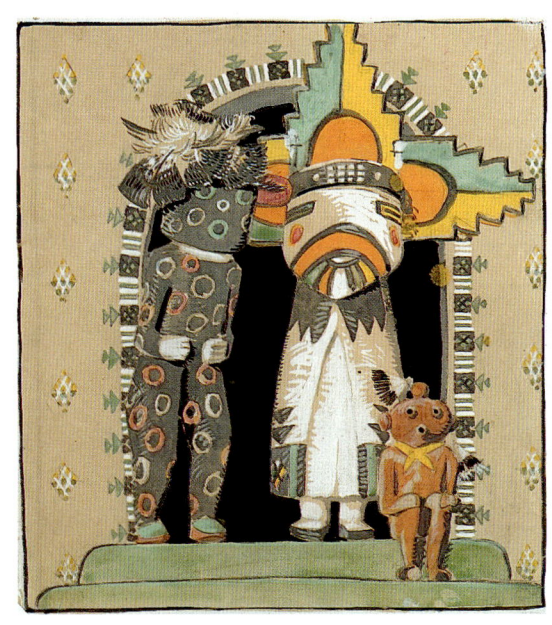

51. UNTITLED (STRANGERS FROM HOPI LAND), 1920
Gouache, 10½ × 9½ in.

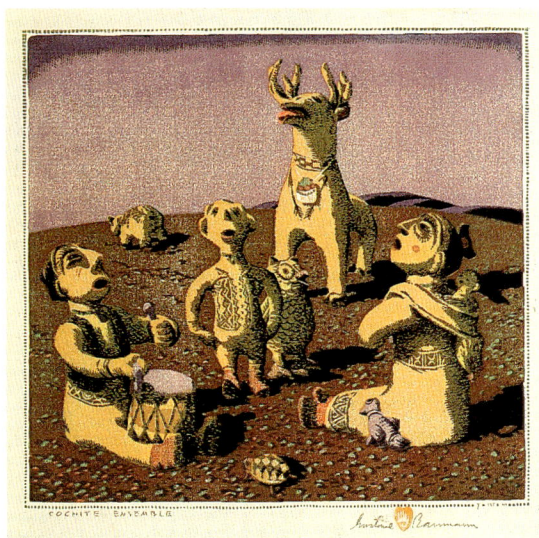

52. COCHITI ENSEMBLE, 1948–1949

Color woodcut, 12¼ × 13¼ in.

namentation. The technical complexity of this print is outstanding, with its myriad colors and intricate designs. This woodcut precisely reproduces the artist's oil painting, now at the Museum of New Mexico, which is titled on the canvas "Pasatiempo." Like the artists of Santa Fe who organized and celebrated the annual Pasatiempo fiesta, Baumann's Kachinas assemble for their own festival, circling around to watch the performance of a troupe of acrobats. The gathering dolls seem to come alive, interacting with each other, taking on human characteristics, and appearing to express their delight in the performance. A childlike tendency to humanize these playthings is common in Baumann's prints of dolls and toys, and reflects something of the artist's character.[43]

Also in the artist's collection were painted and glazed ceramic figurines and dolls, many of them made at nearby Cochiti Pueblo. While the Indian ceramicists sometimes depicted spirits, more often they represented animals and even themselves, usually in a humorous light. Baumann used the statuettes in such prints as *Cochiti Ensemble* (plate 52), which depicts several of these figurines gathered together on a desert bluff to sing to the accompaniment of a drumbeat. Even the deer and owl enthusiastically join in the song while we are left to speculate about the silent bear who ambles off with his head bowed.

Around 1932 the Baumanns embarked on a depression-era adventure when they built and operated their own marionette theater. The artist had first experimented with marionettes during his Indiana years, when he designed and constructed an assembly of puppets that poked fun at typical Hoosiers. He had become discouraged in this earlier effort by his scant knowledge of stagecraft. By 1932, he could call on more than a decade's experience in community theater, and on Mrs. Baumann's considerable talents and experience as a singer and actress. At this time, too, their daughter Ann was five years old, and at first the marionettes were meant to amuse her. In truth, as the artist admitted, the hobby also allowed him to return to the playful hours of childhood.[44] Baumann designed and carved the marionettes, made many of the costumes, and wrote most of the scripts for their plays, but he was never a puppeteer. He also constructed a miniature stage with changeable sets, designed to be portable for touring purposes. Mrs. Baumann polished the scripts, composed the songs, directed the productions, and manipulated marionettes while providing their voices. Several family friends also were recruited and trained as puppeteers. The troupe presented a limited number of public performances, but for the most part the theater enjoyed its finest reception in the Baumann home at Christmastime.

Over two decades the artist created sixty-five different marionettes, some of them representing the Baumanns themselves.[45] At least

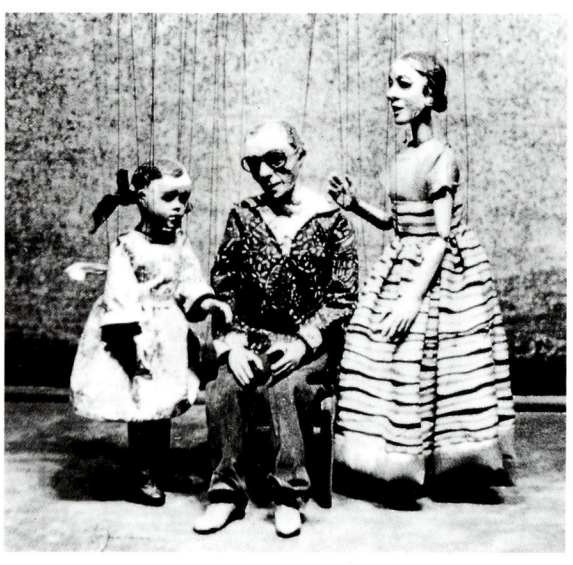

The Baumann family marionettes:
Ann, age four, Gus, and Jane, ca. 1933.

twice during the mid-1930s the marionettes made their way into woodcuts (plate 53). Eventually, they and their traveling gear required so much room that the artist was forced from his studio and into a small detached building he constructed away from the house. Though popular, the puppets never fulfilled one of their maker's original expectations, to furnish supplementary income. They turned out instead to be rather an expensive hobby. Nevertheless, the troupe provided an exciting family enterprise for years, and joyful memories for the puppeteers and their audiences. The last public performance of the Baumann marionettes was in Santa Fe at the Museum of International Folk Art in 1959.

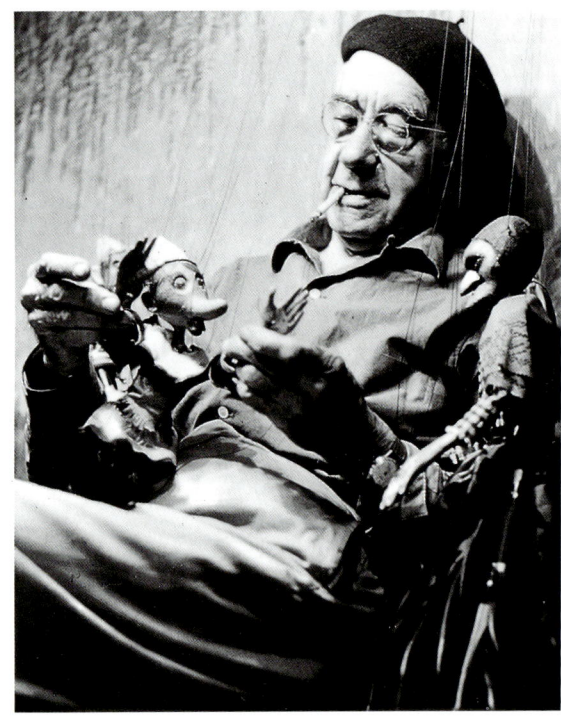

The artist with el duende *and*
the Old Lady, two marionettes from the
Baumann Marionette Theater, ca. 1959.

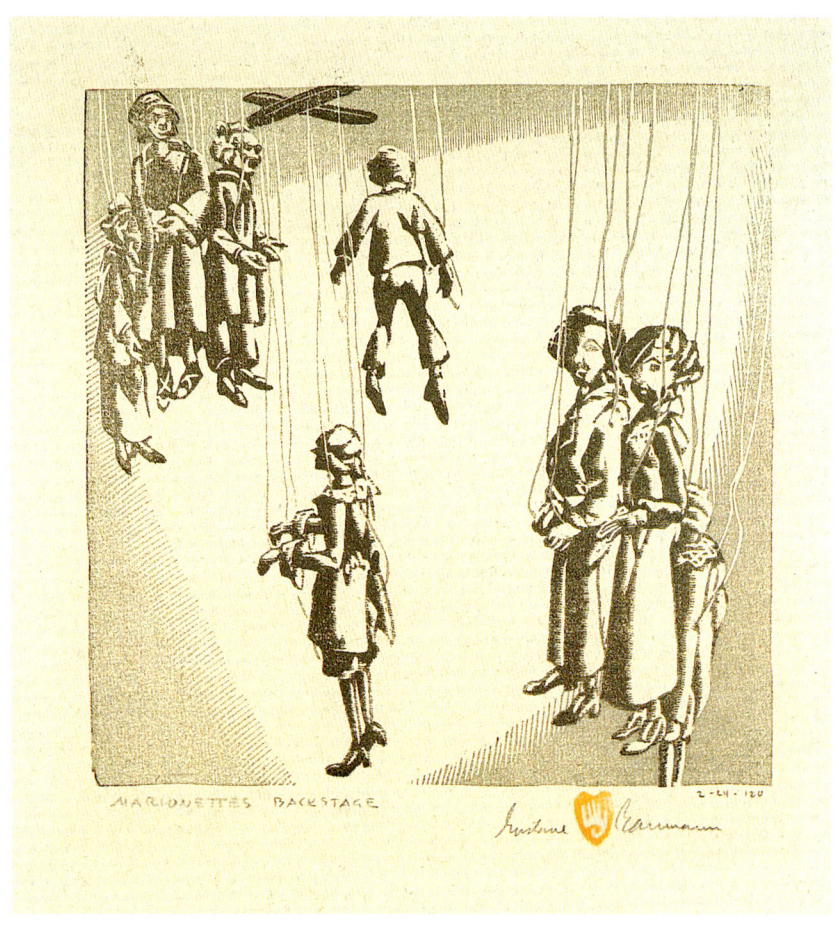

53. MARIONETTES BACKSTAGE, *ca.* 1935
Color woodcut, 8×8⅛ in.

The exceptional size and range of Baumann's woodcut production resulted from his working at printmaking as a full-time job. He was in the studio first thing almost every morning, pausing regularly for rejuvenating breaks and family meals, and he often worked late into the night. Friends and customers saw the prints only in the hospitable setting of the house, never in the workshop, which was the artist's private domain. The three-room shop was organized for efficiency and comfort, with separate areas for woodworking, painting, and printing. Baumann acquired his expertise through years of patient practice and refinement, and derived as much enjoyment from the involved processes of carving and printing his color woodcuts as he did from the aesthetic inspiration and experience of designing them. Describing the demands of his chosen art, he wrote that color woodcut requires "sharp tools, a complete disregard for time and considerable patience in waiting."[46]

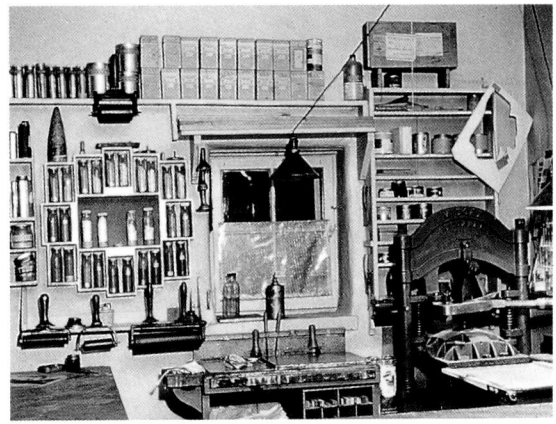 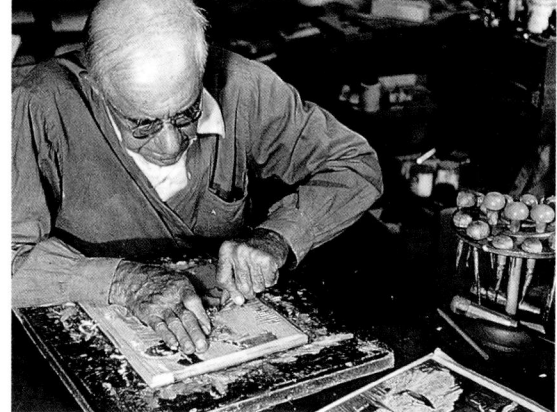

The studio at 409 Camino de las Animas, ca. 1960.   *Cutting the block for* Taos Placita, *ca. 1960.*

When American color-relief prints enjoyed a faddish nationwide explosion in the first quarter of this century, Baumann was a luminary. During this period several different printmaking methods came to the fore, the most popular of which derived from the centuries-old Japanese technique. In this process a separate carved block generally was used to print each hue. Watercolors were applied to the blocks with brushes and could be subtly blended and shaded on the printing surface while wet. The artist printed by hand, rubbing the back of the sheet with a stiff pad or wooden spoon. This process was popular for its ease and economy, its soft color and tonal subtlety. Many other methods of color-relief printmaking also became available in this period, including linoleum block printing and the single-block, white-line woodcut technique.[47] Nevertheless, Baumann never strayed from his traditional European process, which utilized a set usually of five carved blocks, oil- and varnish-based inks, and a mechanical press to do the printing. Like most American artists of the day, he undertook every stage of the process himself. Private and solitary in his work, he never employed students or assistants in the studio.

Baumann began each print with a full-color sketch in gouache, usually executed on site in the mountain, desert, or pueblo. The size of this model was transferred precisely onto the blocks, and in his mature prints of the West he often made sketches about thirteen inches square, the largest size that could comfortably fit into his press. The gouaches often were executed on gray or tawny brown papers, similar in tone to the printing paper that the artist preferred, but usually thicker and more absorbent. The pliancy of this soft paper allowed him to press hard and firmly emboss the sheet with a sharp pencil when he traced the finished composition to transfer its design to the first block.

54. SPRING BLOSSOMS

PROGRESSIVES, MARCH 1950

Color woodcut, 12⅝ × 13⅜ in. (series of 17)

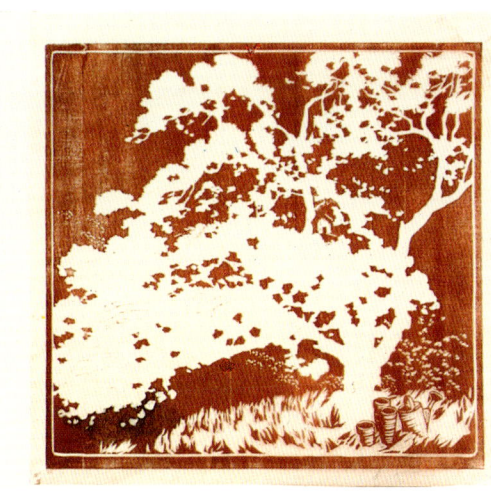

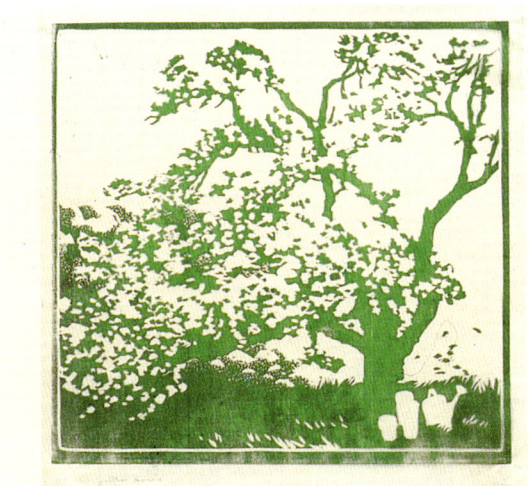

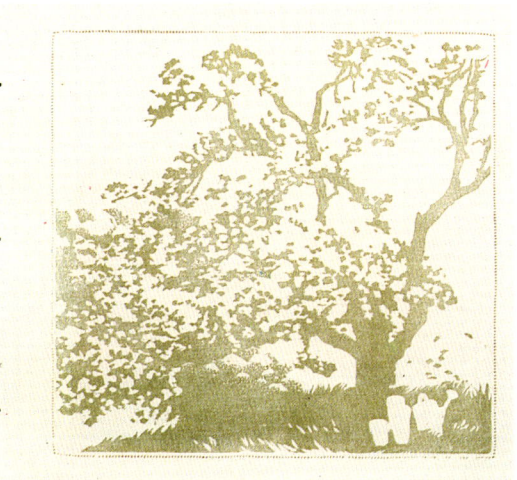

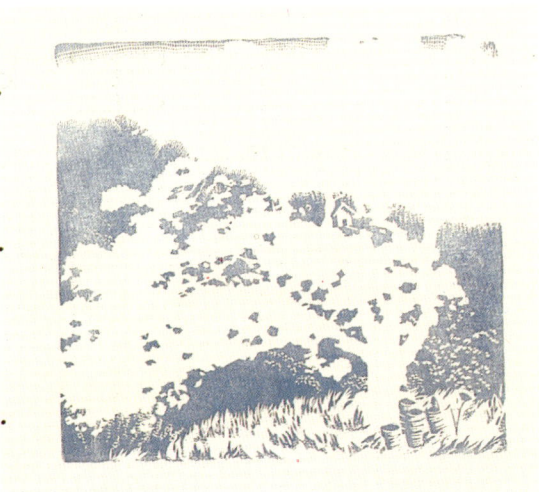

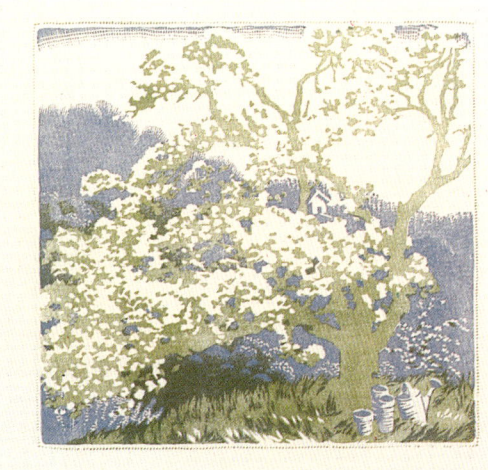

Baumann made his printing blocks of basswood, a material that is relatively soft and easy to work. He carved with steel knives and gouges, and was fastidious about keeping his tools sharp, keening their edges often with slip stones and a leather strop. All of the blocks in a set were made of precisely the same dimensions, which helped to achieve correct registration when they were placed in a jig on the bed of the Reliance Midget press, a small machine designed for the hobbyist printer to use with movable type. Baumann made his own inks, grinding and mixing dry pigments with a varnish base according to his own recipes. Through years of experience he developed a comprehensive understanding of ink chemistry, for each pigment behaved differently and some could not be mixed or overprinted by some others.[48] Baumann skillfully adjusted the saturation and viscosity of his inks so that they would remain on the surface of his sized, linen-content paper. He used brayers to apply ink to the blocks, at some times aiming for thin, transparent films of color, and at others applying a thick, impervious coat. Normally, the artist began by matching his ink hues to the naturalistic colors of his gouache model. This drawing was only a general guide, and not followed slavishly. During printing he continuously tried to improve the look of his prints by adjusting colors, and even altered his designs by recutting, adding, or subtracting blocks within an edition. Therefore, despite their seemingly conscientious numbering, Baumann's editions are not always uniform.

The artist printed on fine laid papers made of cotton or linen. While he used sheets with the Gladbach watermark for his earlier woodcuts, most of those made in Santa Fe during the 1920s and 1930s were printed on a distinctive, oatmeal-colored paper made in Germany to the artist's specifications and watermarked with his own heart-and-hand seal. After the mill for this paper was destroyed in World War II, Baumann printed primarily on laid papers of German or Dutch manufacture.[49]

Generally the artist pulled a maximum of one hundred twenty-five impressions of each print, but he never produced an entire edition at once. He made woodcuts according to demand, producing impressions as they were needed for sale or exhibition, or when he found the time. He often preserved files with progressive color proofs for his own reference, ideally along with the gouache model and what would now be called a *bon à tirer* ("good to print") proof, a perfect example from the edition that Baumann could later use as a guide. Many of the prints in the collection of the Museum of Fine Arts in Santa Fe were such model impressions that the artist had retained for his own use. To keep track of the numbers of prints within ongoing editions, Baumann devised his own system of inscription,[50] though despite all good intentions he often strayed from the plan.

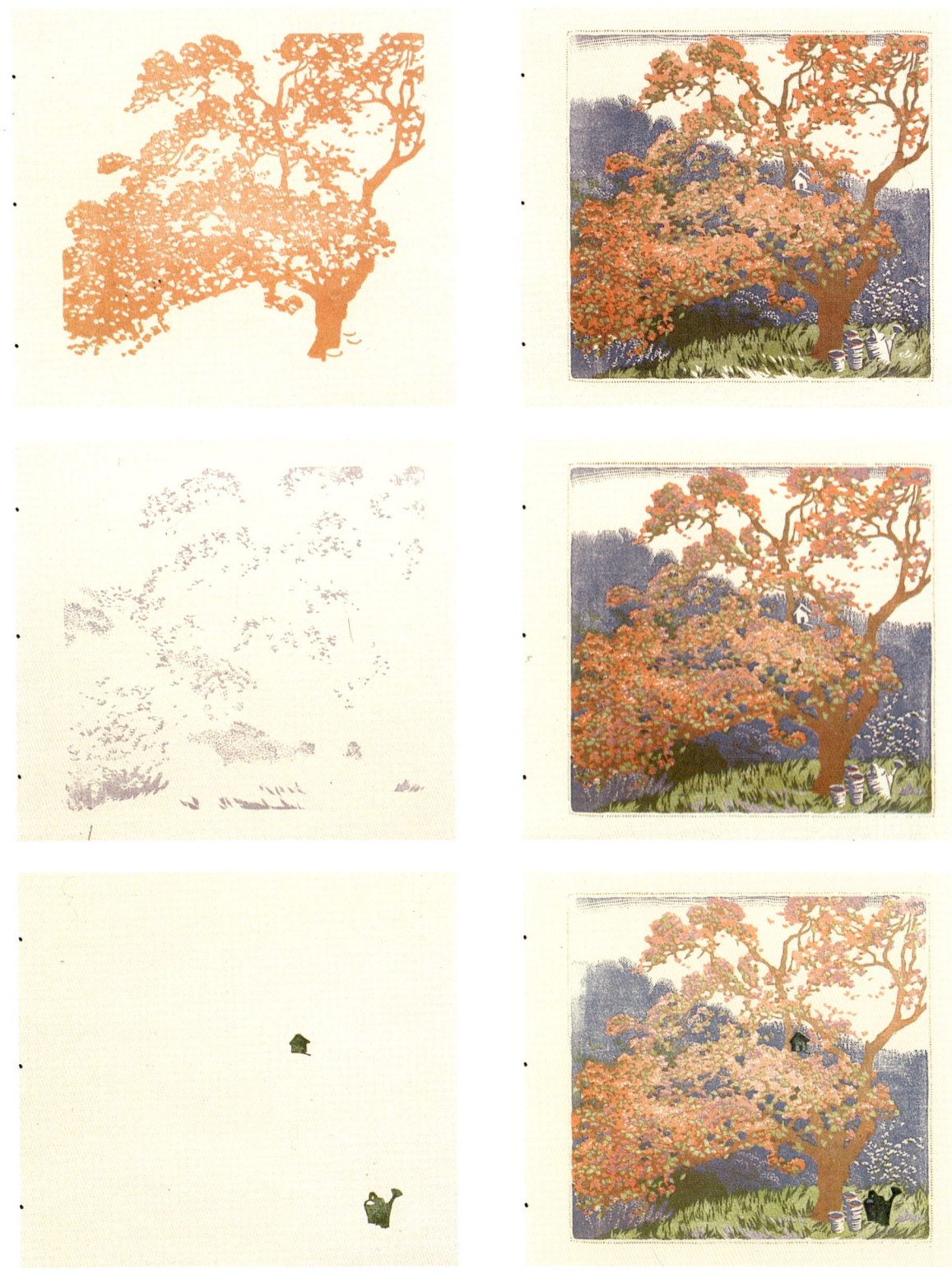

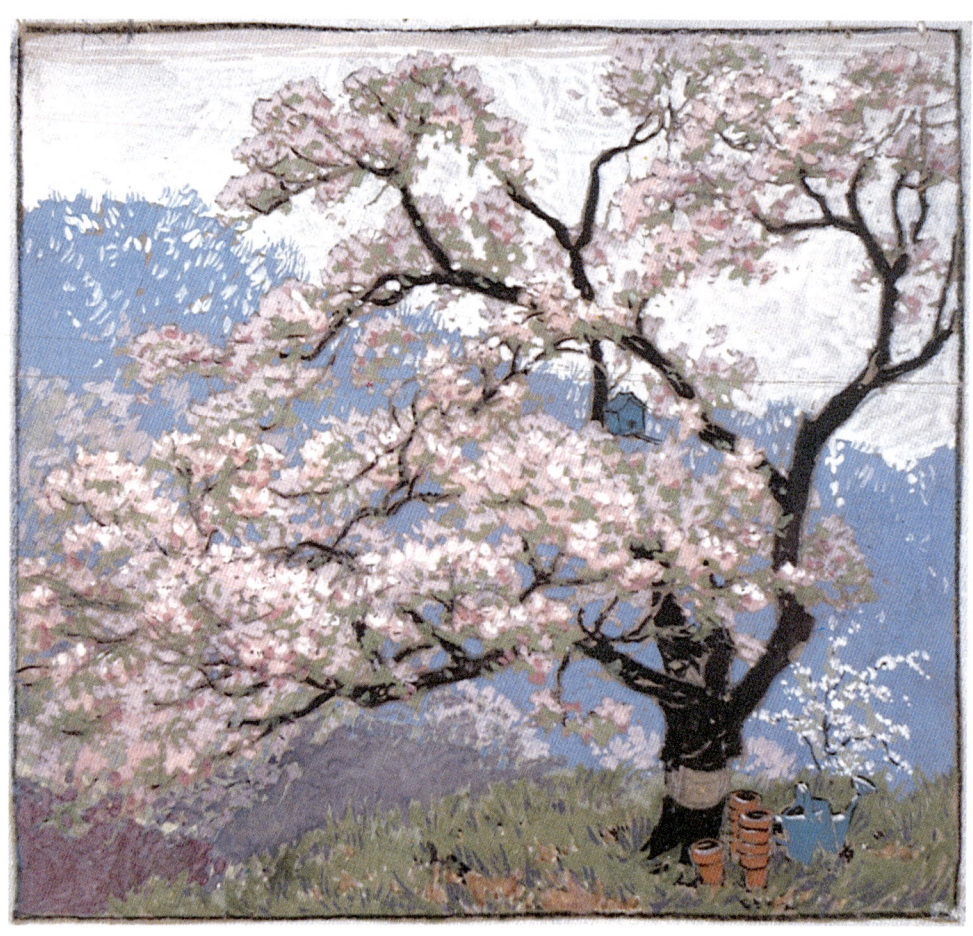

55. SPRING BLOSSOMS, *ca.* 1950

Gouache, 11⅞ × 12¾ in.

After the 1930s, it seems that Baumann no longer mounted ambitious sketching expeditions to gather new material. Although his prints reflect further travels in the West, through New Mexico and to Colorado, Texas, and California, these landscapes tend to be the exception to the work of this period. Review of the dated prints suggests that generally he stayed closer to home, often reprinting from his repertoire of earlier blocks.

Several of the prints from this period include florals and cozy domestic interiors reflective of Baumann's happy home-life. His affection for his daughter Ann is apparent in references to her in his writings, and in a handful of prints. Baumann regularly produced woodcut holiday greeting cards, and several of these incorporate Ann's ideas or poems. One Christmas card from about 1932 translated into woodcut her drawings of Santa Claus and a self-portrait. The artist's receptivity to childish play and to fresh perceptions is evident in *Rain* (plate 56), a woodcut of about

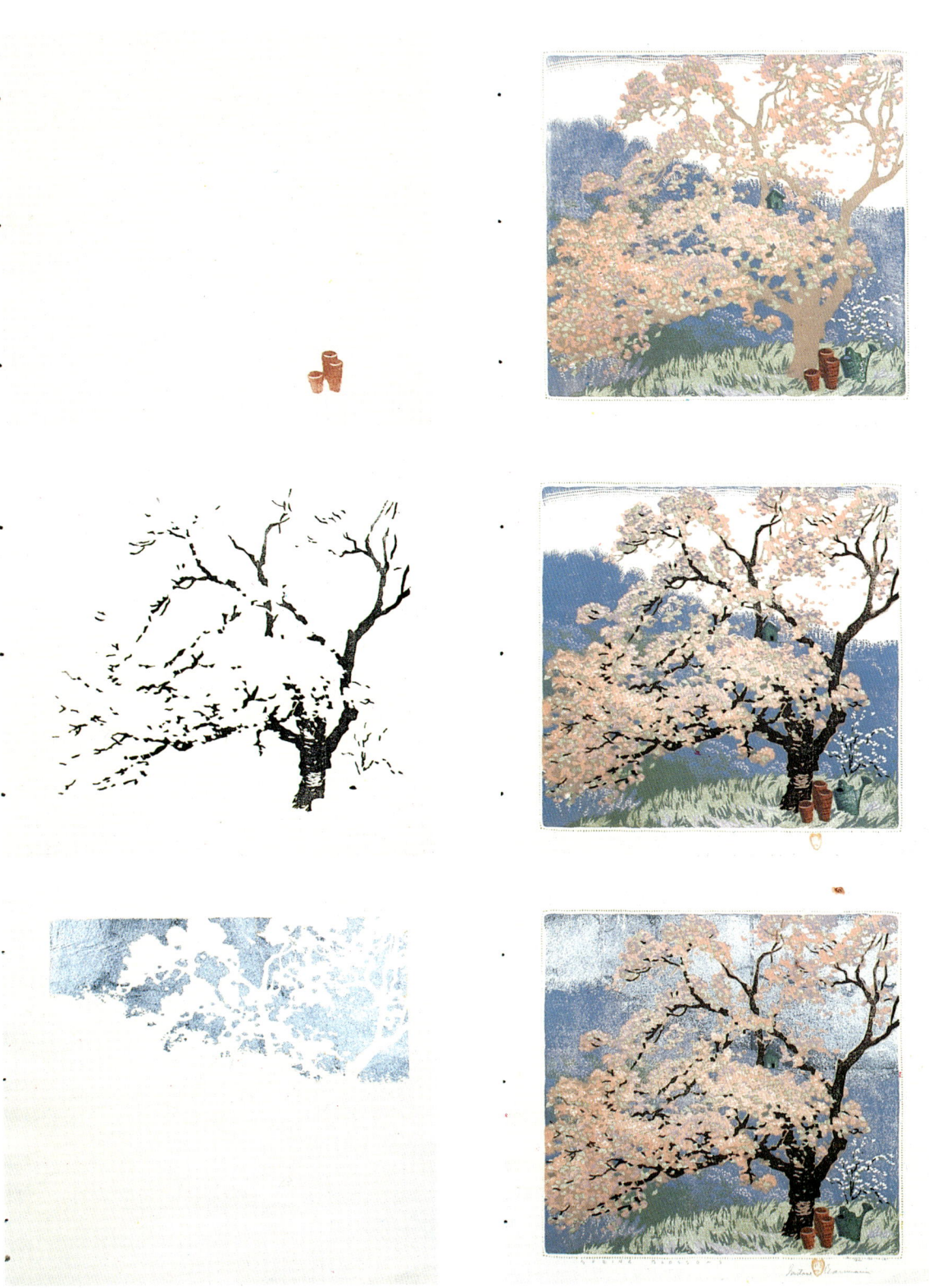

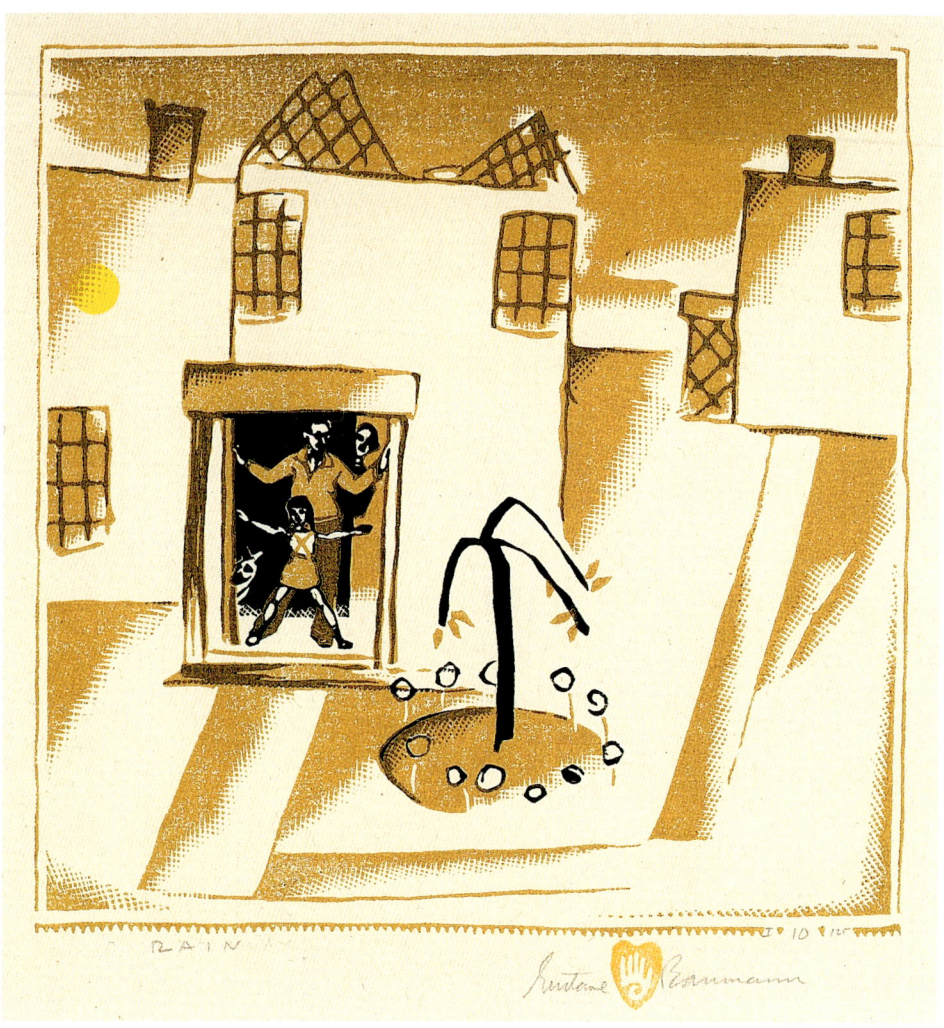

56. RAIN, *ca.* 1935

Color woodcut, 8⅛ × 8⅛ in.

1937 that depicts the Baumann family waiting for rain in the doorway of their home. The print's style combines the simplicity of children's art with the formal distortions and emotional directness of German expressionist printmaking.

Baumann made imaginative use of Native American art in two handsome prints of 1948, based on Pueblo potsherds. One, *Night Ceremony* (plate 57), depicts not a still life of painted Indian vessels, but the abstract decorative patterns taken from the fragments of many pots, overlayered and jigsawed together to make a design montage. Printed in tones of gray and black, and finished with silver leaf, the palette of *Night Ceremony* simulates the jet black and burnished luster of Santa Clara Pueblo pottery. Using the same set of blocks and another color scheme, Baumann

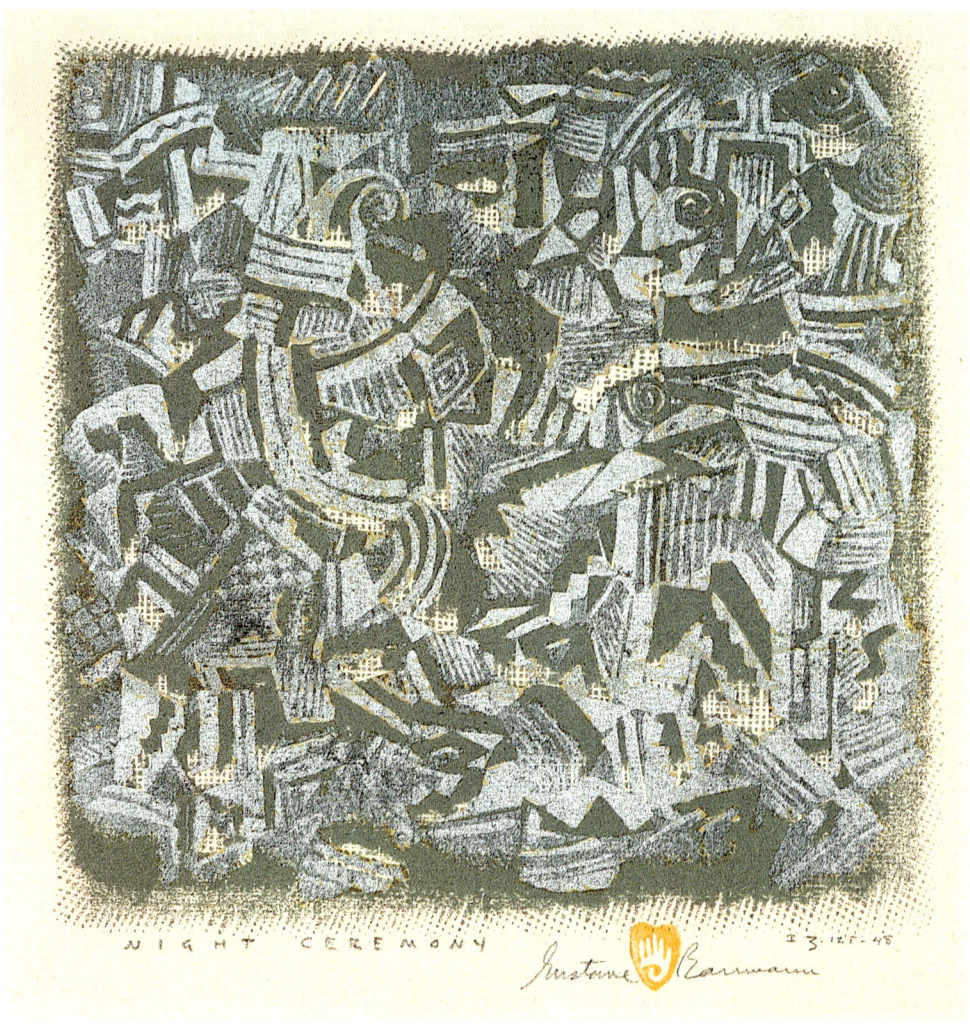

57. NIGHT CEREMONY, 1948
Color woodcut, 8⅛ × 8¼ in.

achieved a slightly different effect in a print titled *Fire Dance*.[51] The artist was knowledgeable about Southwest Native American decorative design, particularly that of the Pueblo peoples. He often used these designs in his own drawings, and he decorated his home with ornamentation incorporating this formal vocabulary. However, aside from the vignettes of *Frijoles Canyon Pictographs*, these designs appear only in this tiny group of prints. While plans had been expressed to produce a book about southwestern Indian pottery designs, illustrated with woodcuts, the idea never came to fruition.[52]

Although he was not a churchgoer, Baumann believed deeply in God and the essential values of Christianity, and in his own private way he was a spiritual man. It meant a great deal to him

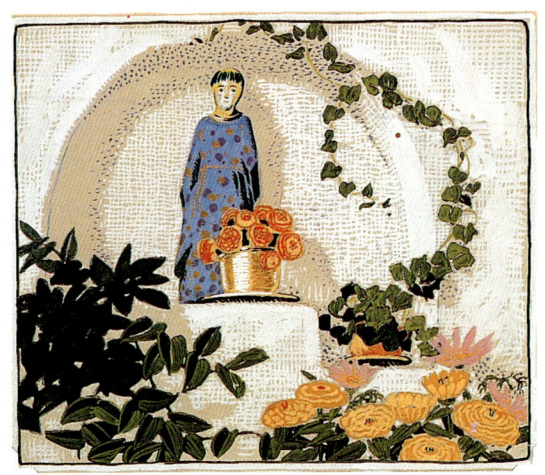

58. UNTITLED (EL SANTO), 1919

Gouache, 9⅛ × 11 in.

to execute two important projects of religious art in his career. In the early 1930s he took it upon himself to restore one of Santa Fe's most revered religious artifacts from the Spanish period, a painted and gilded carved-wood sculpture of the standing Virgin of the Rosary, which today remains enshrined in the Cathedral of St. Francis. Probably created around 1625, this figure is thought to have been brought to New Mexico in 1680 by Benavides and the first Spanish settlers. Thus, she has long been known as *La Conquistadora*.[53] For generations this icon had played an important part in Santa Fe's annual fiesta celebrating the festival of Corpus Christi, when it was carried through the city streets to the Rosario Chapel.

Baumann set out to restore the icon, whose surfaces were cracked and chipped and its most delicate extremities broken off.[54] He worked for a month in his studio, painstakingly cleaning the sculpture, carving and replacing its broken fingers, and restoring flaked areas of paint and gold leaf. Eventually the Virgin appeared much as she would have in the seventeenth century. After the restoration, Baumann made a replica of the statuette, which he donated to the cathedral and its community. This facsimile would be used in the church's annual celebrations, saving the original icon from the perils of further movement. The replica was blessed in the Fiesta Mass, and first carried in its procession in 1935.

Baumann began an even more ambitious ecclesiastical project in 1943, for the Episcopal Church of the Holy Faith in Santa Fe. The building was designed by the New York architect Wilfred Edwards Anthony, under commission from the philanthropist Mrs. Benjamin Talbot B. Hyde. Mrs. Hyde engaged Baumann to design and execute a carved and gilt wooden *reredos*, the screen above and behind the altar. The altarpiece represents Christ enthroned in heaven, flanked by panels depicting the evangelists Paul and John, who are surrounded by figures representing four races of humanity, and a host of angels. The artist executed this work on site in the church. Occasionally, when he needed models, he called upon his friends, including the rector, C. J. Kinsolving III, who were made to strike poses required at the moment, often at odd hours. The artist completed the project in about two years, and the altarpiece was dedicated on August 12, 1945.[55]

Baumann enjoyed a long, distinguished, and comfortable retirement. During the latter part of his career, following World War II, the volume of his print production waned as he applied his energies to other activities. During the last thirty years of his life, he averaged about one new print a year. It was during this period that he routinely reprinted new versions of old prints, sometimes producing variant states by altering blocks or changing their coloration, and by inscribing them with new, alternative titles. He still enjoyed working outdoors, making gouache paintings in his garden or at the pueblos, some of which studies were made into color woodcuts. However, most of these represent isolated exercises, and the prints resulting from them were fairly conventional.

Tares (plate 59), a woodcut produced in 1952, exemplifies Baumann's enduring powers as a craftsman. His steady hand and intricate carving still matched the subtlety of his perception. By overprinting layers of ink in progressively darker grays, superimposed finally by rich black, the artist achieved an illusion of these slender stalks as freestanding and resilient. Yet the way in which he dissolved the background with hatching at the edges of his composition denies this artifice. This intimate still life reveals the intricate beauty of a common weed, the sort of wonder that often goes unnoticed. Here the artist captured a fleeting and delicate balance of line and form. The tiny yellow flowers dry and shrivel before us, and the downy white spheres will dissolve in a moment as the wind scatters their seeds on a thousand weightless silken parachutes. If this is an image of transience, it is also one of regeneration and the comforting cycles of nature and of life.

Baumann was named an honorary fellow of the Fine Arts School of American Research in Santa Fe in 1952, the year that a retrospective exhibition of his prints was mounted at the New Mexico Museum of Fine Arts, a full thirty-five years after his first exhibition there. At the same time, a comprehensive body of Baumann's work was donated to the museum, including more than three hundred objects, among them one hundred seventy color woodcuts.

In the years following, the printmaker continued to work contentedly. During the 1960s, he even dabbled with abstraction in his paintings and prints. He had always maintained a good-natured respect for nonobjective art, cherishing the work of Paul Klee and others. His understanding of abstraction deepened with interest in Native American and children's art.[56] Nevertheless, Baumann found it nearly impossible to free his work of references to concrete visual experience. He made a handful of exploratory prints, such as *Torrey Pine* (1961) and *Hidden Meaning* (1962), but these efforts were diversions. He never seriously confronted the challenges and possibilities of abstract woodcuts.

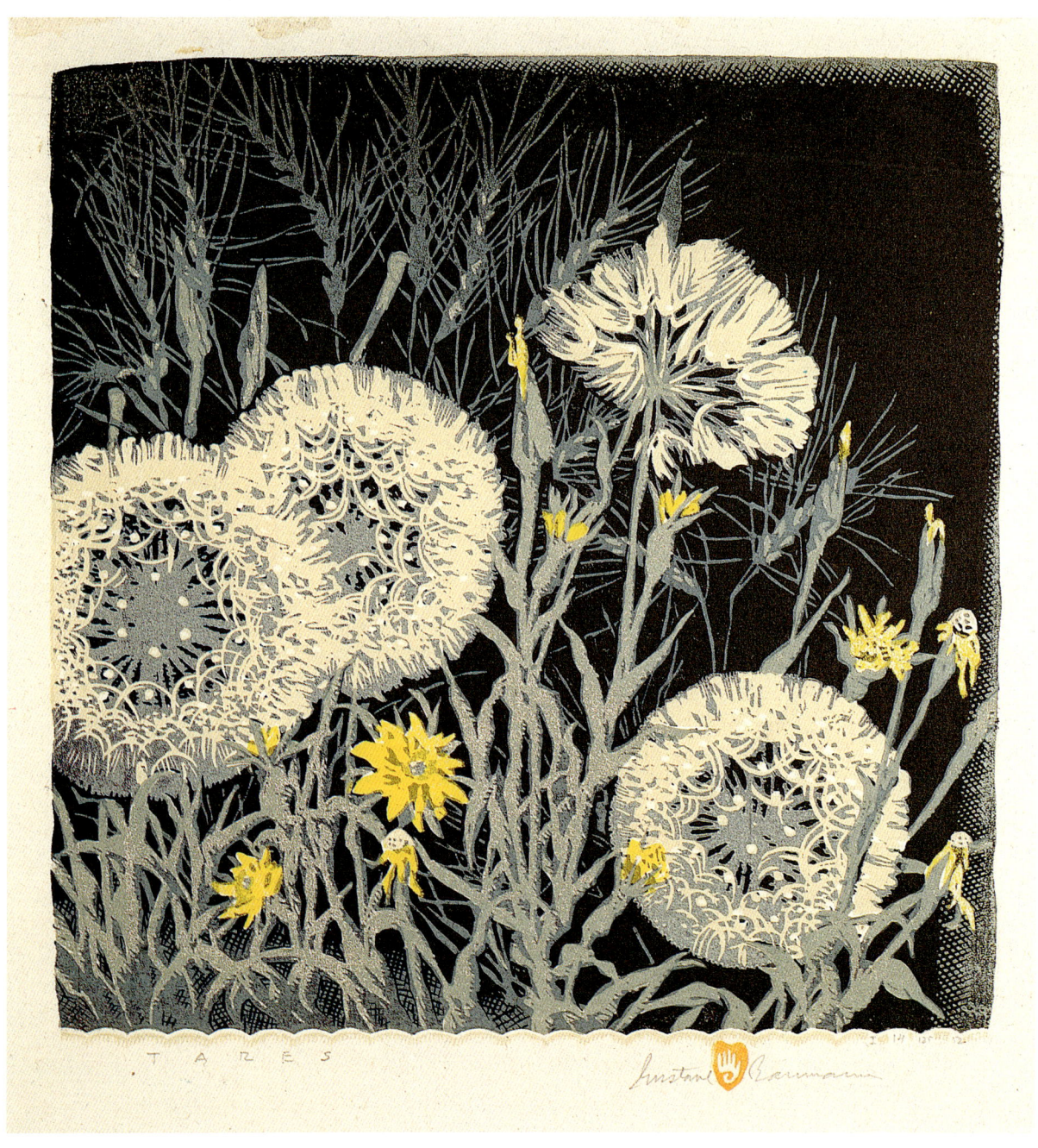

59 · TARES, 1952

Color woodcut, 12¾ × 12½ in.

Baumann's prints always remained proudly oriented to craft. The great achievement of his career was that he was able to delight people by the melding of his craftsman's skill with the sustained inspiration he drew from the beauty of nature, the venerable traditions of Native

American culture, and a prevailing sense of good humor, all of which he discovered and nourished in the American West during the years of his artistic maturity. Beyond the inarguable allure of his images and his obvious skill in rendering them, Baumann captured the quiet contemplation of solitude that increasingly came to characterize his life. It is this sensation that reverberates in his art. Most of Gustave Baumann's prints succeed in sharing with the viewer something of the comfortable contentment of the artist's own personality.

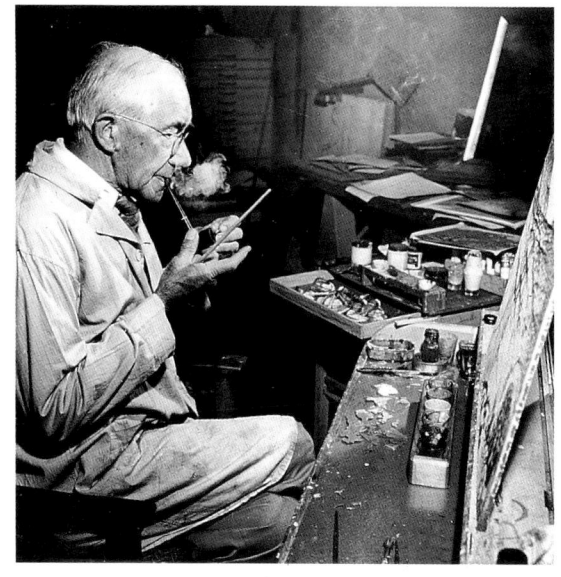

Baumann at his easel, ca. 1952.

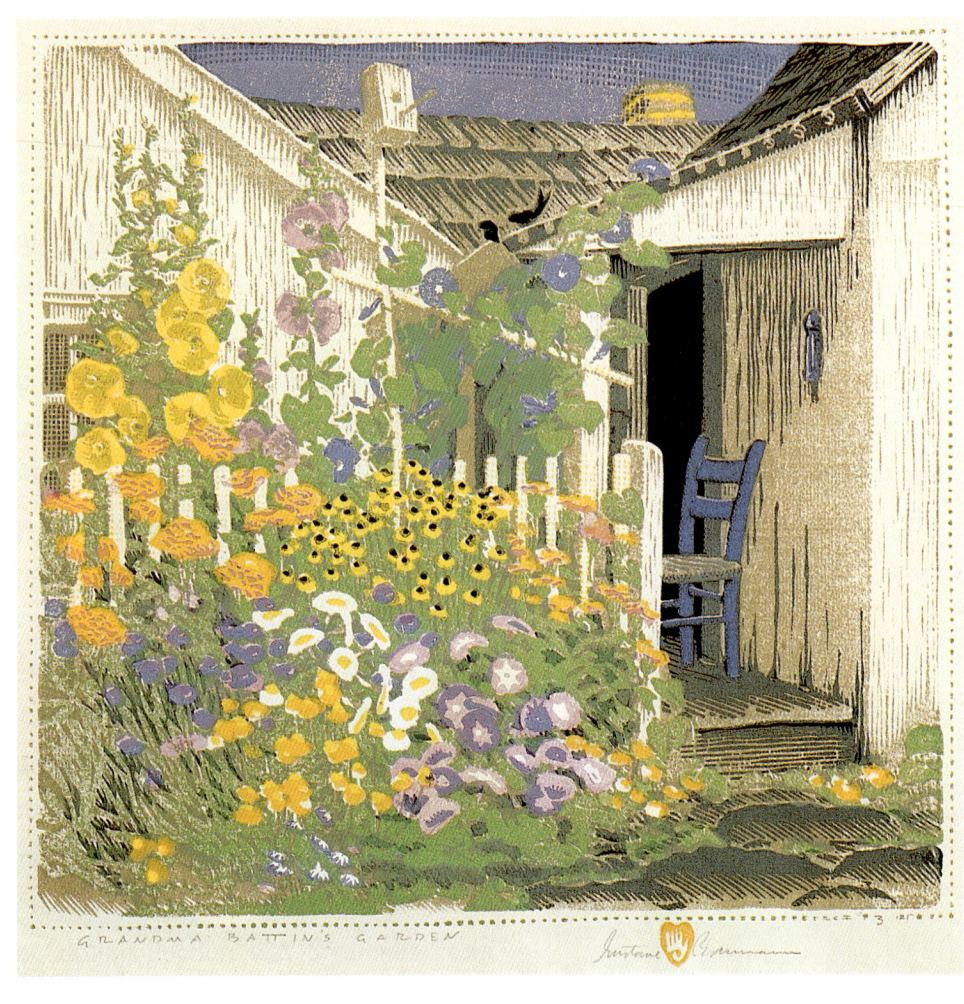

GRANDMA BATTIN'S GARDEN

60. GRANDMA BATTIN'S GARDEN (HOOSIER GARDEN), 1926

Color woodcut, 12 × 13 in.

GOUACHES
AND
WOODCUTS
1905–1952

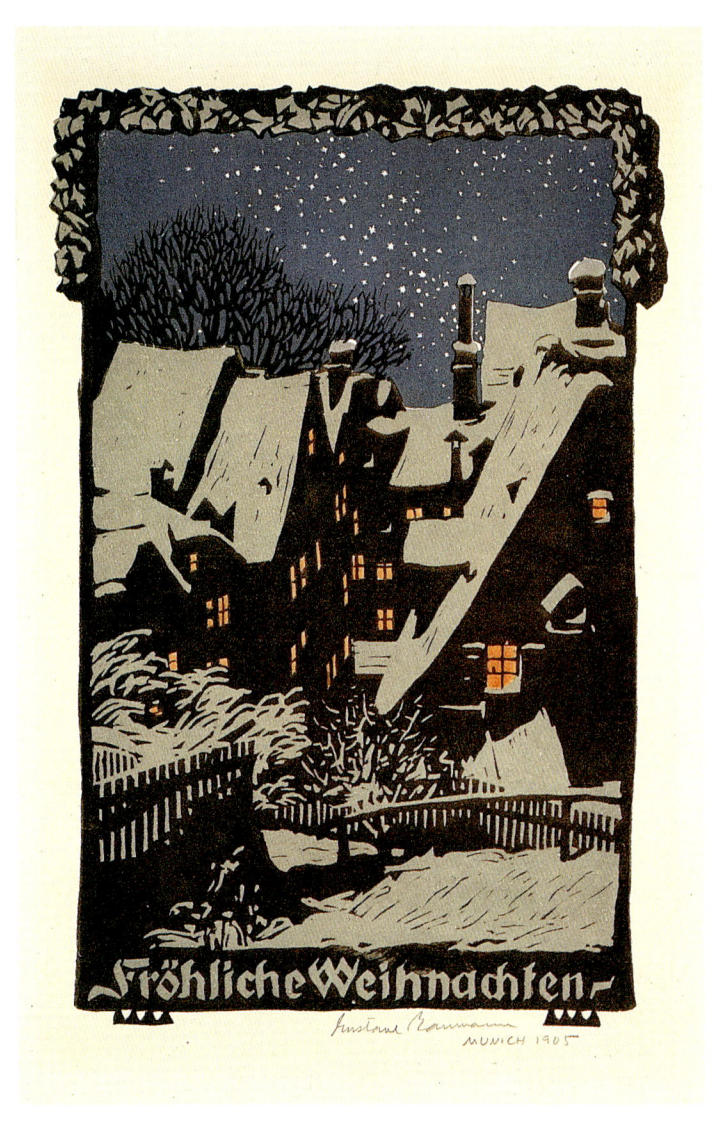

61. FRÖHLICHE WEIHNACHTEN – MUNICH, 1905

Color linocut, 9¾×6½ in.

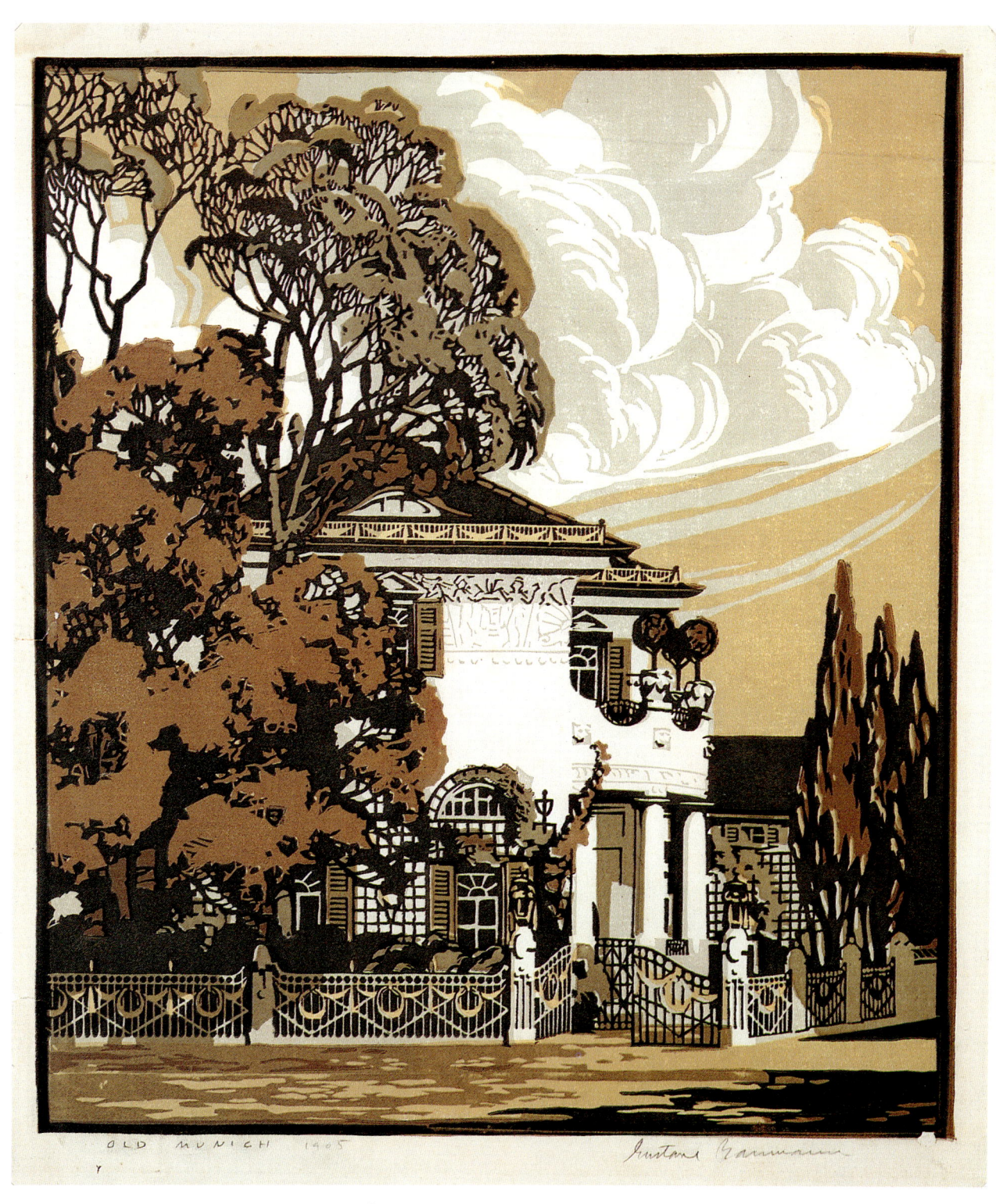

62. OLD MUNICH, 1905

Linocut, 18⅞ × 16½ in.

63. MUNICH MAY, 1905

Pencil, 9½ × 10¾ in.

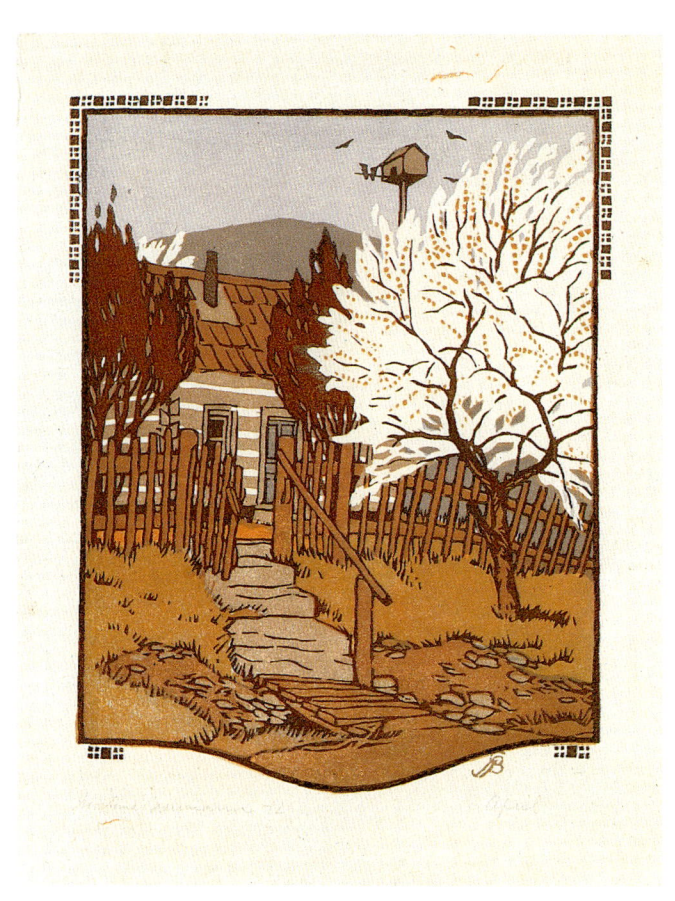

64. ALL THE YEAR ROUND (APRIL), 1912

Color woodcut, 8×6⅛ in.

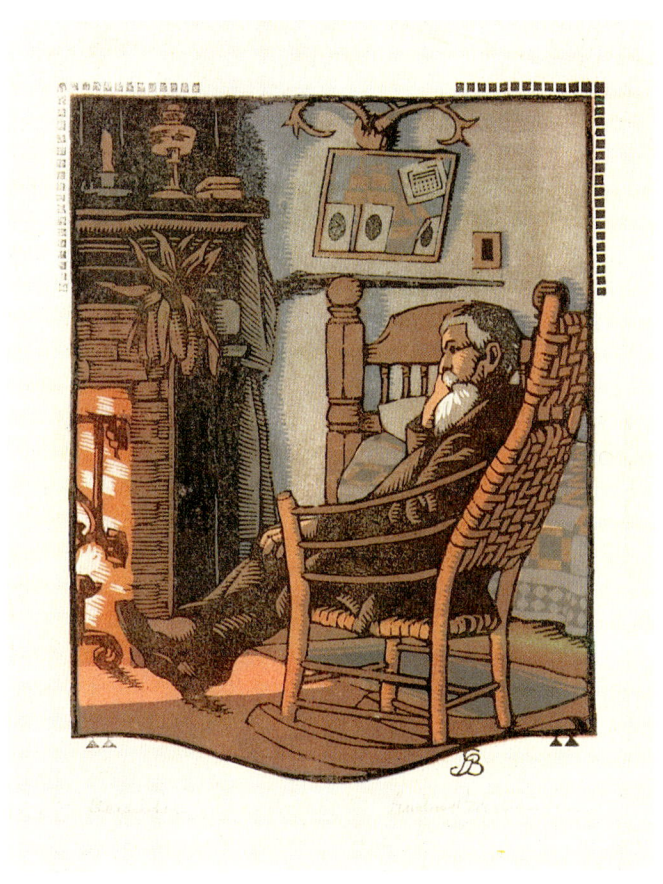

65. ALL THE YEAR ROUND (DECEMBER), 1912

Color woodcut, 8×6½ in.

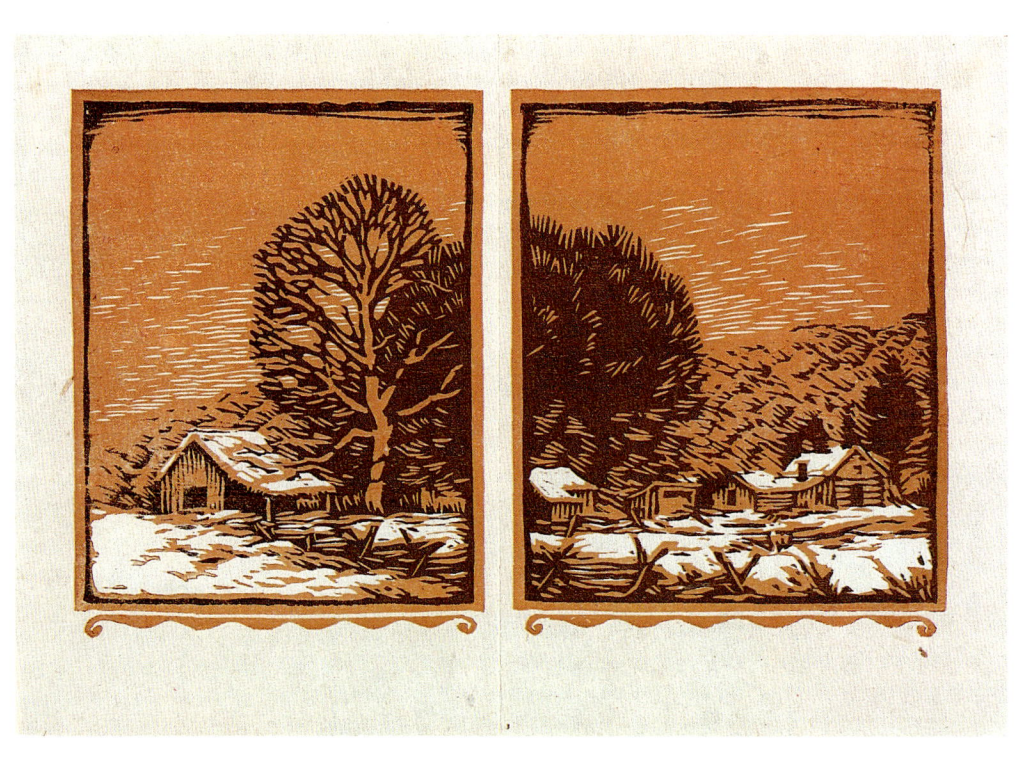

66. UNTITLED, *ca.* 1912

Color woodcut, 6×8¾ in.

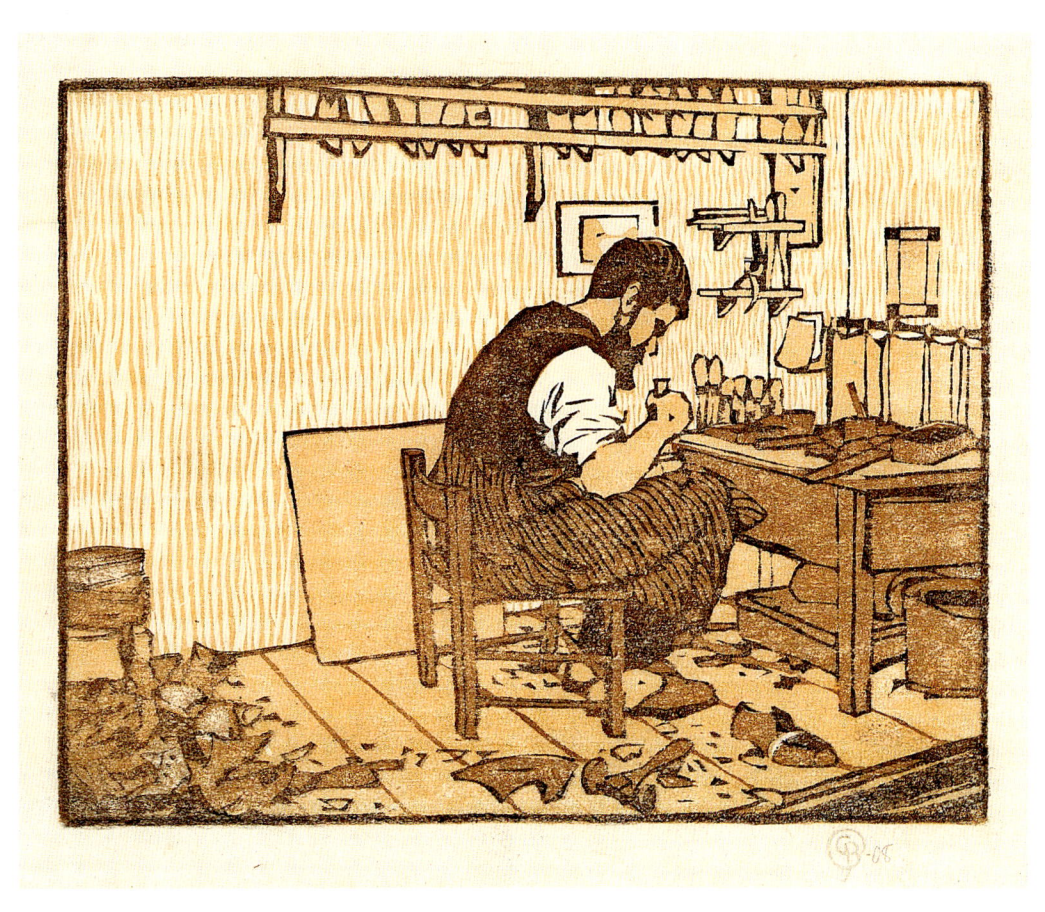

67. THE COBBLER, 1908

Color woodcut, 7×9 in.

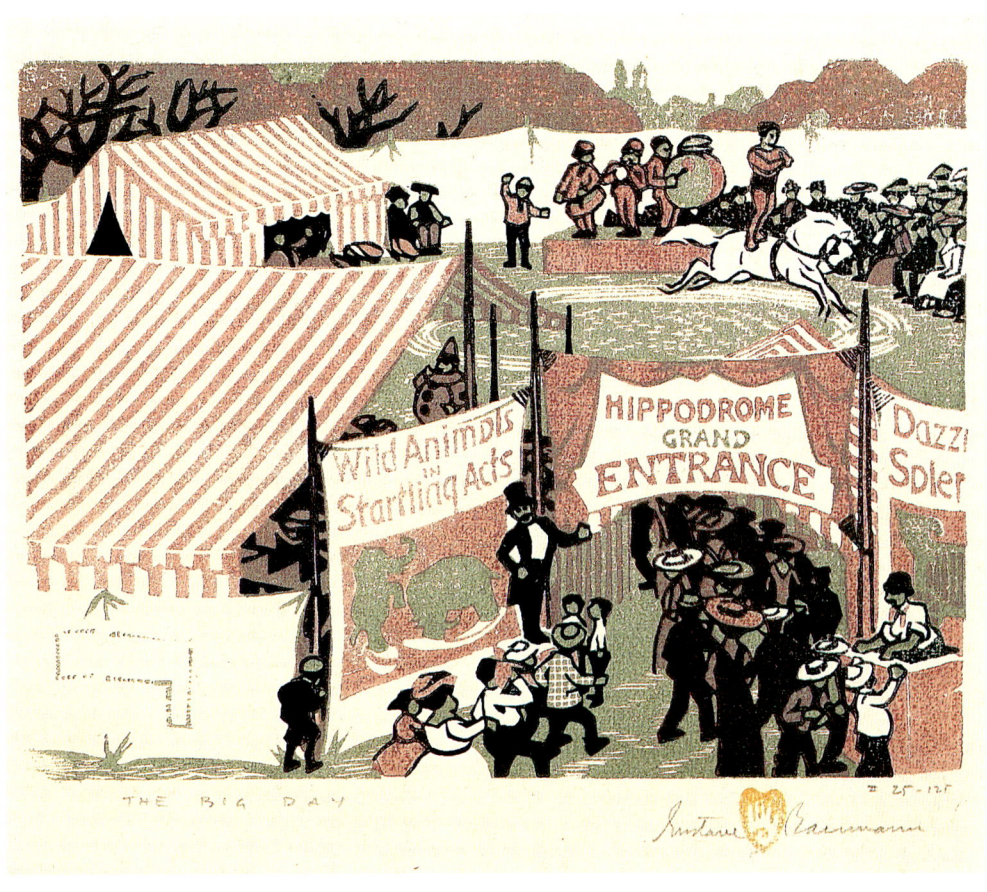

68. THE BIG DAY (COUNTRY CIRCUS), 1909

Color woodcut, 6¾×9¼ in.

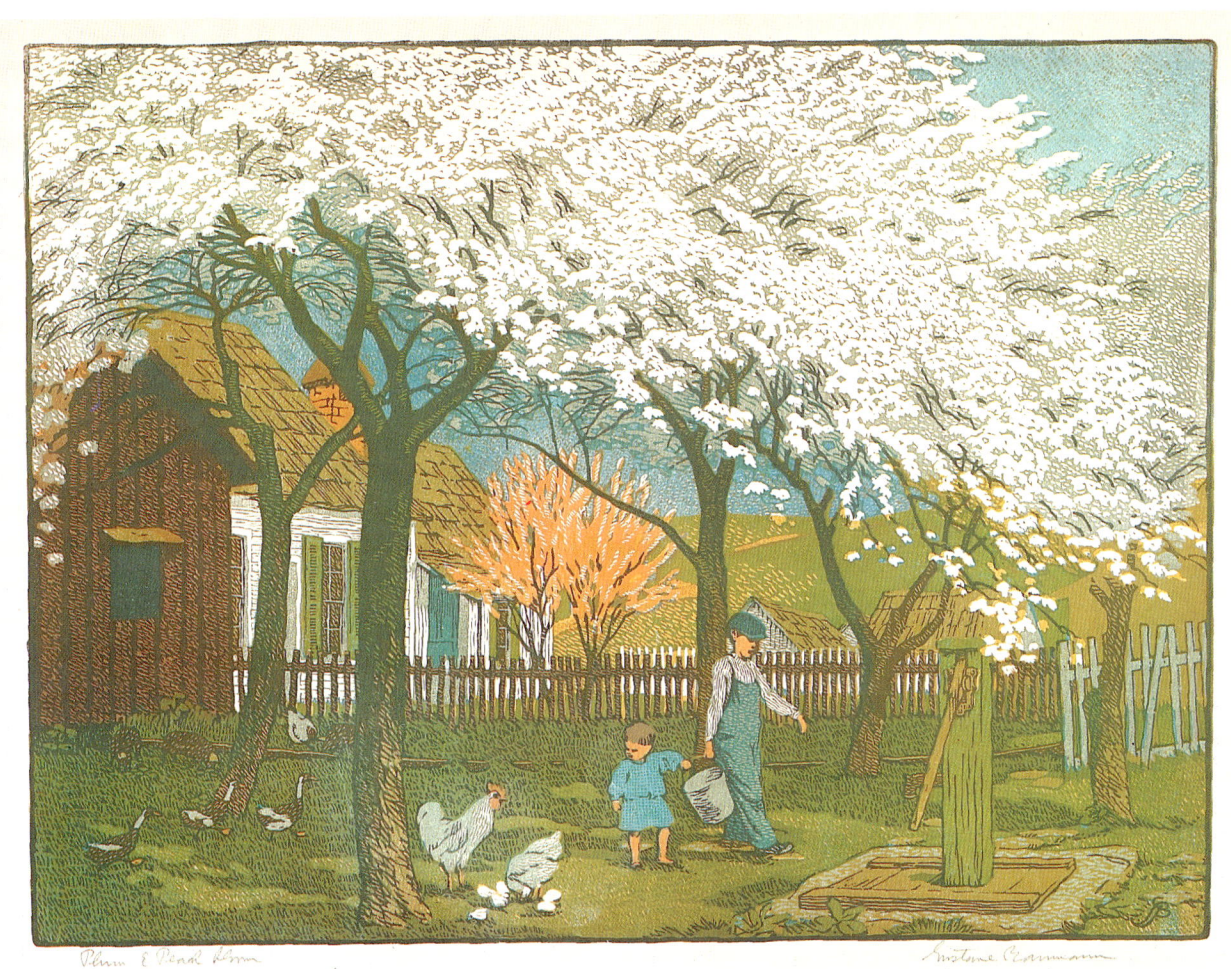

69. PLUM AND PEACH BLOOM, 1911–1913

Color woodcut, 19¾ × 26⅝ in.

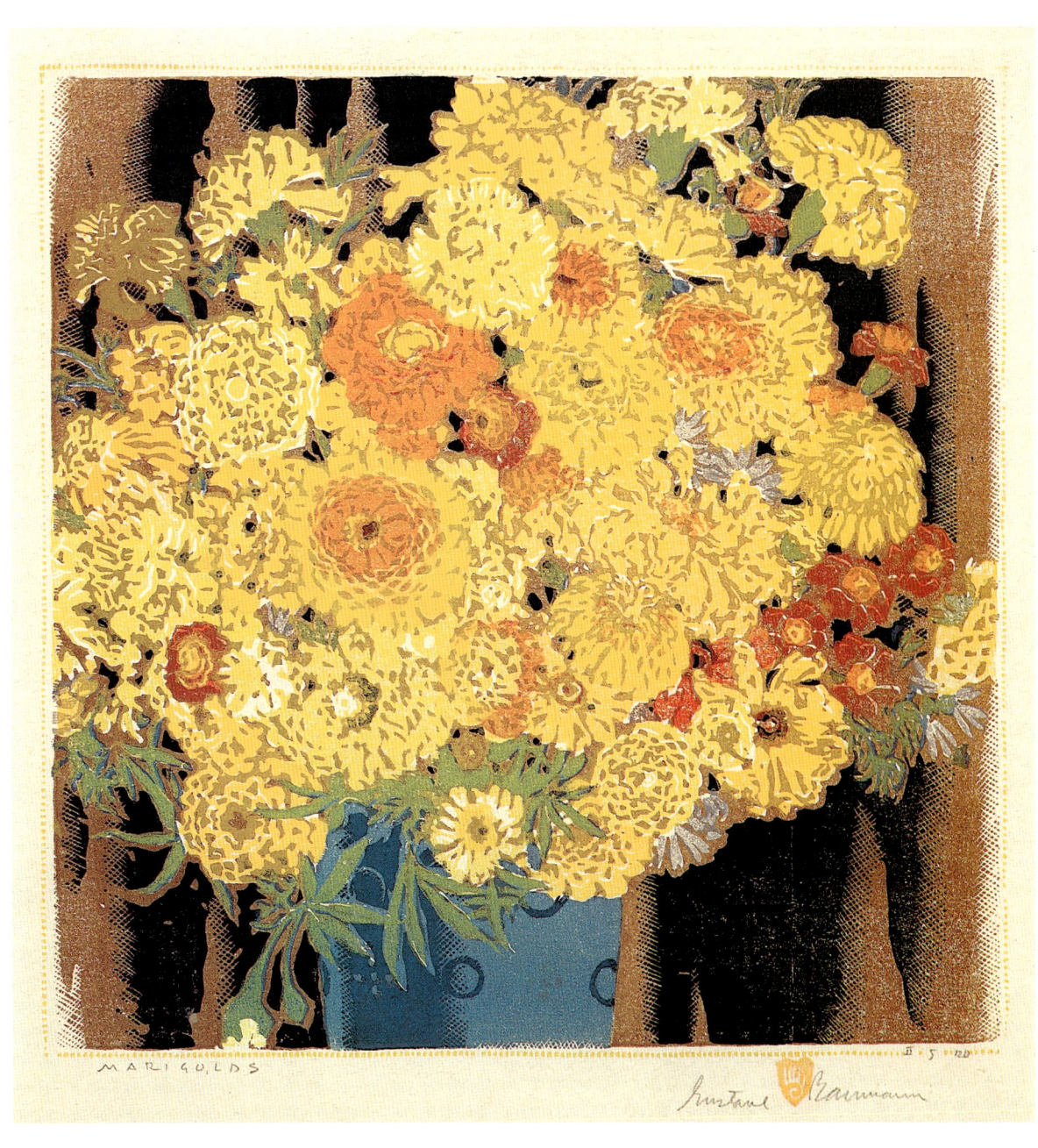

70. MARIGOLDS, 1915–1916

Color woodcut, 12¾ × 12¾ in.

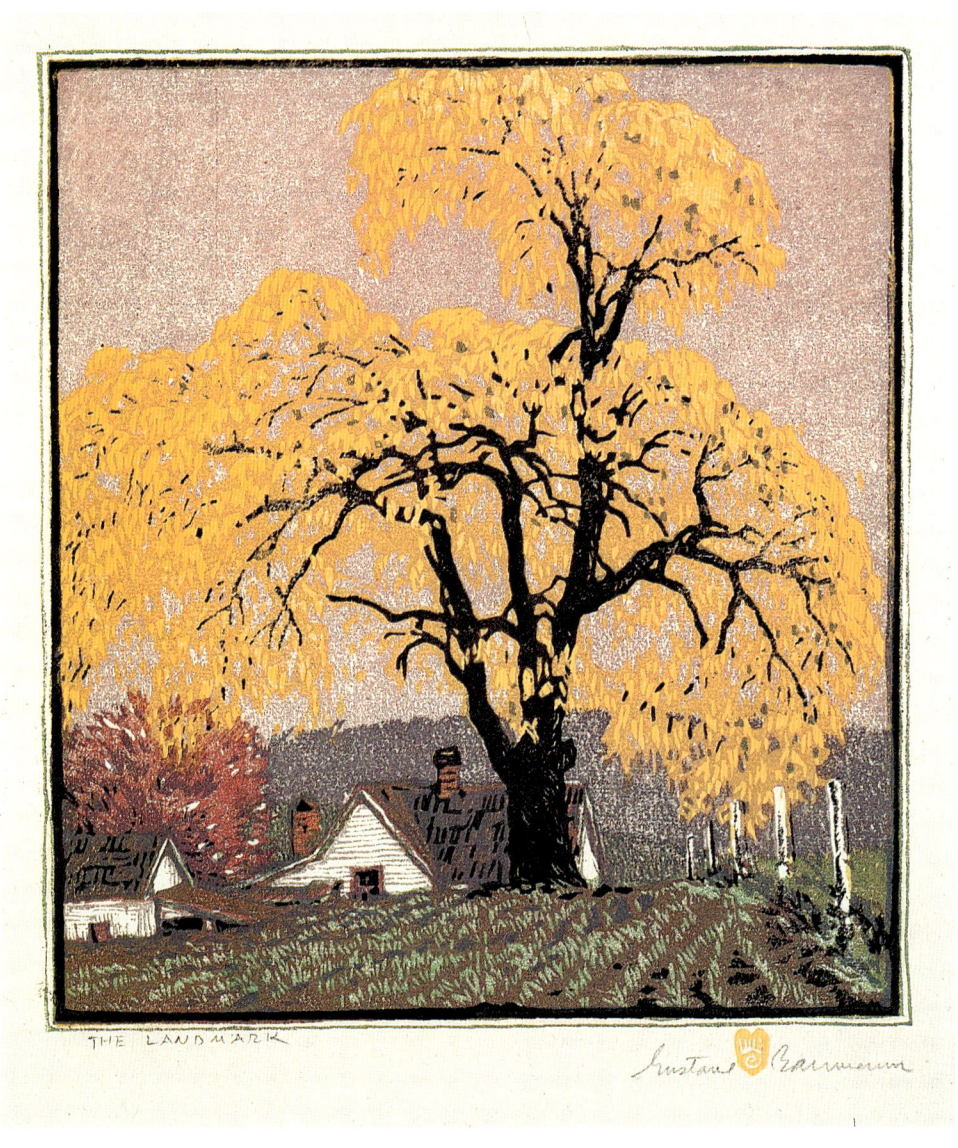

71. THE LANDMARK, 1916

Color woodcut, 10⅞ × 9⅞ in.

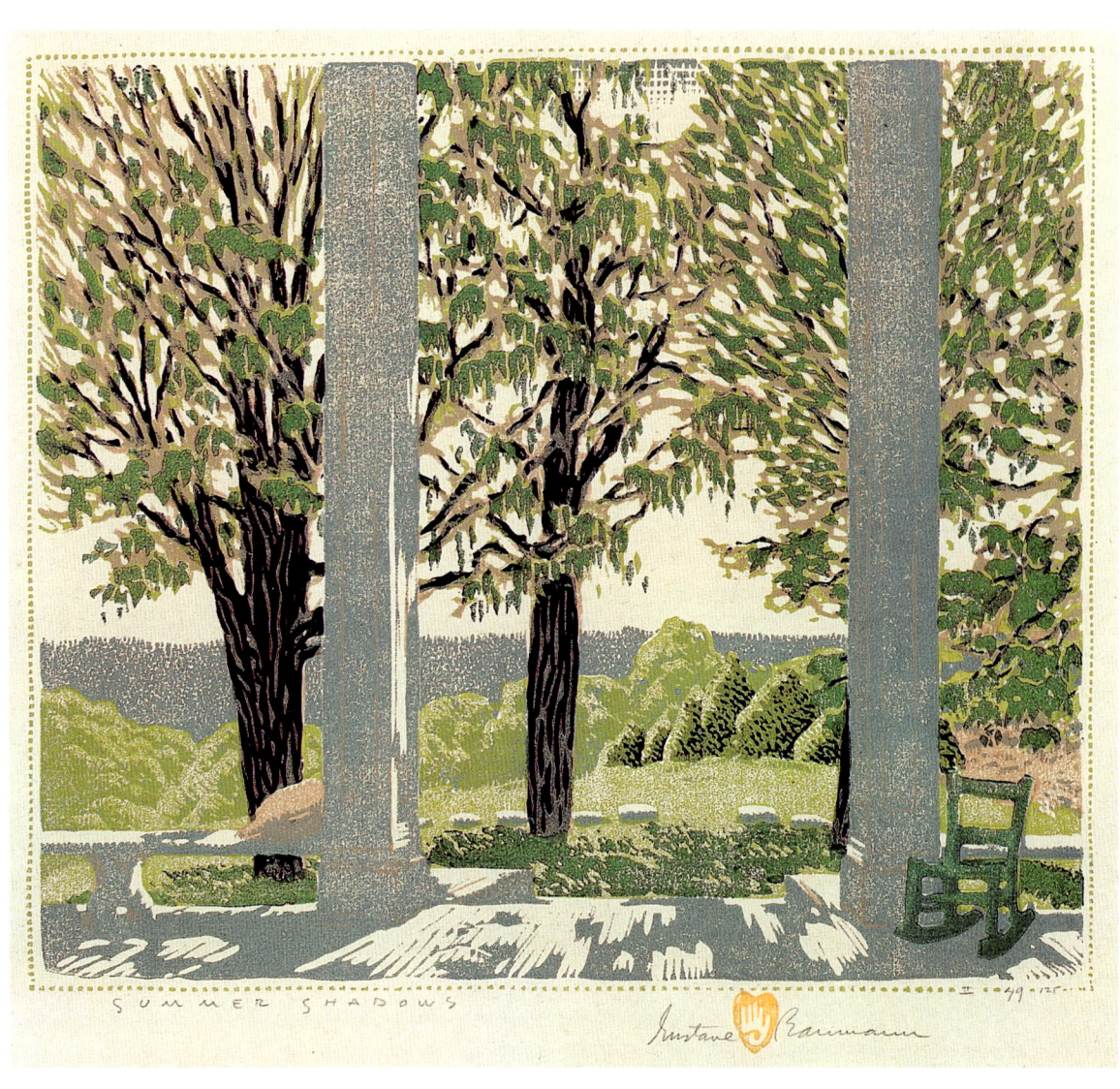

72 . SUMMER SHADOWS, 1917

Color woodcut, 9⅝ × 11¼ in.

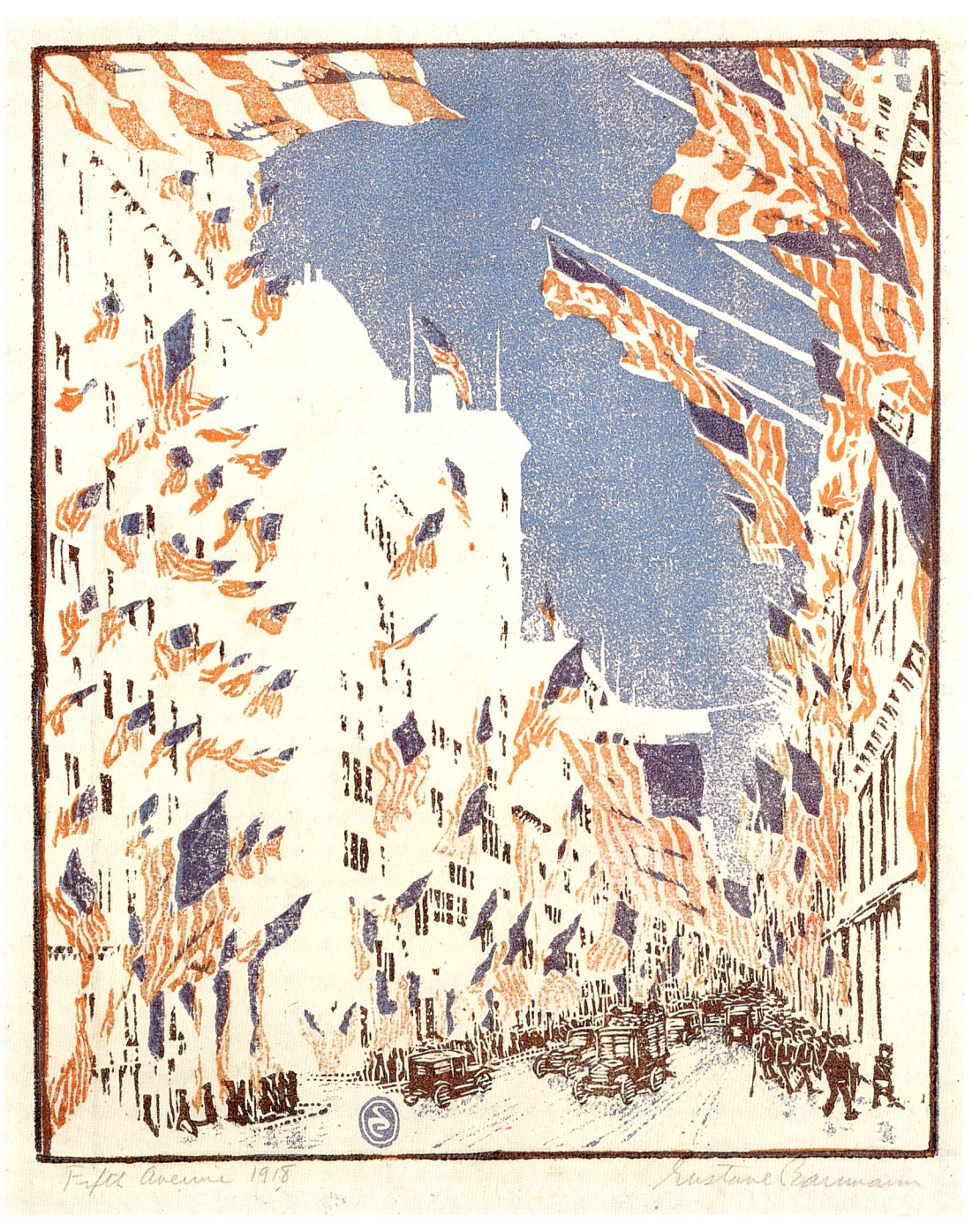

73. FIFTH AVENUE, 1917

Color woodcut, 13¼×11¼ in.

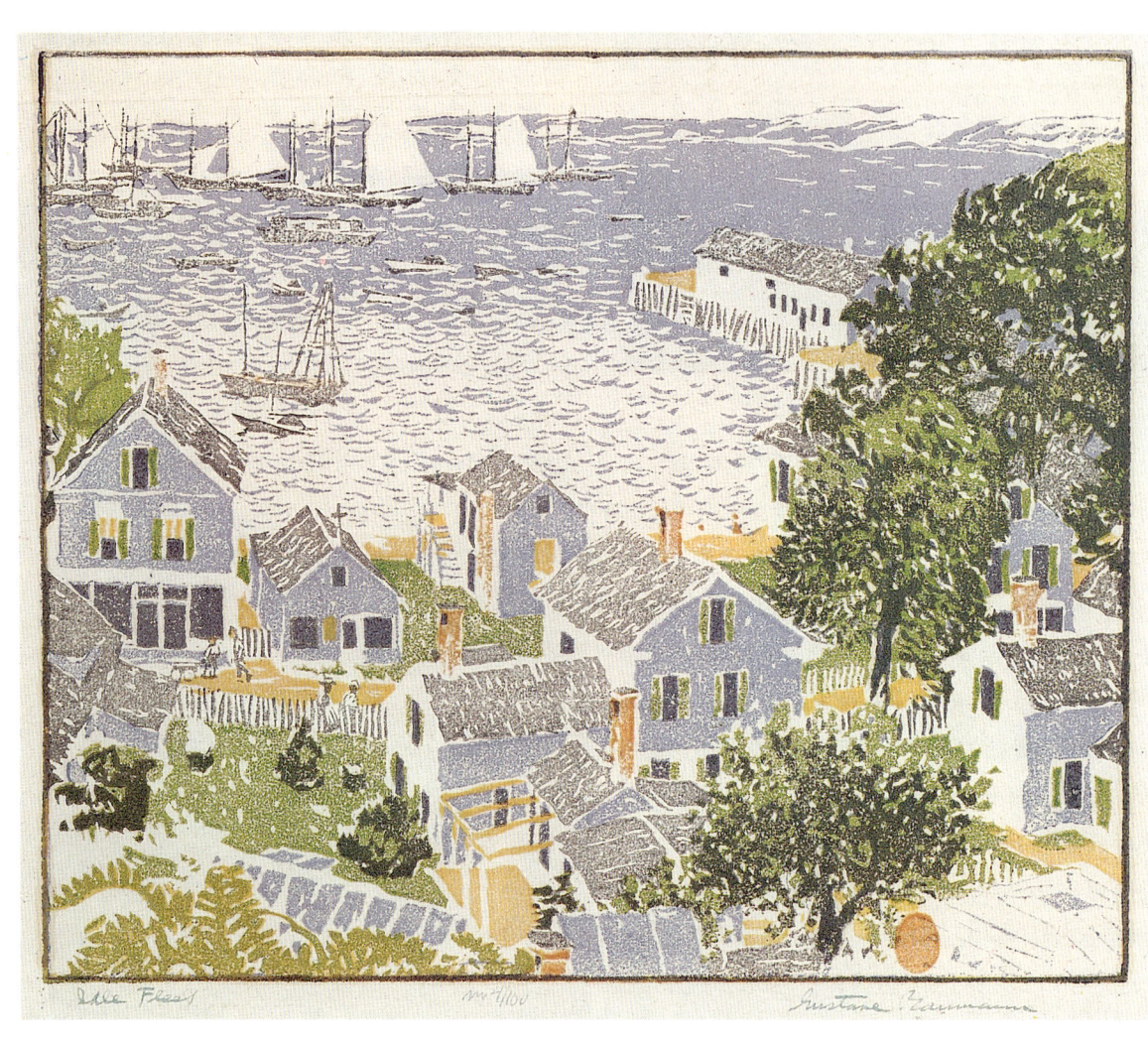

74 . IDLE FLEET , 1917

Color woodcut, 10⅞ × 13¼ in.

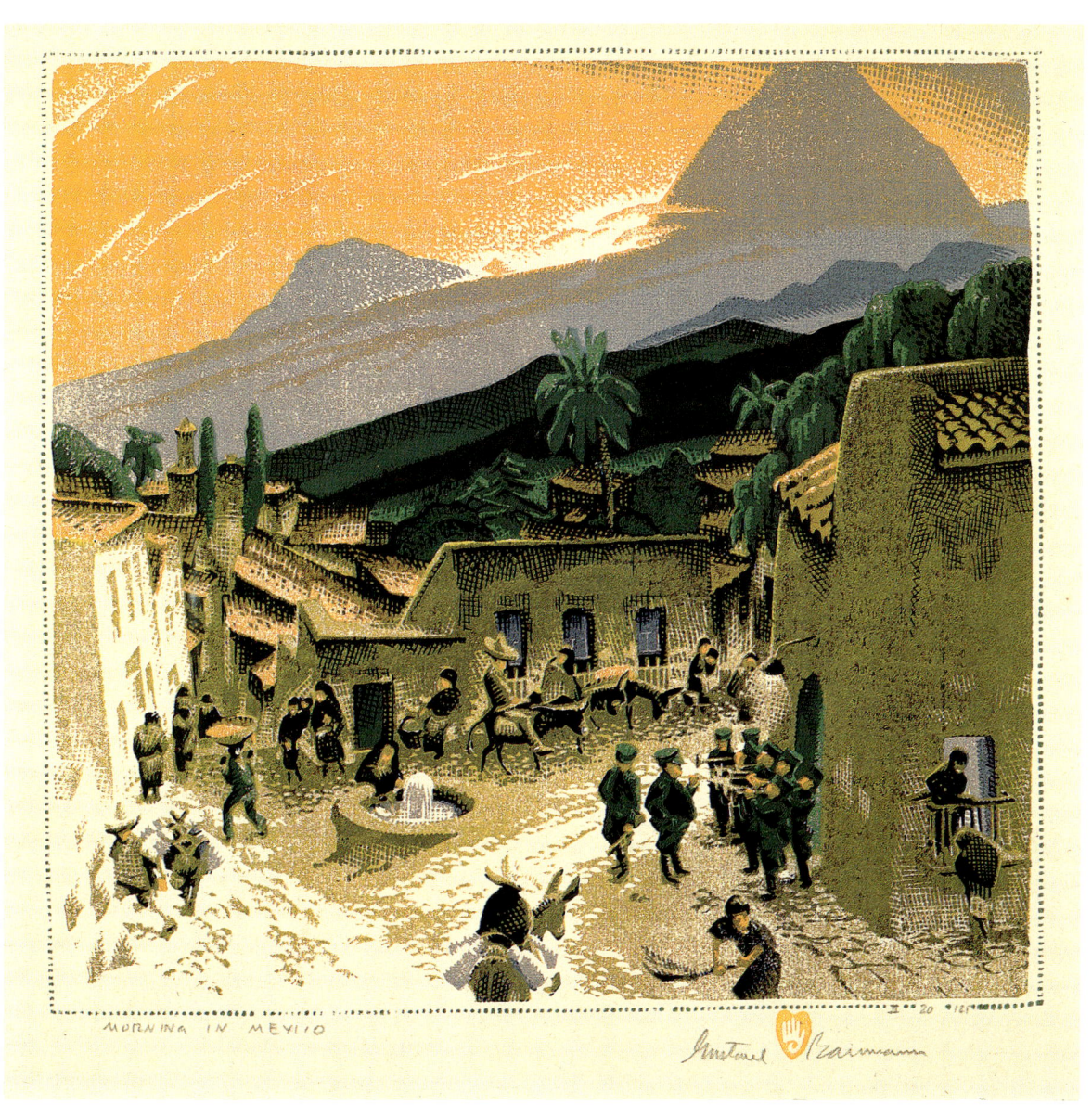

75 · MORNING IN MEXICO, 1917

Color woodcut, 12 × 13 in.

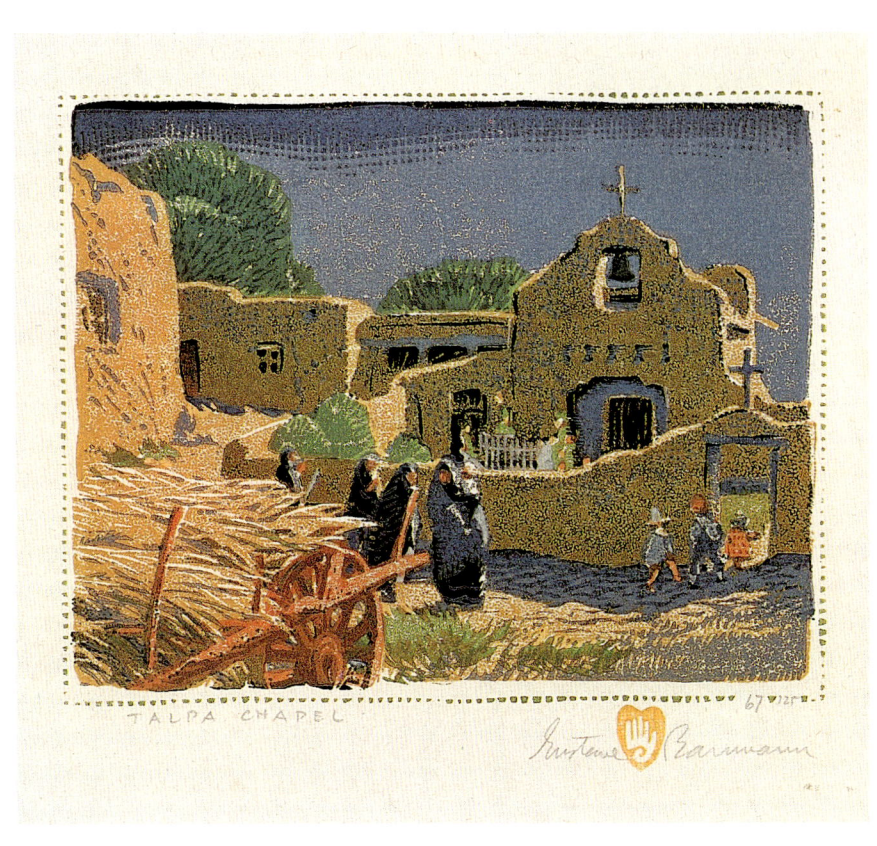

76. TALPA CHAPEL, *ca.* 1920

Color woodcut, 5¾ × 7½ in.

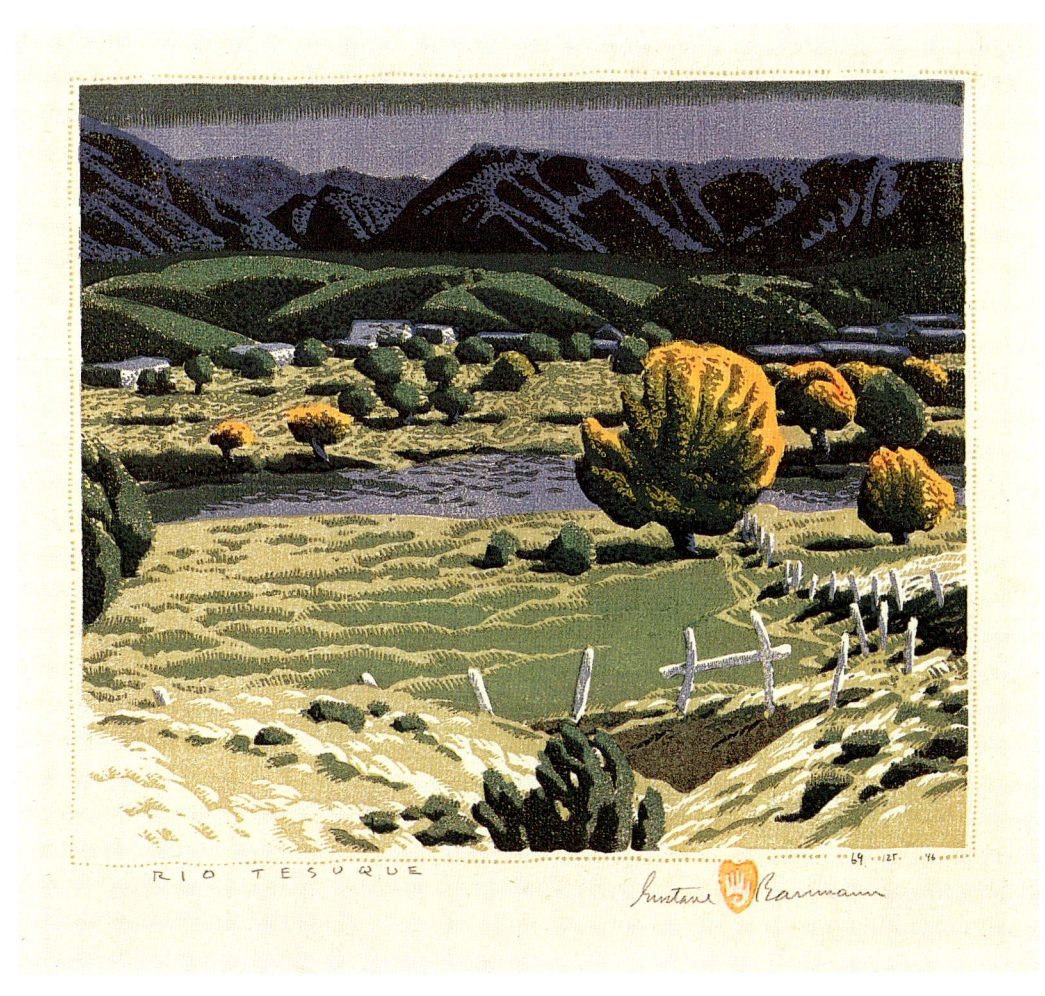

RIO TESUQUE

77. RIO TESUQUE, 1939

Color woodcut, 9¼ × 11 in.

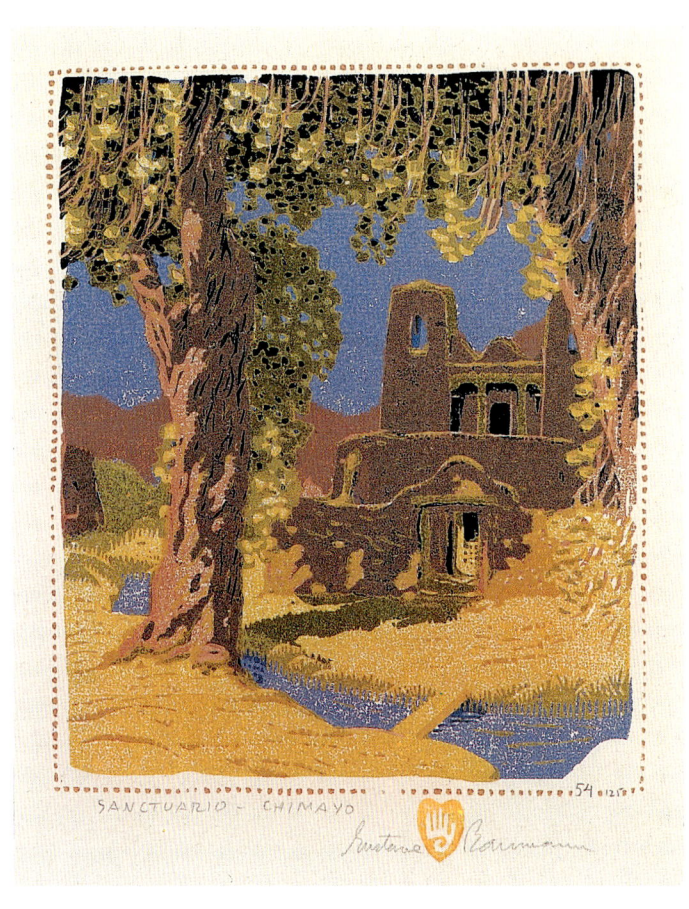

78. SANCTUARIO – CHIMAYO, 1924

Color woodcut, 7¼×6 in.

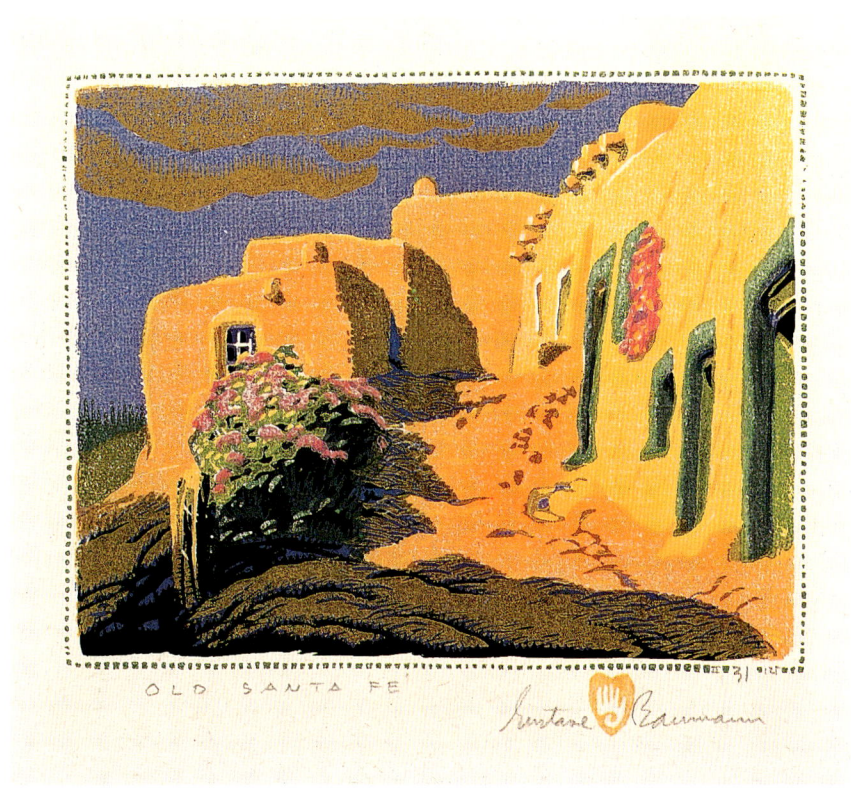

79. OLD SANTA FE, 1924

Color woodcut, 6×7⅝ in.

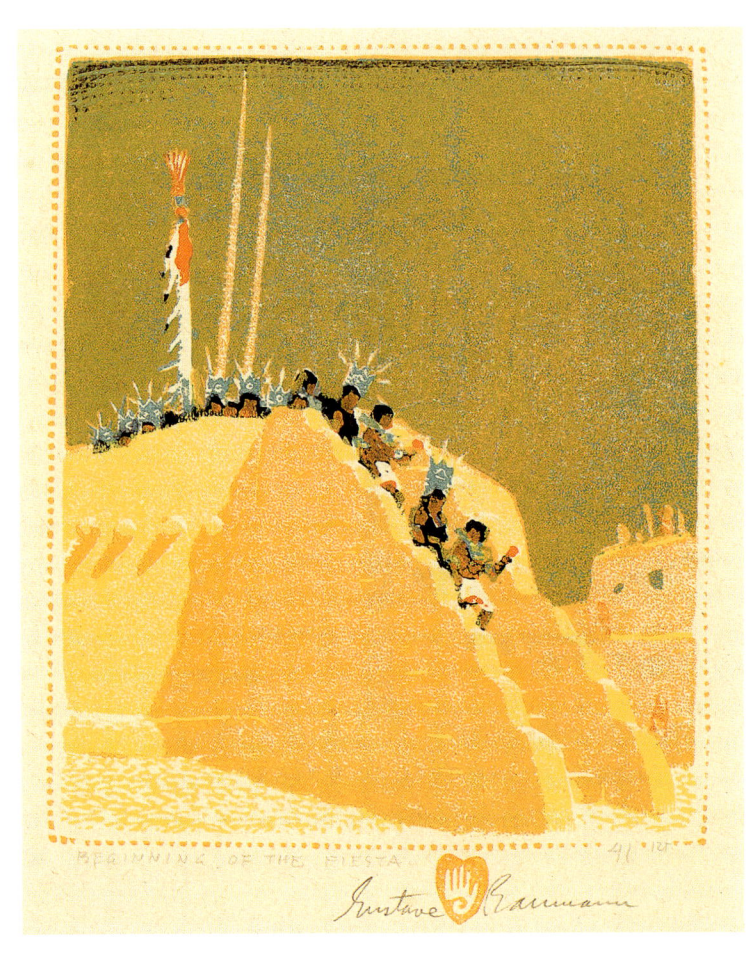

80. BEGINNING OF THE FIESTA, *ca.* 1920

Color woodcut, 7¼×6⅛ in.

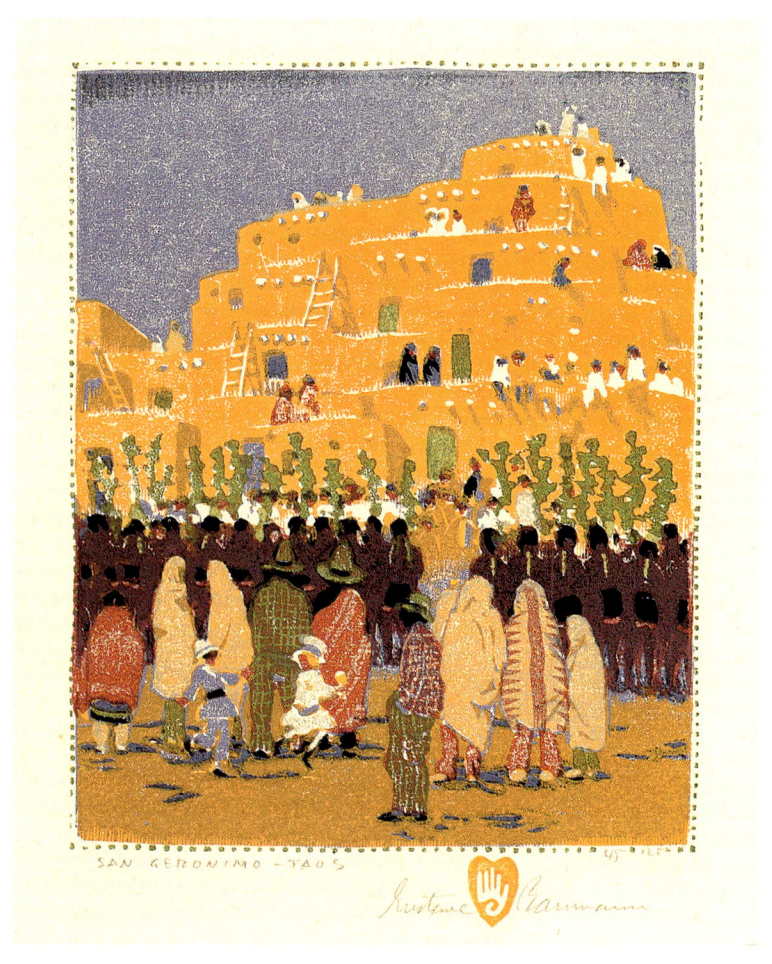

81. SAN GERONIMO – TAOS, 1924

Color woodcut, 7×6 in.

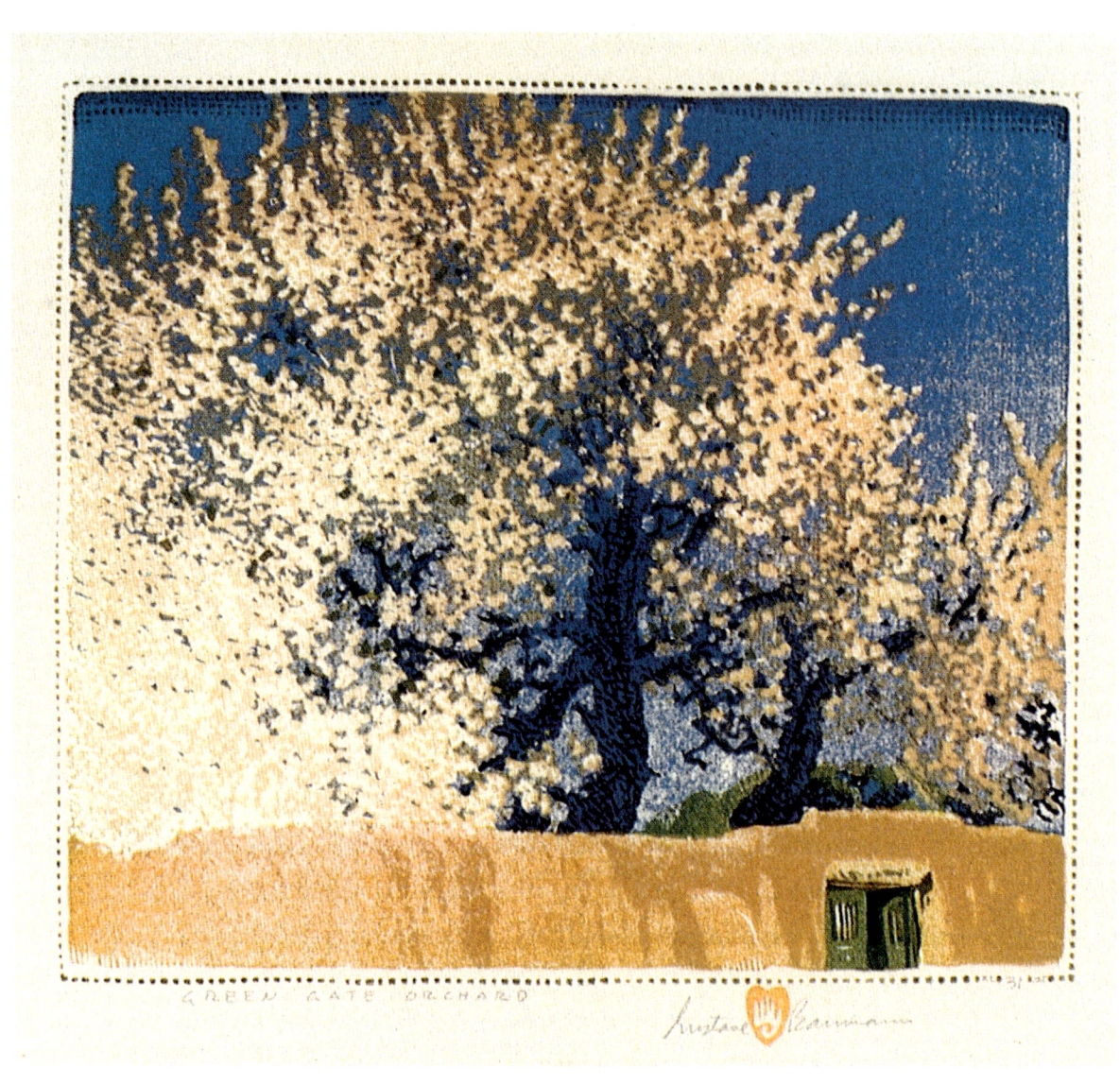

GREEN GATE ORCHARD

82. GREEN GATE ORCHARD, 1923

Color woodcut, 9½ × 11⅛ in.

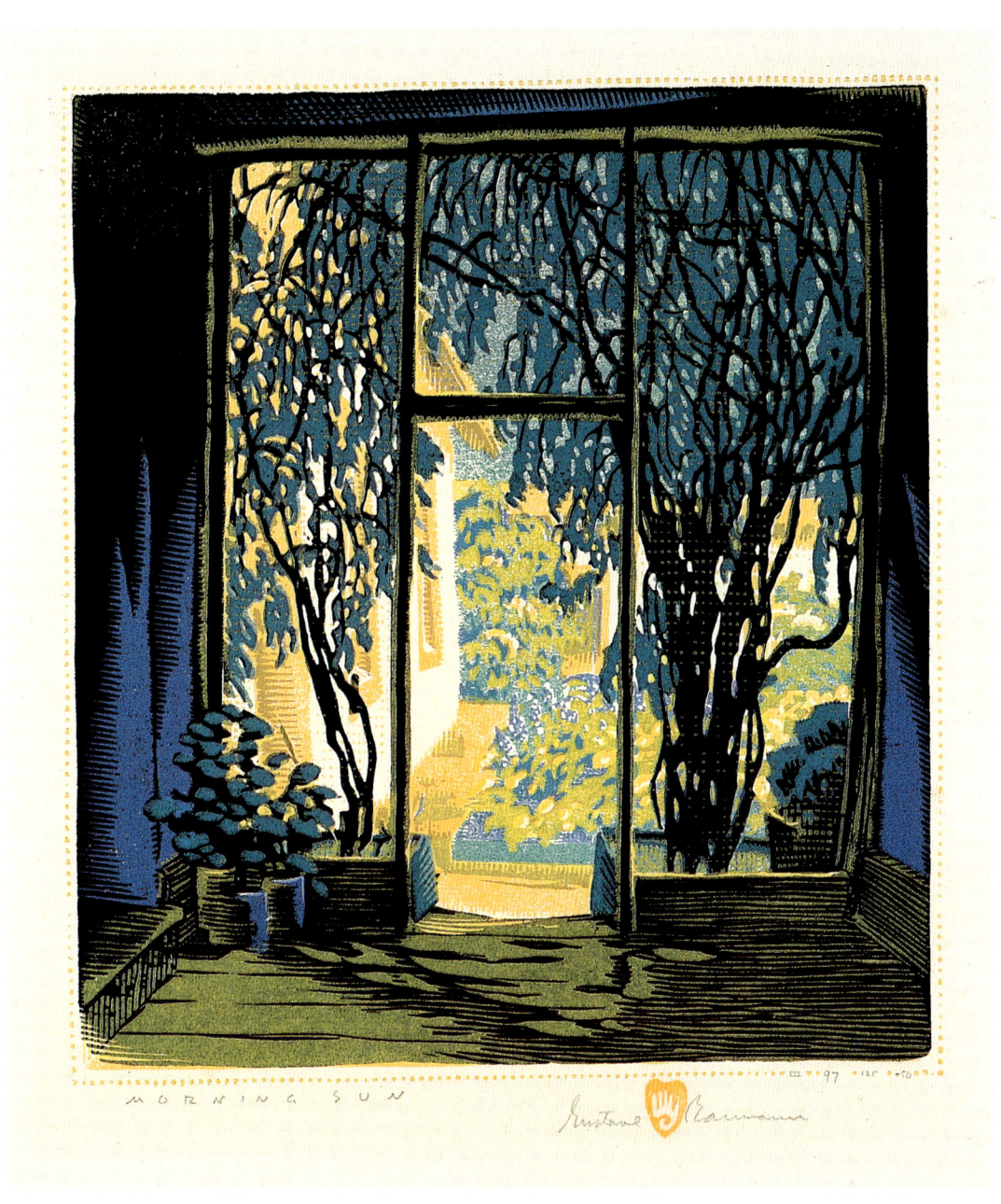

MORNING SUN

83. MORNING SUN, 1932

Color woodcut, 10¾×9⅝ in.

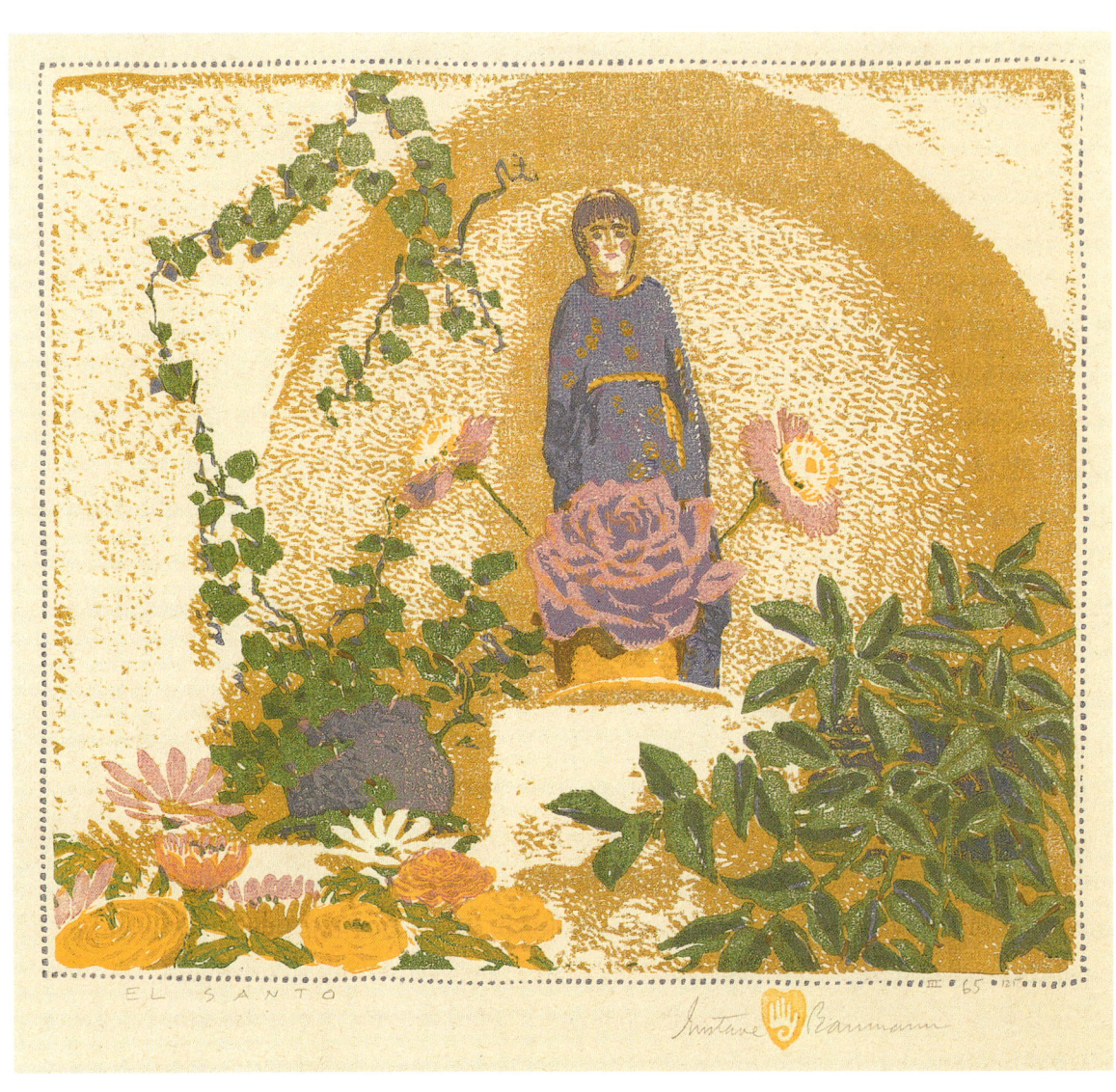

84. EL SANTO, 1919

Color woodcut, 9½ × 11¼ in.

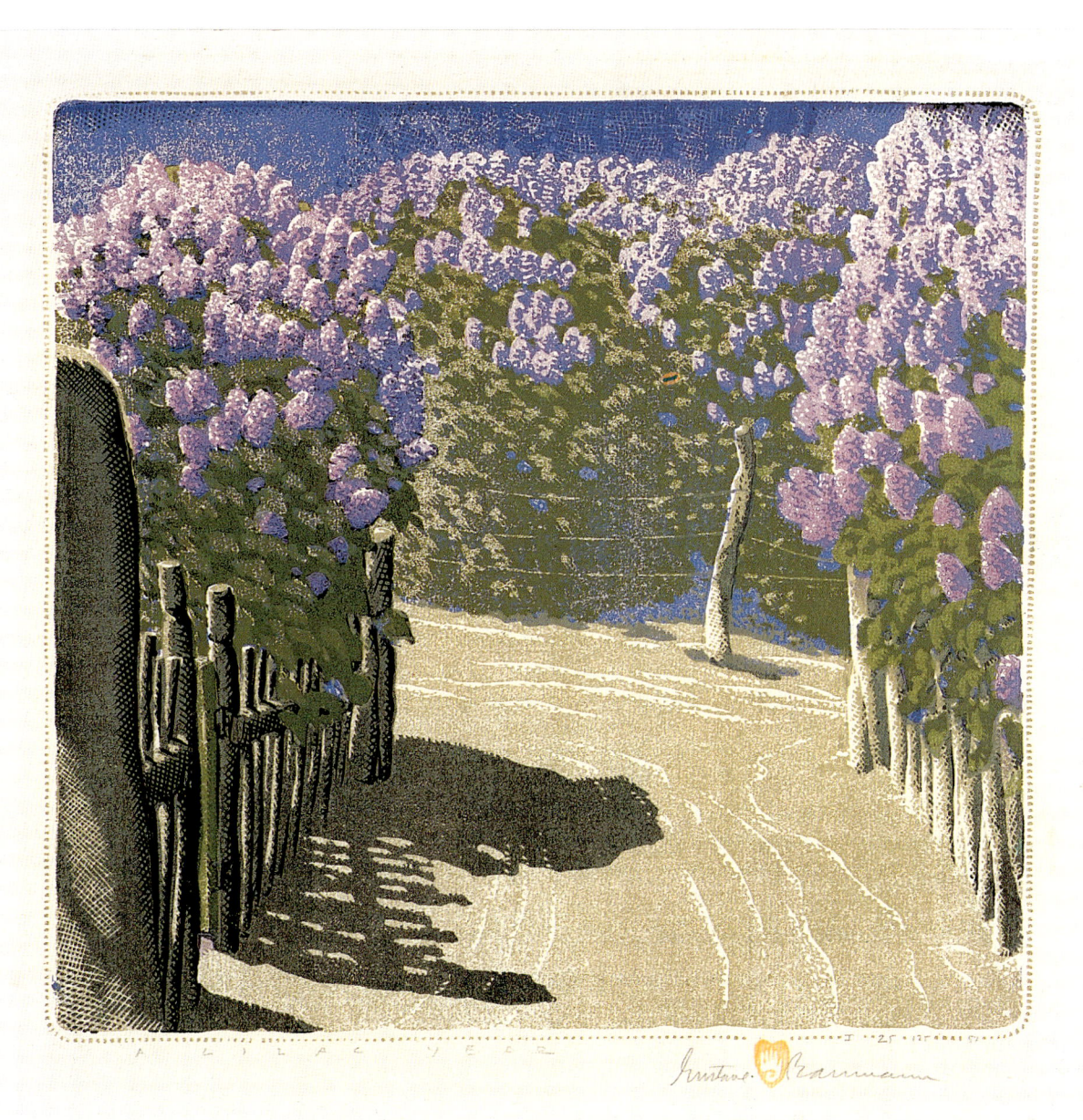

85. A LILAC YEAR, 1949

Color woodcut, 12¼ × 13³⁄₁₆ in.

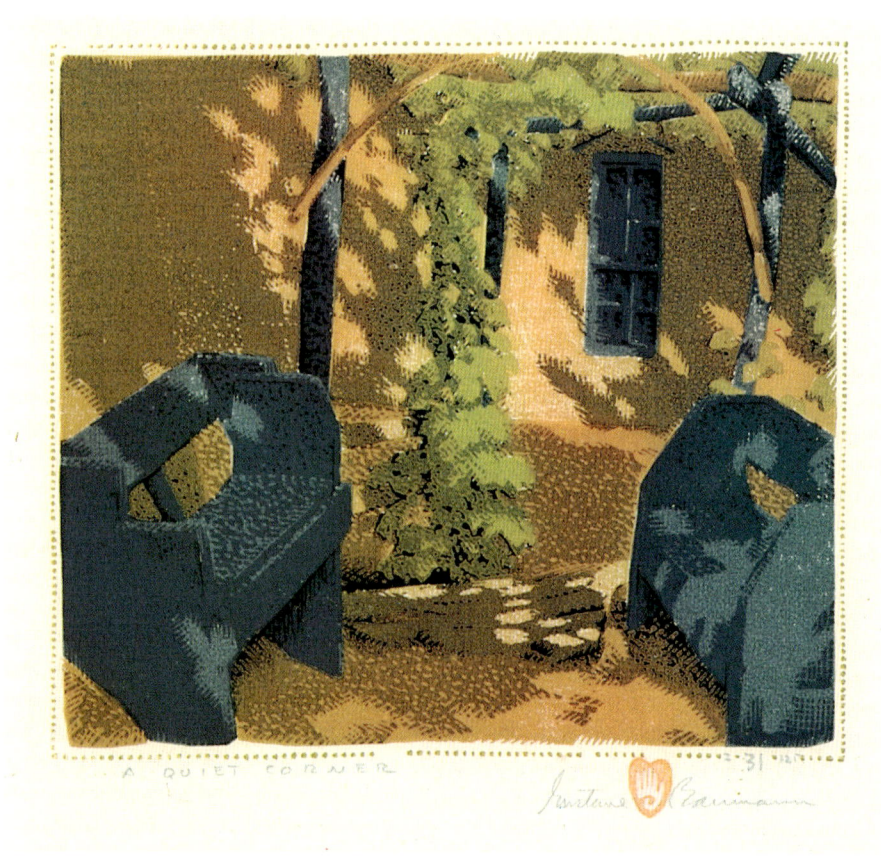

86. A QUIET CORNER, 1918

Color woodcut, 7⅞ × 7⅞ in.

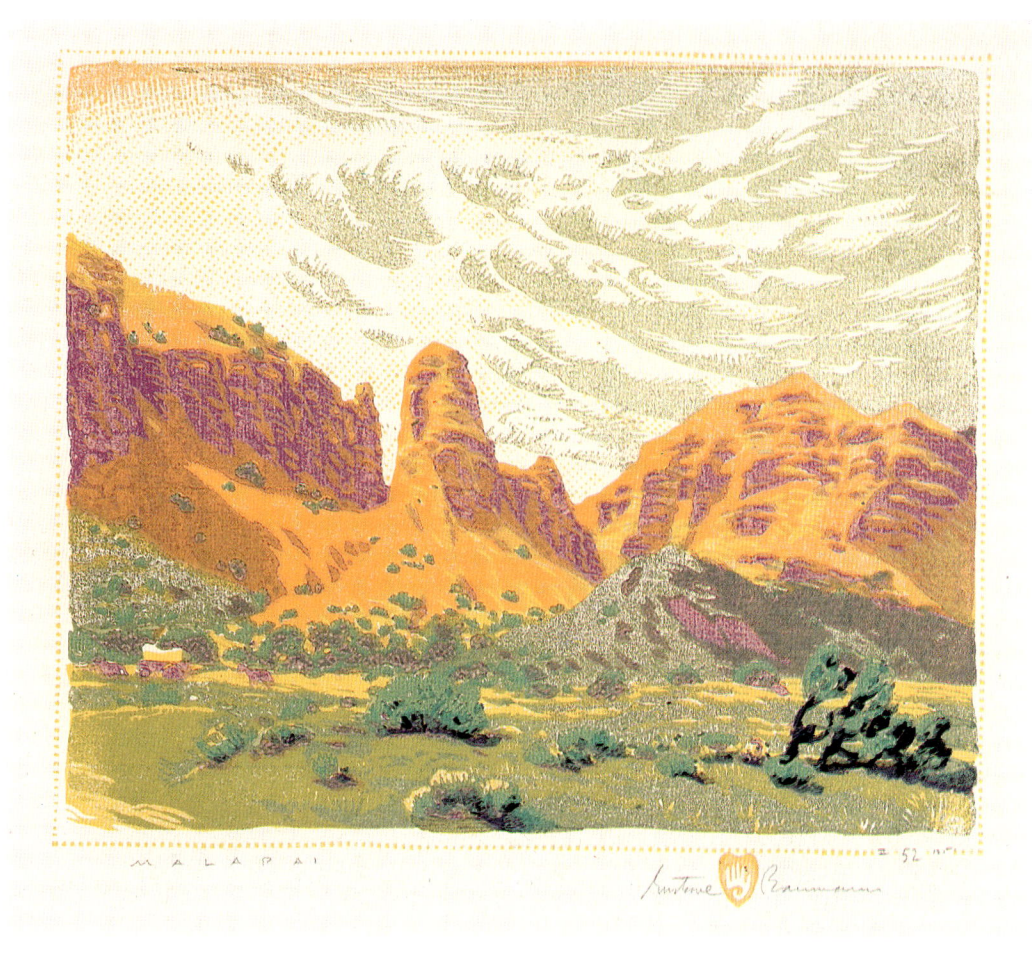

87. MALAPAI, *ca.* 1930

Color woodcut, 9¼ × 11⅛ in.

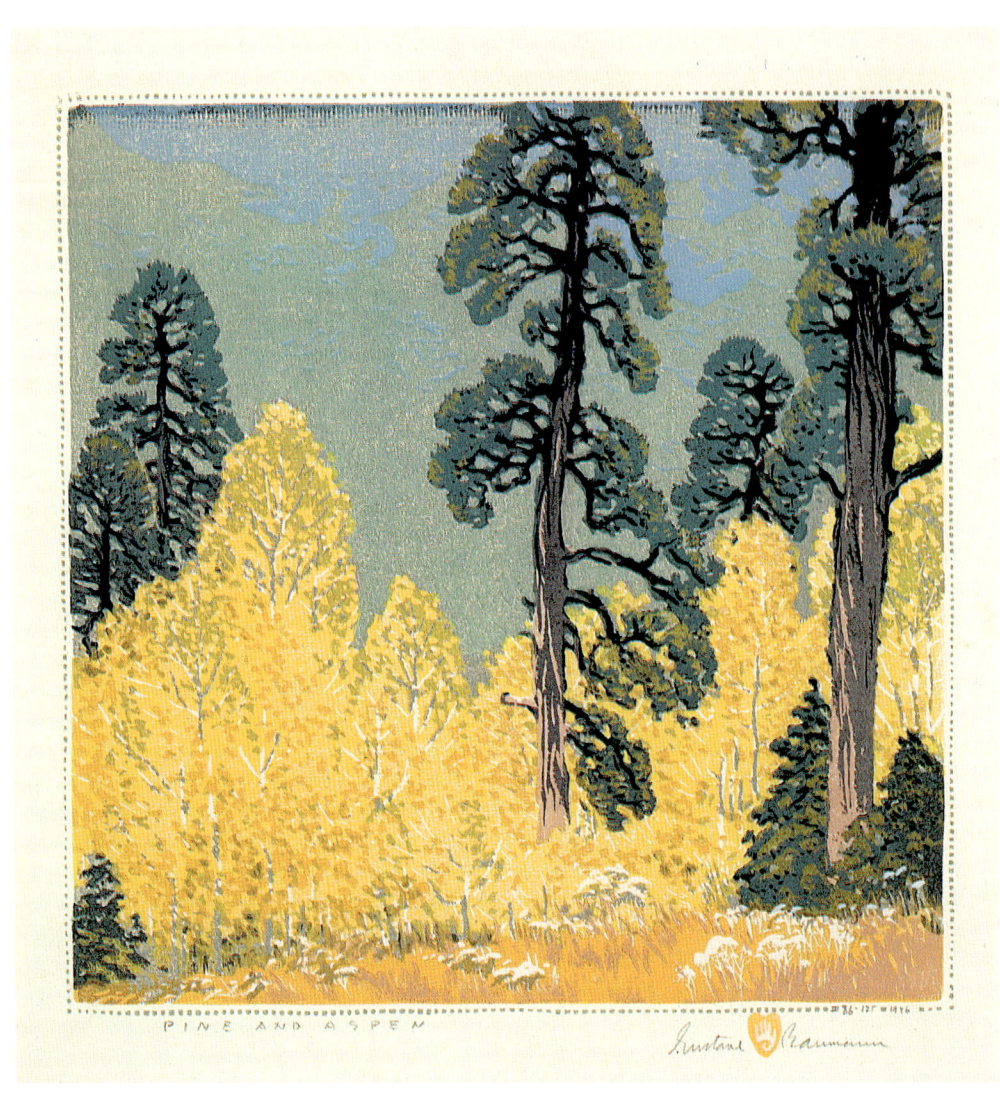

88. PINE AND ASPEN, *ca.* 1920

Color woodcut, 13 × 12¾ in.

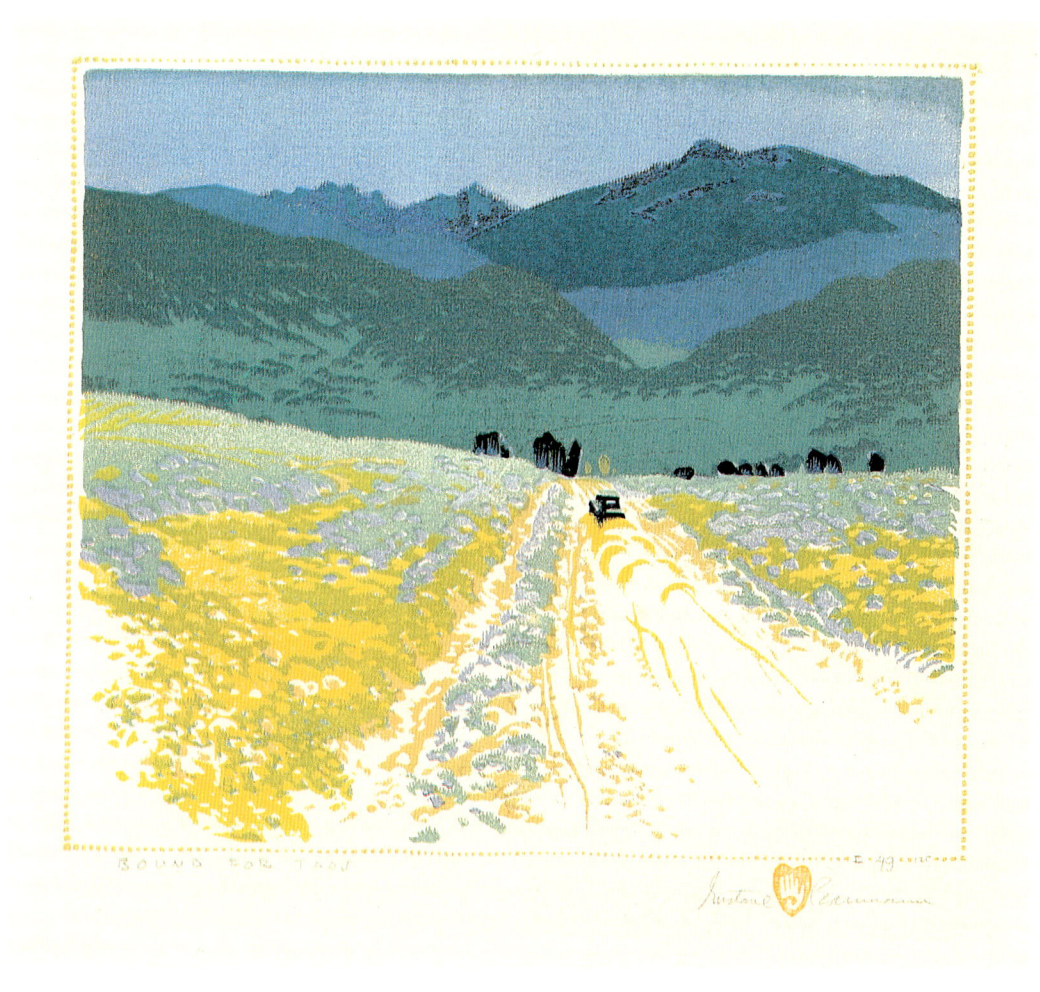

89. BOUND FOR TAOS, 1930

Color woodcut, 9¼ × 10¾ in.

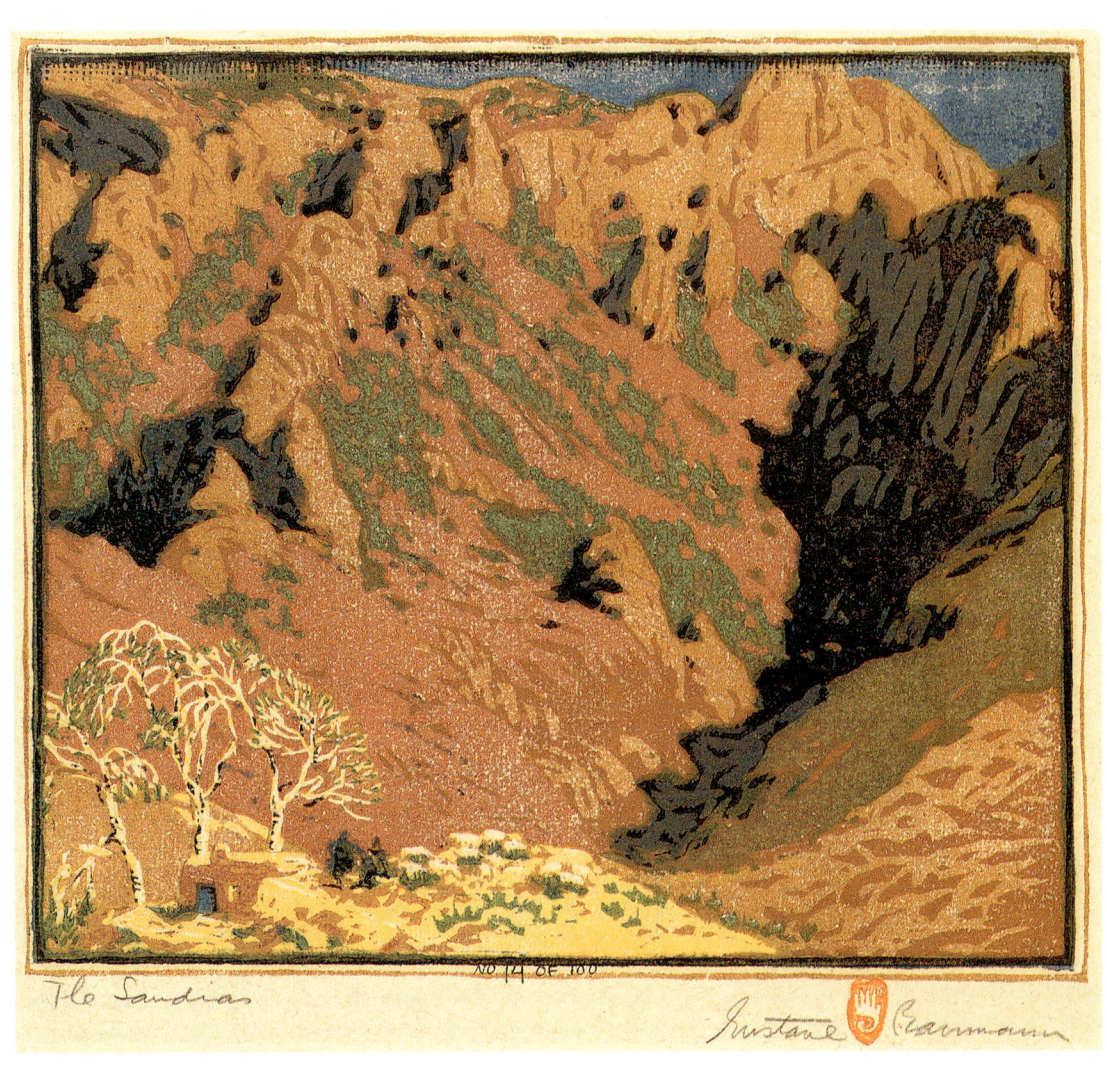

The Sandias   NO. 14 OF 100   Gustave Baumann

90. THE SANDIAS, 1928

Color woodcut, 9¼ × 11 in.

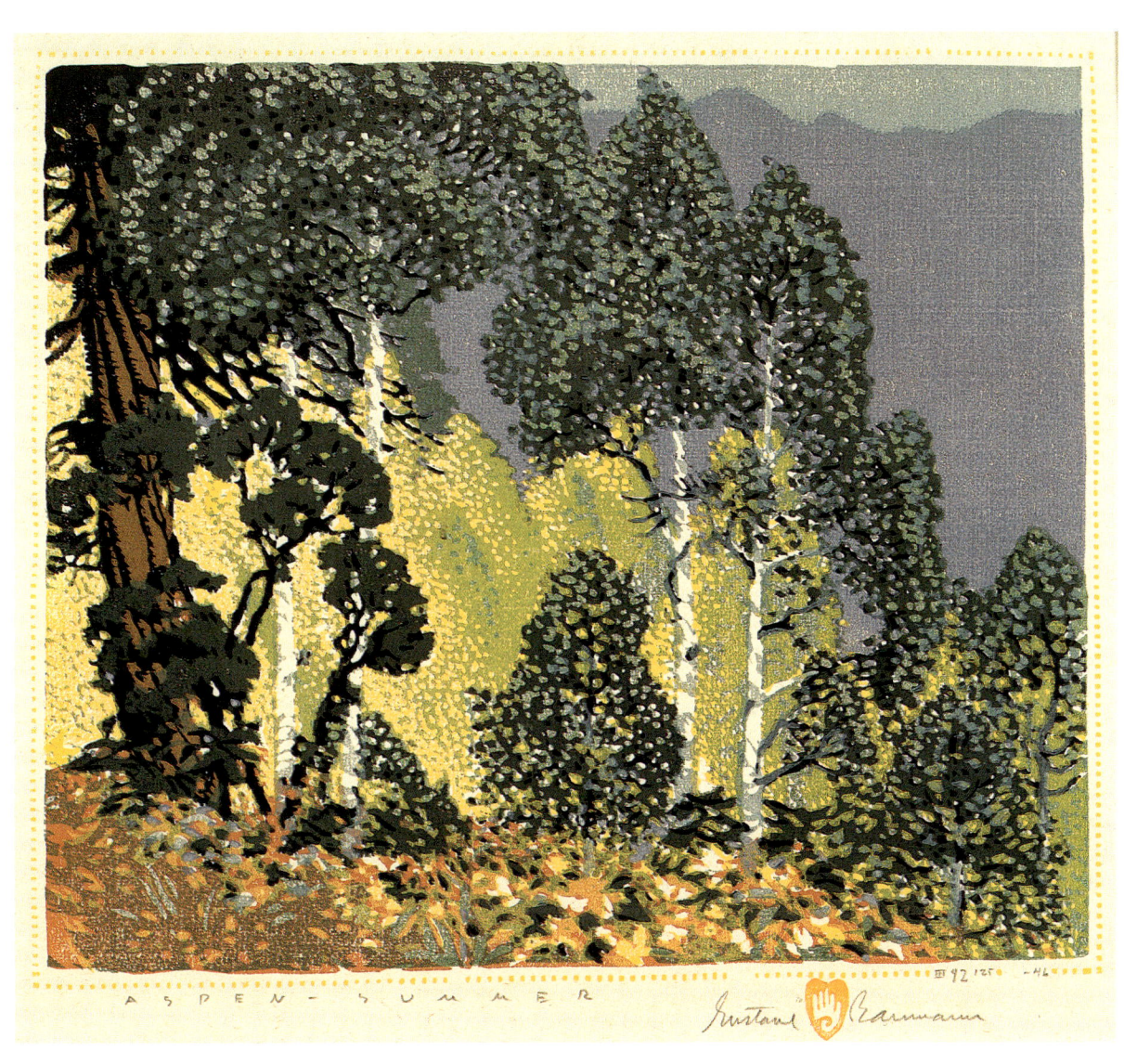

91. ASPEN – SUMMER, 1920

Color woodcut, 9¼×11 in.

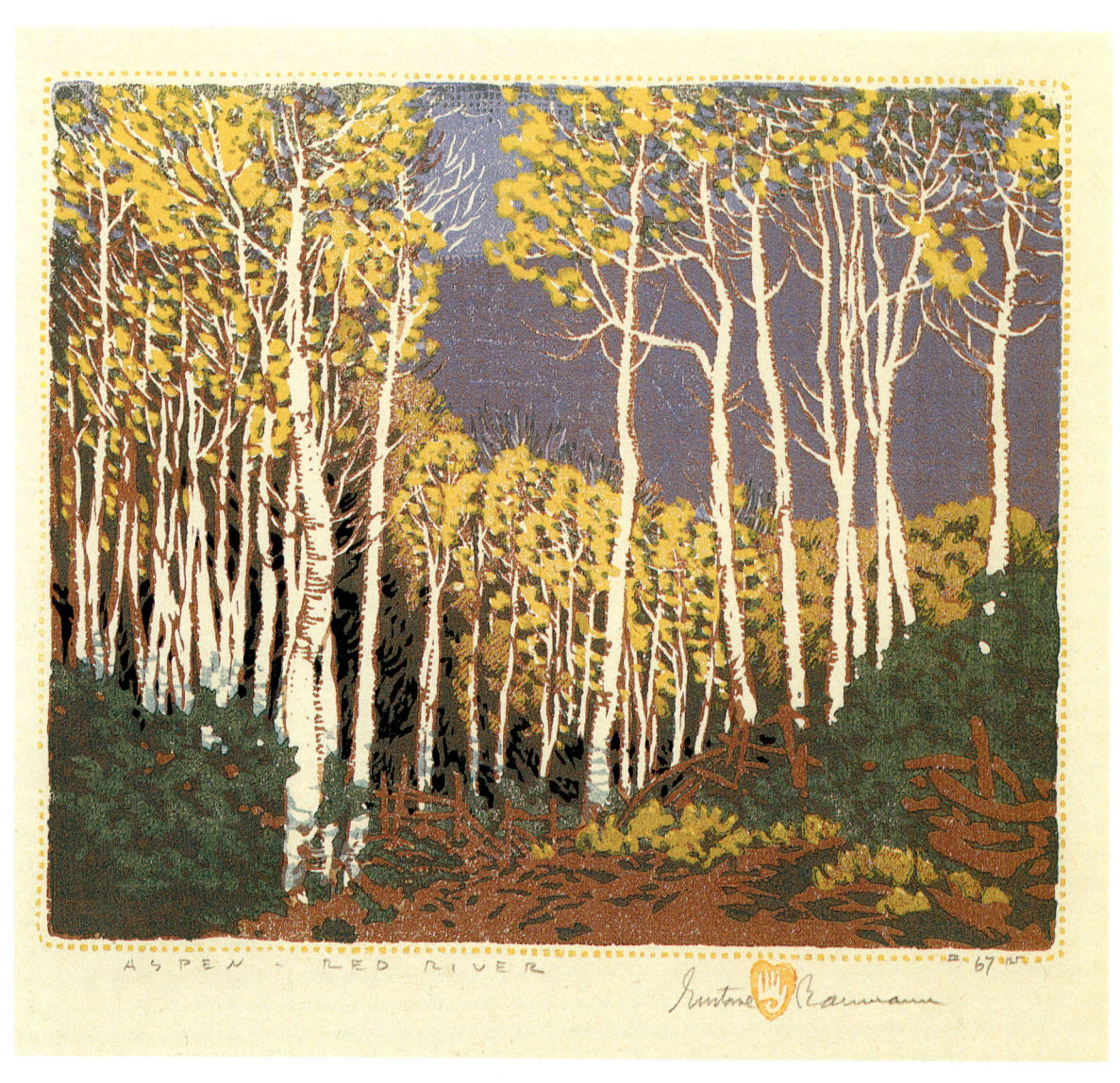

92 . ASPEN – RED RIVER, 1925

Color woodcut, 9×11 in.

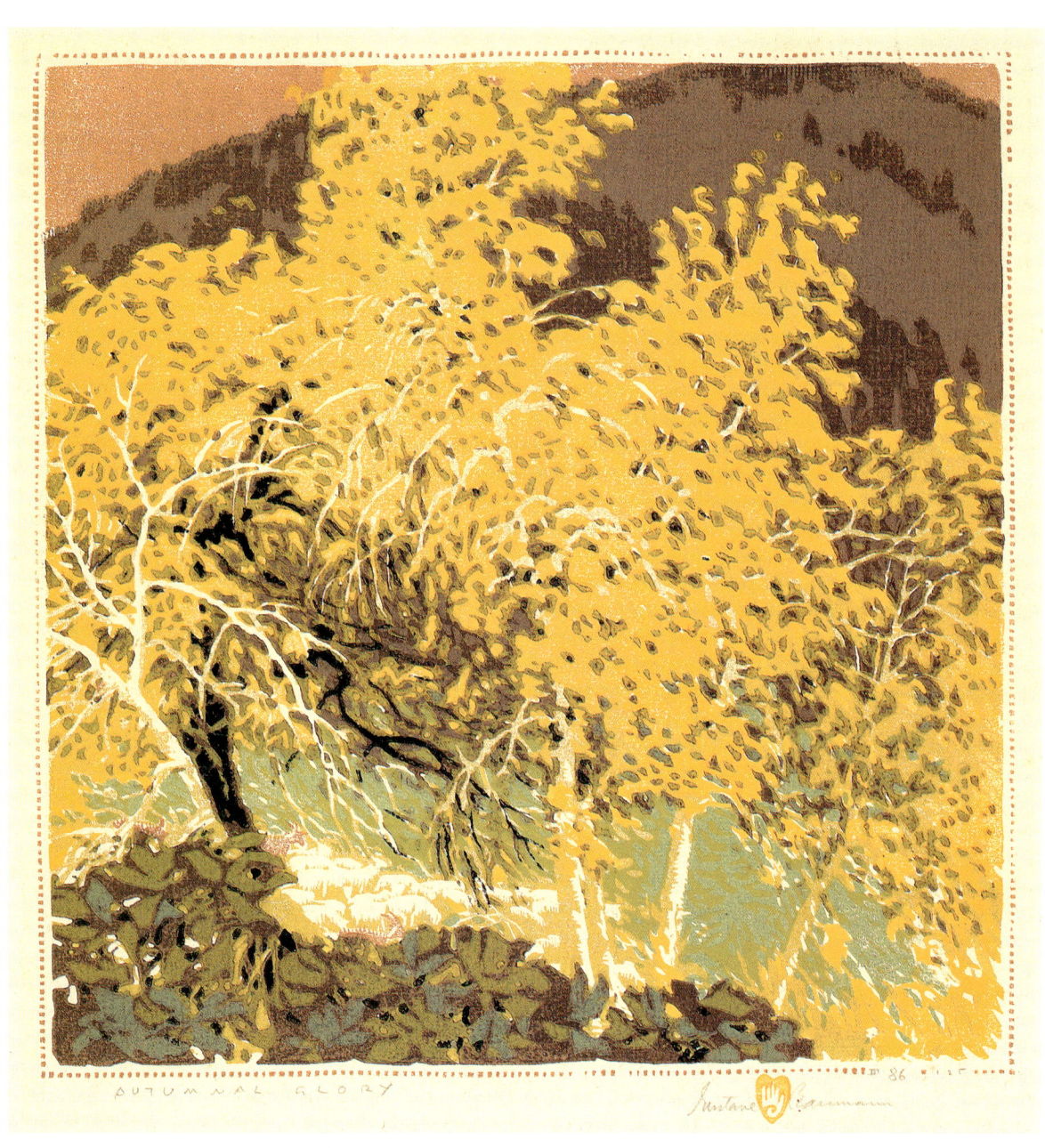

AUTUMNAL GLORY

93. AUTUMNAL GLORY, 1917

Color woodcut, 12½ × 12½ in.

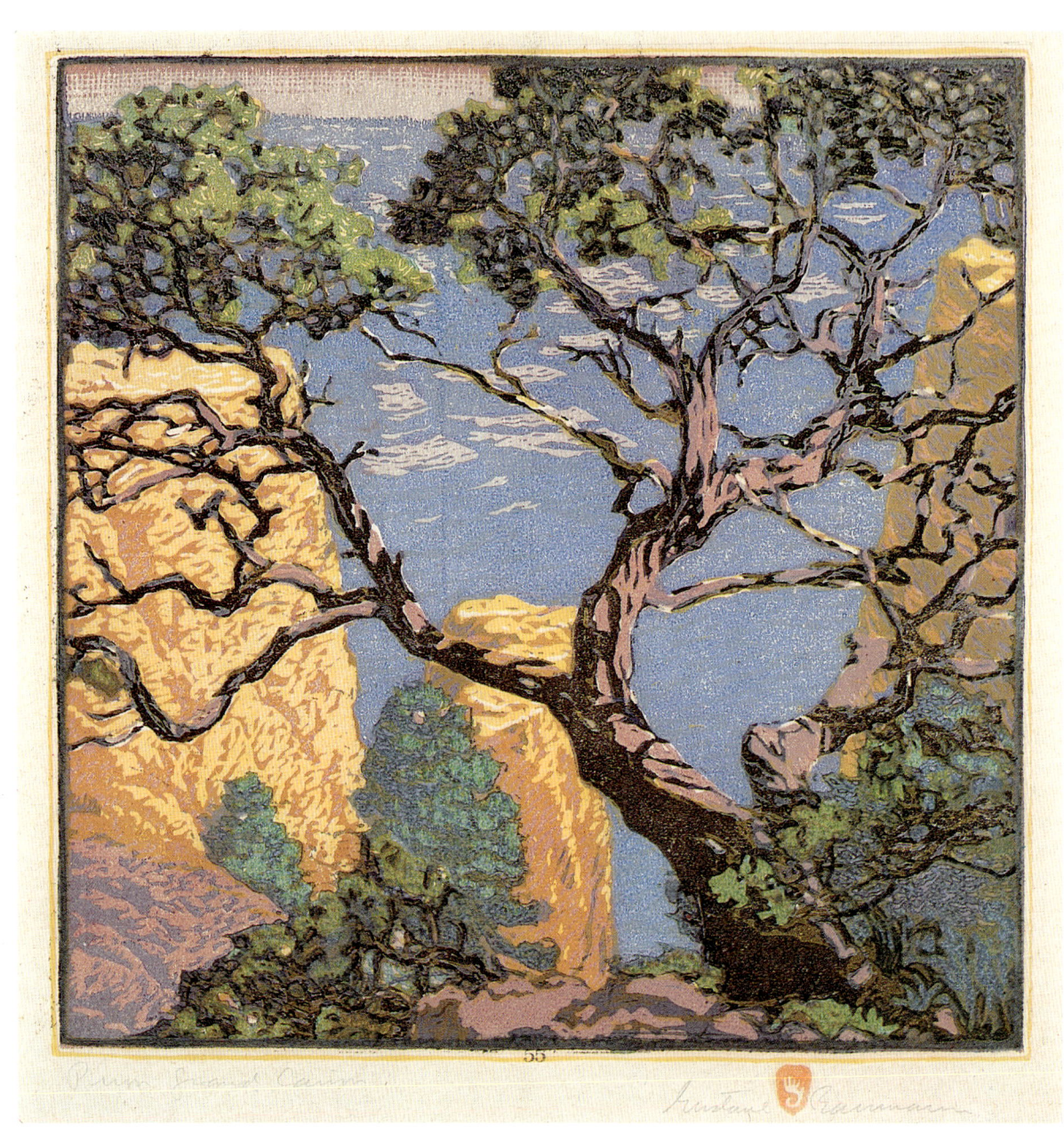

94 · PIÑON – GRAND CAÑON, 1921

Color woodcut, 13 × 12⅞ in.

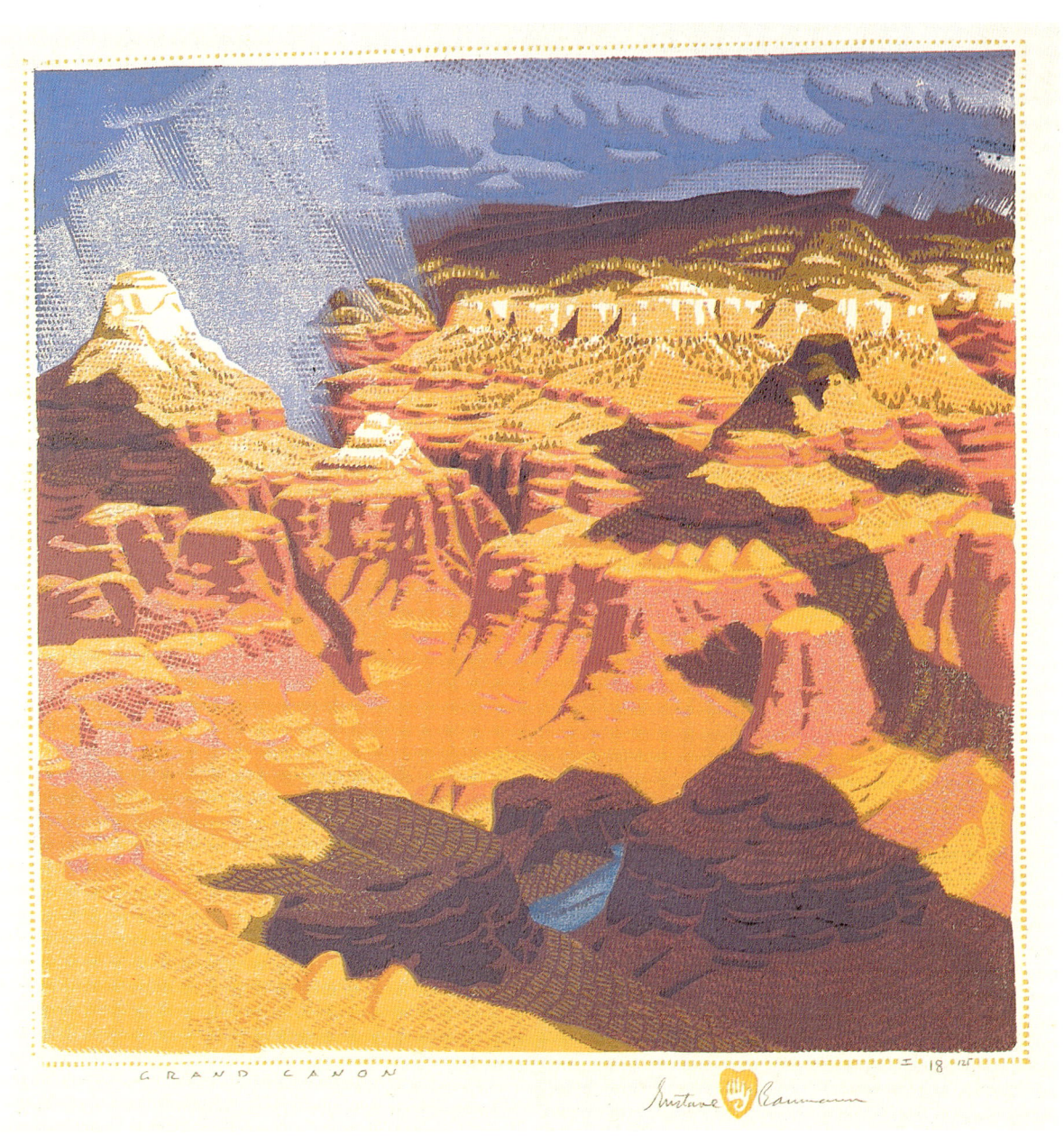

GRAND CAÑON

95. GRAND CAÑON, *ca.* 1930S

Color woodcut, 12⅝ × 12⅞ in.

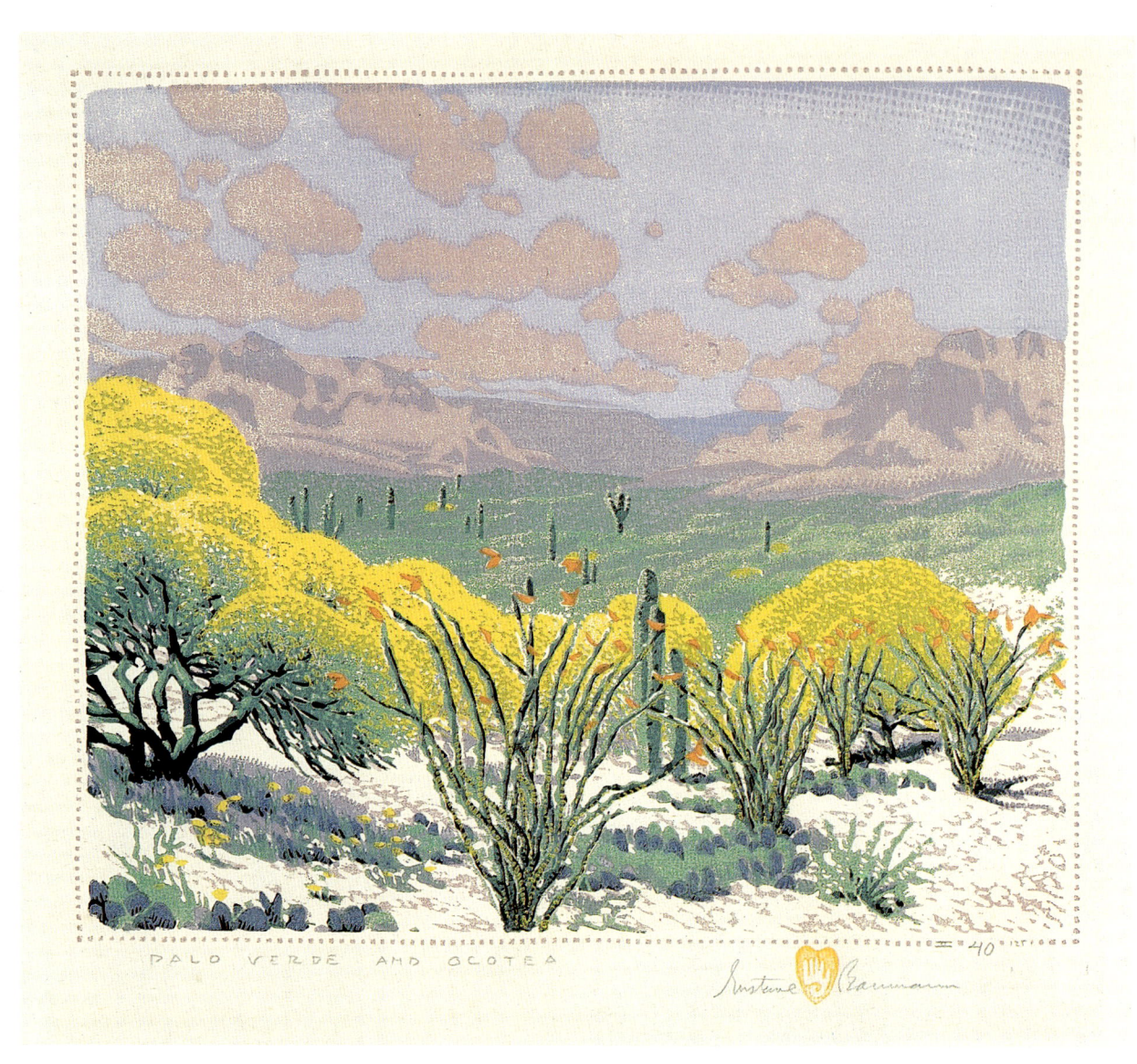

PALO VERDE AND OCOTEA

96. PALO VERDE AND OCOTEA, 1924

Color woodcut, 9⅜ × 11¼ in.

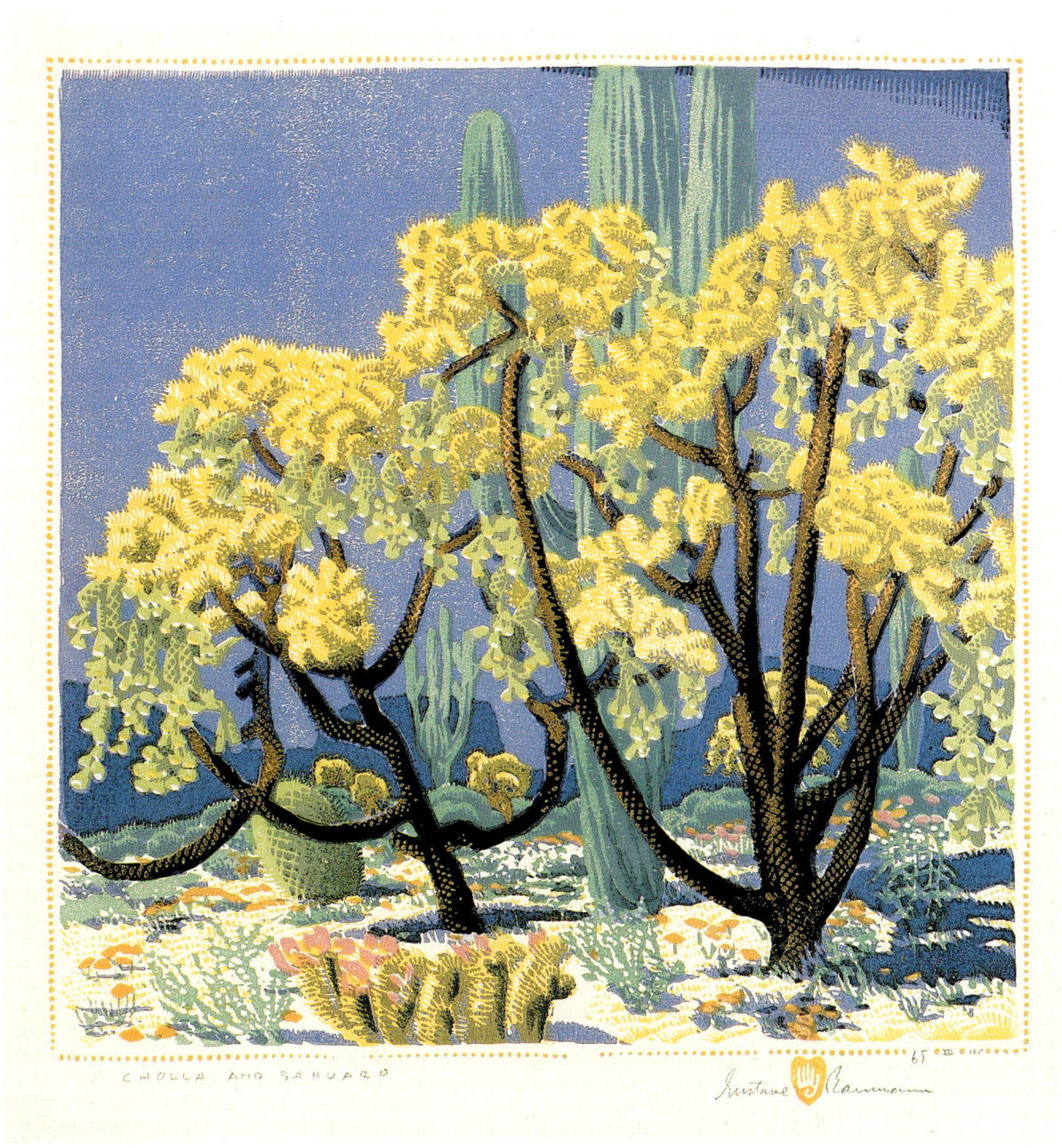

CHOLLA AND SAHUARO

97. CHOLLA AND SAHUARO, 1924

Color woodcut, 12⅝ × 12¾ in.

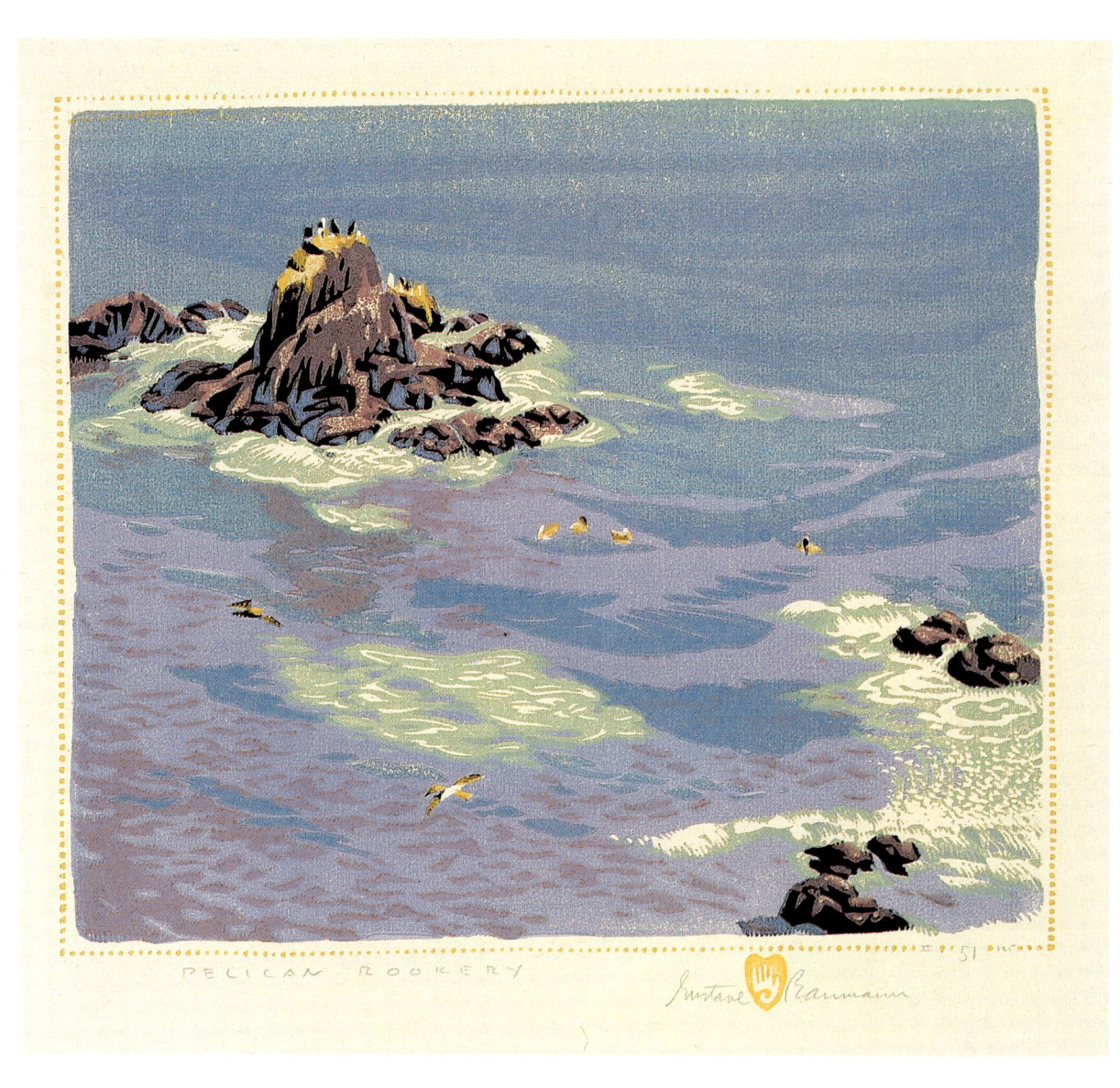

PELICAN ROOKERY

98. PELICAN ROOKERY, *ca. mid-* 1920s

Color woodcut, 9½ × 11⅜ in.

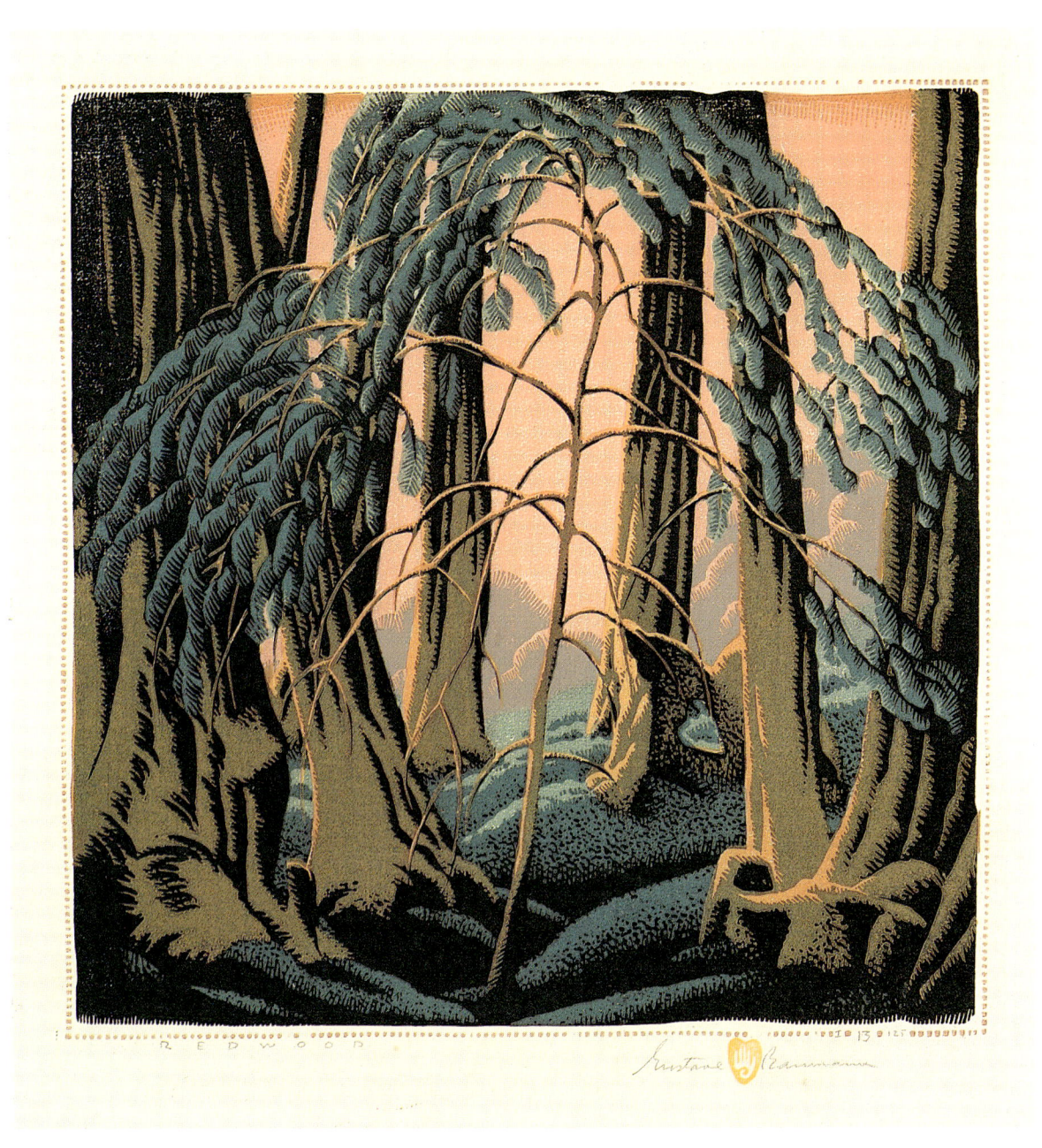

99. REDWOOD, 1928

Color woodcut, 12⅞ × 12¾ in.

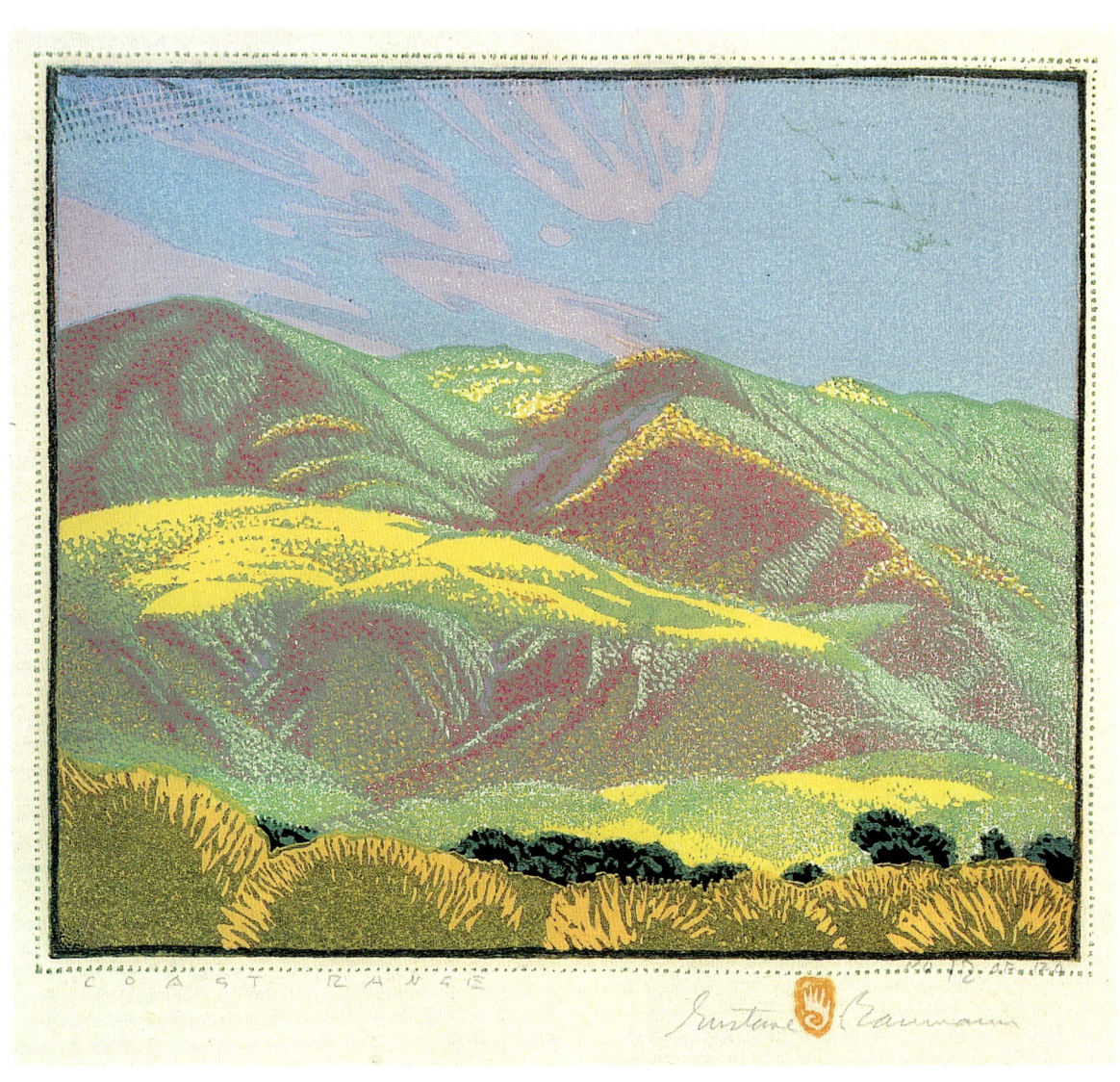

100. COAST RANGE, *ca. mid*-1920s

Color woodcut, 9½ × 11⅜ in.

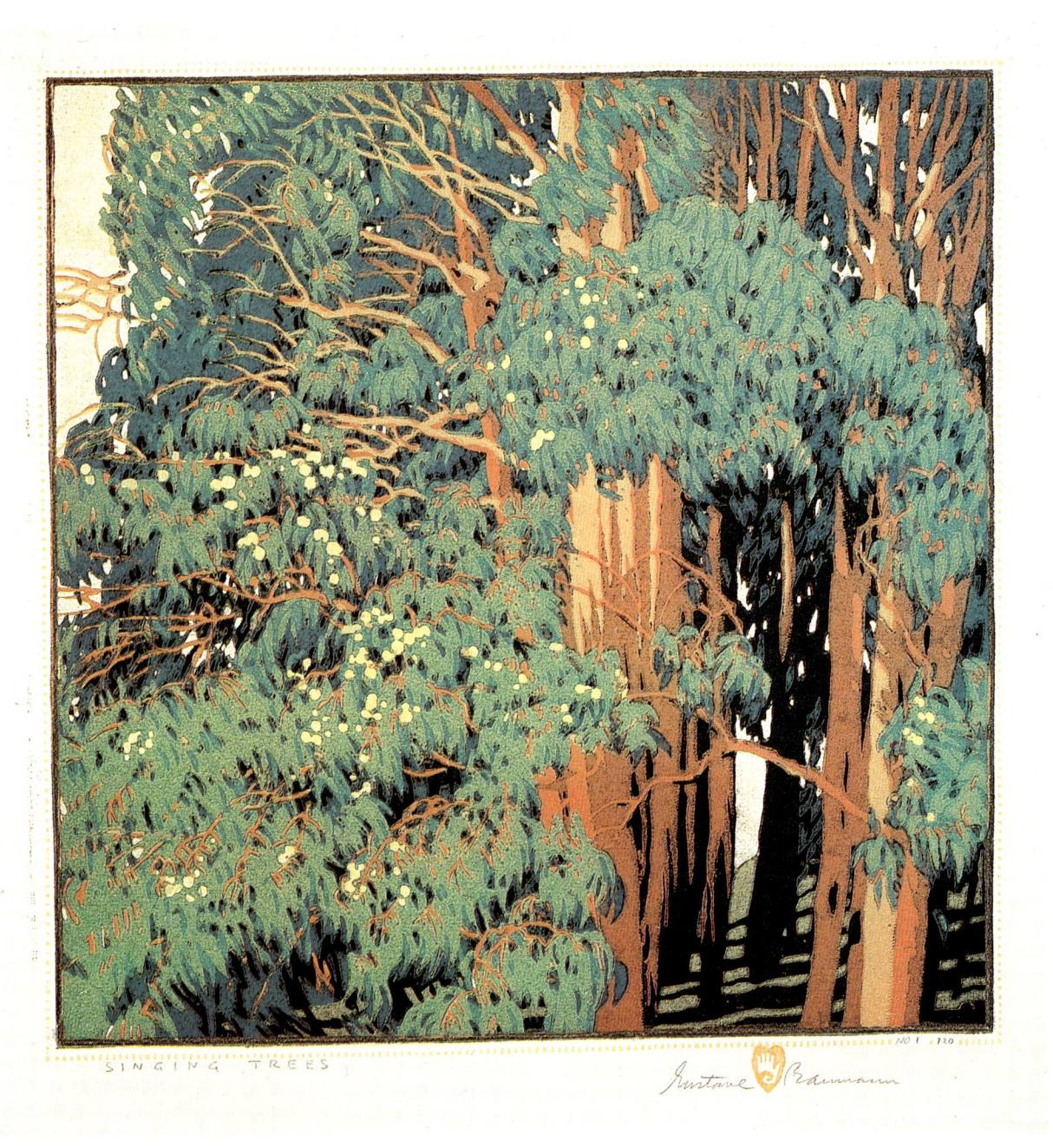

SINGING TREES

101. SINGING TREES, 1928

Color woodcut, 12½ × 12½ in.

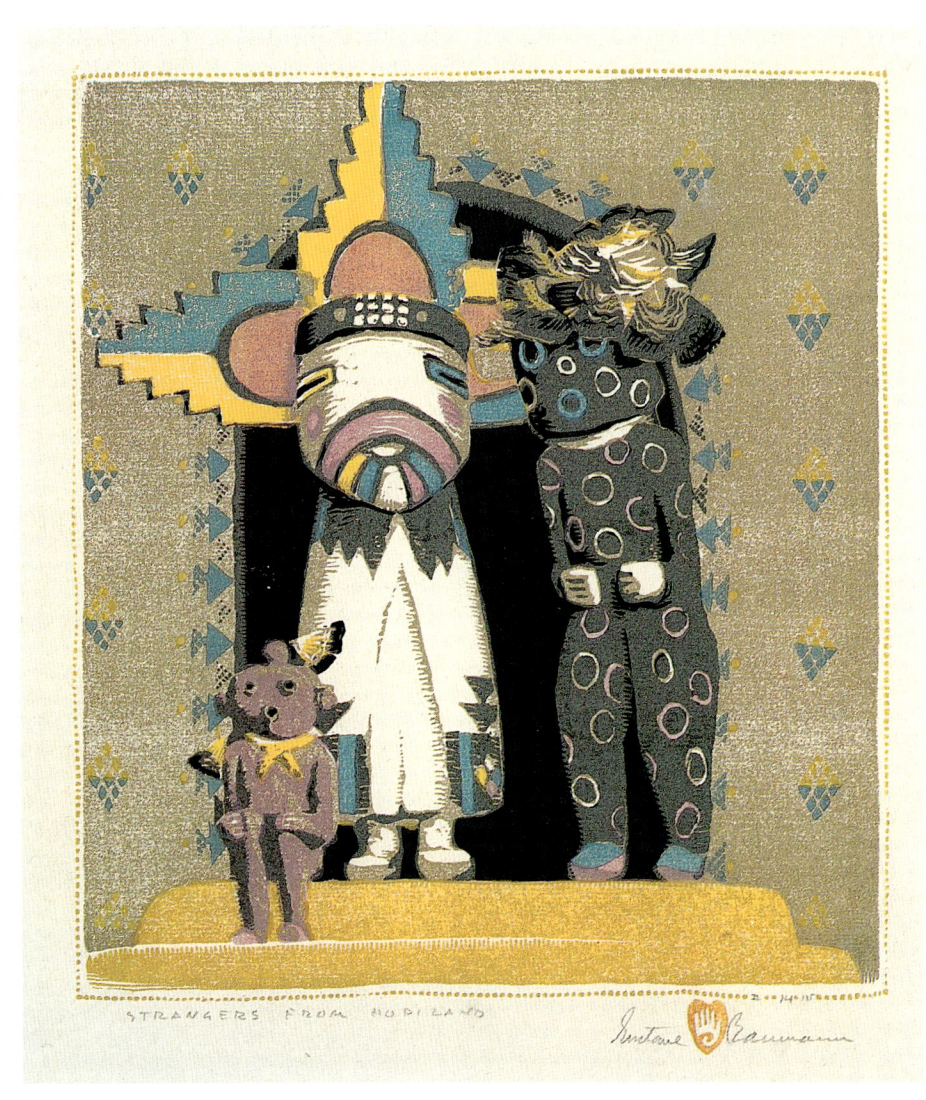

STRANGERS FROM HOPI LAND

102. STRANGERS FROM HOPI LAND, 1920–1921

Color woodcut, 10¾×9¾ in.

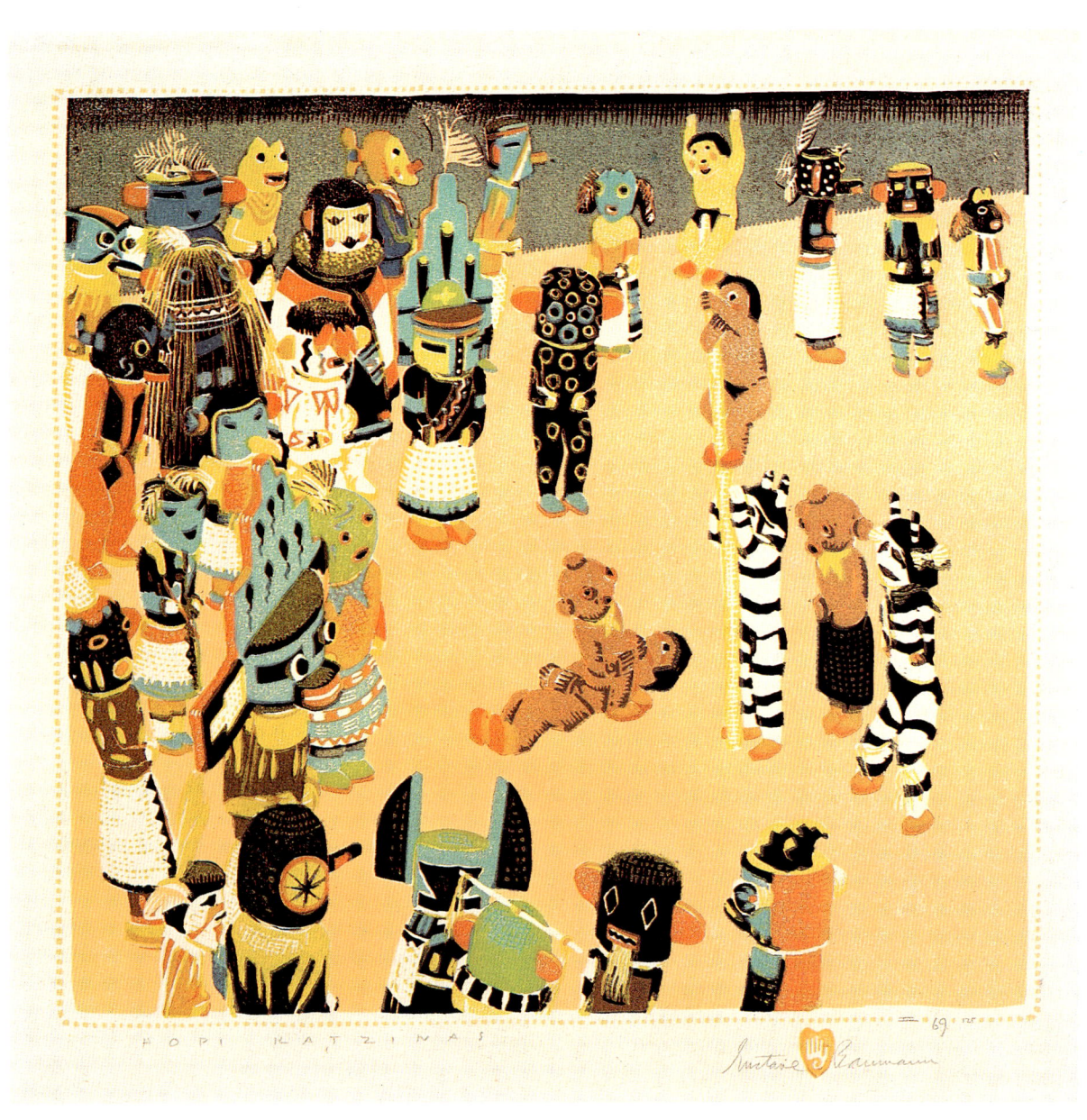

103. HOPI KATZINAS, 1925

Color woodcut, 12¼ × 13¼ in.

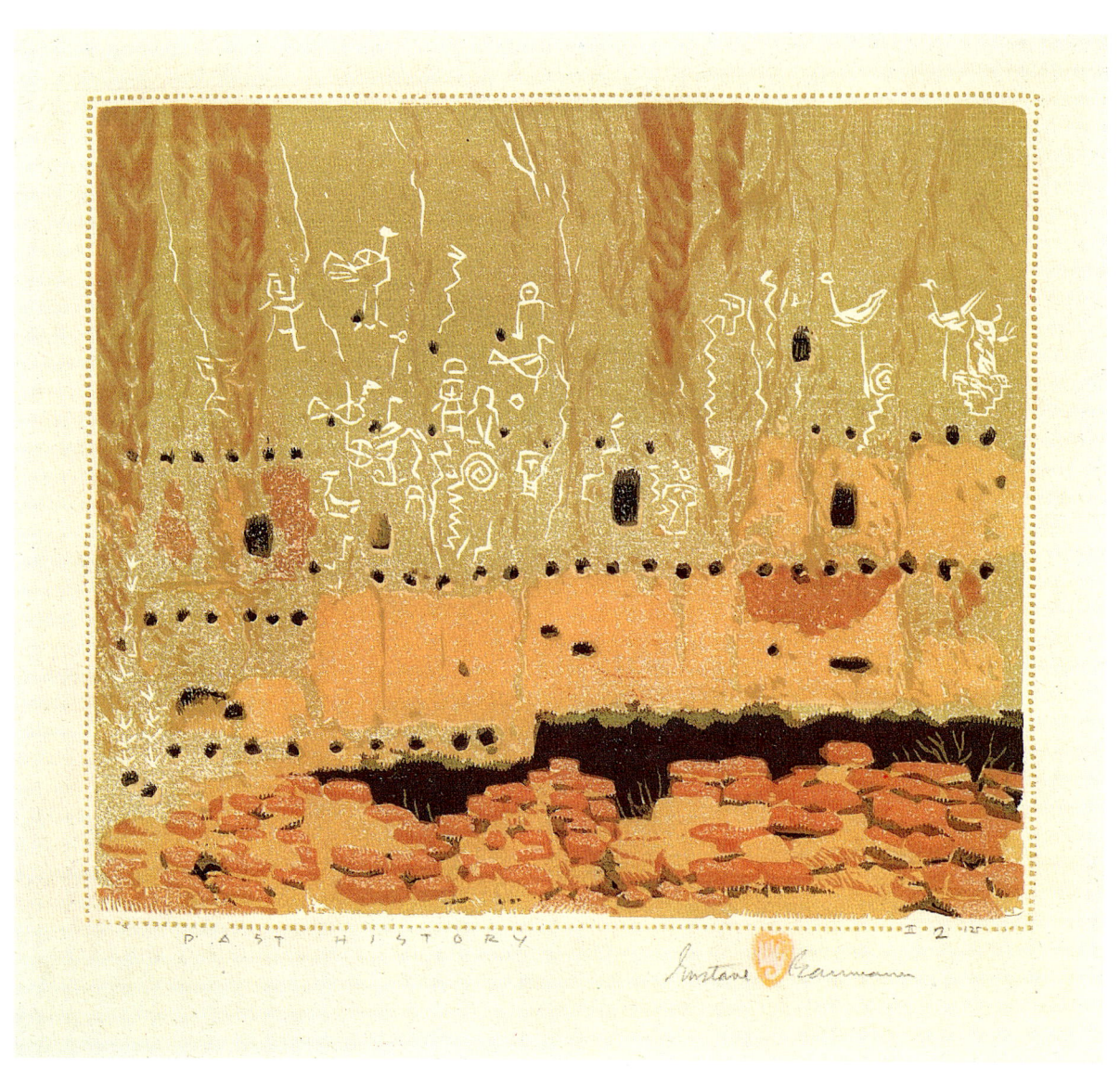

104. PAST HISTORY, 1946

Color woodcut, 9¼ × 10⅞ in.

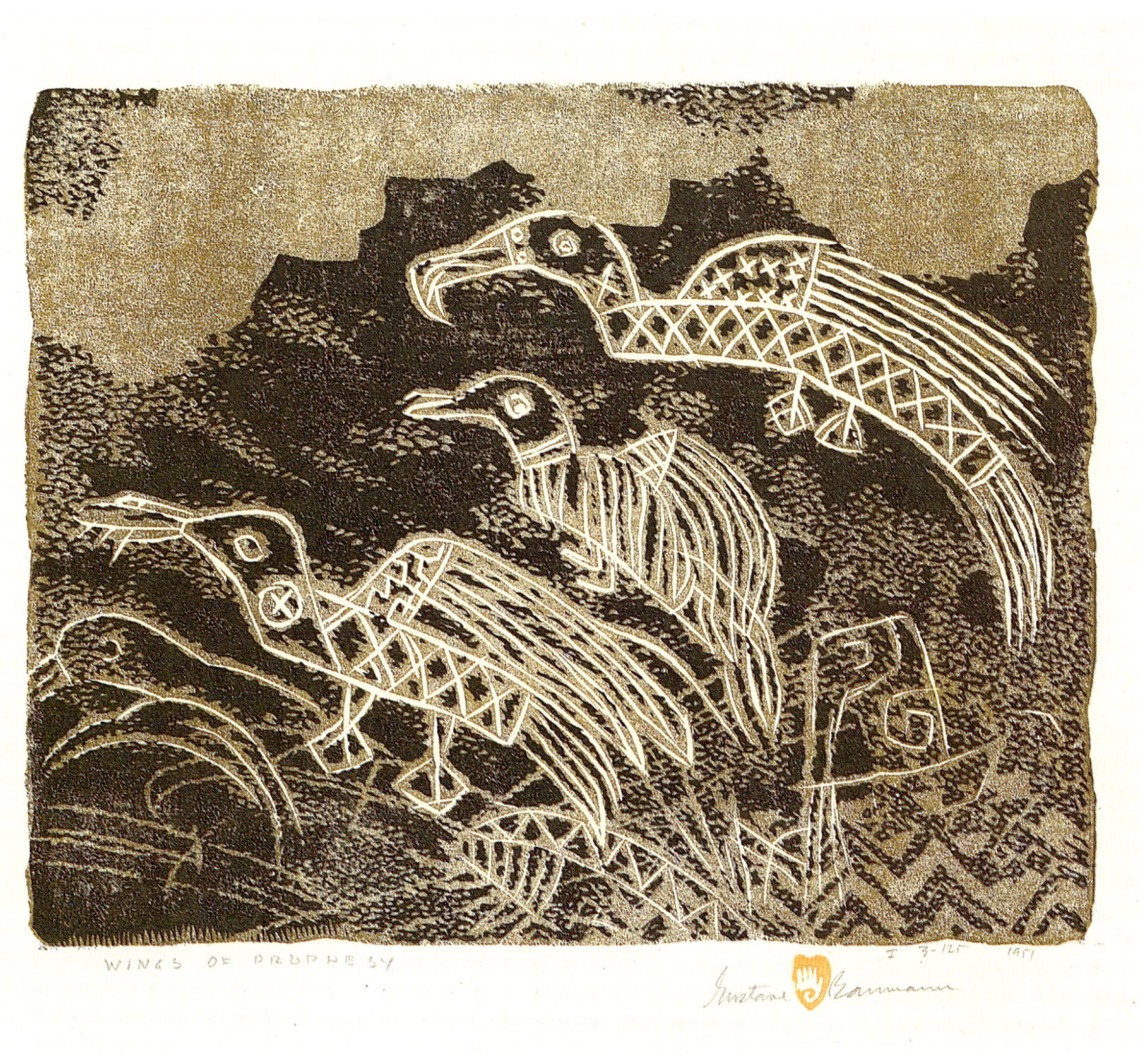

WINGS OF PROPHESY

Gustave Baumann 1941

105. WINGS OF PROPHESY, 1941

Color woodcut, 9¾ × 12½ in.

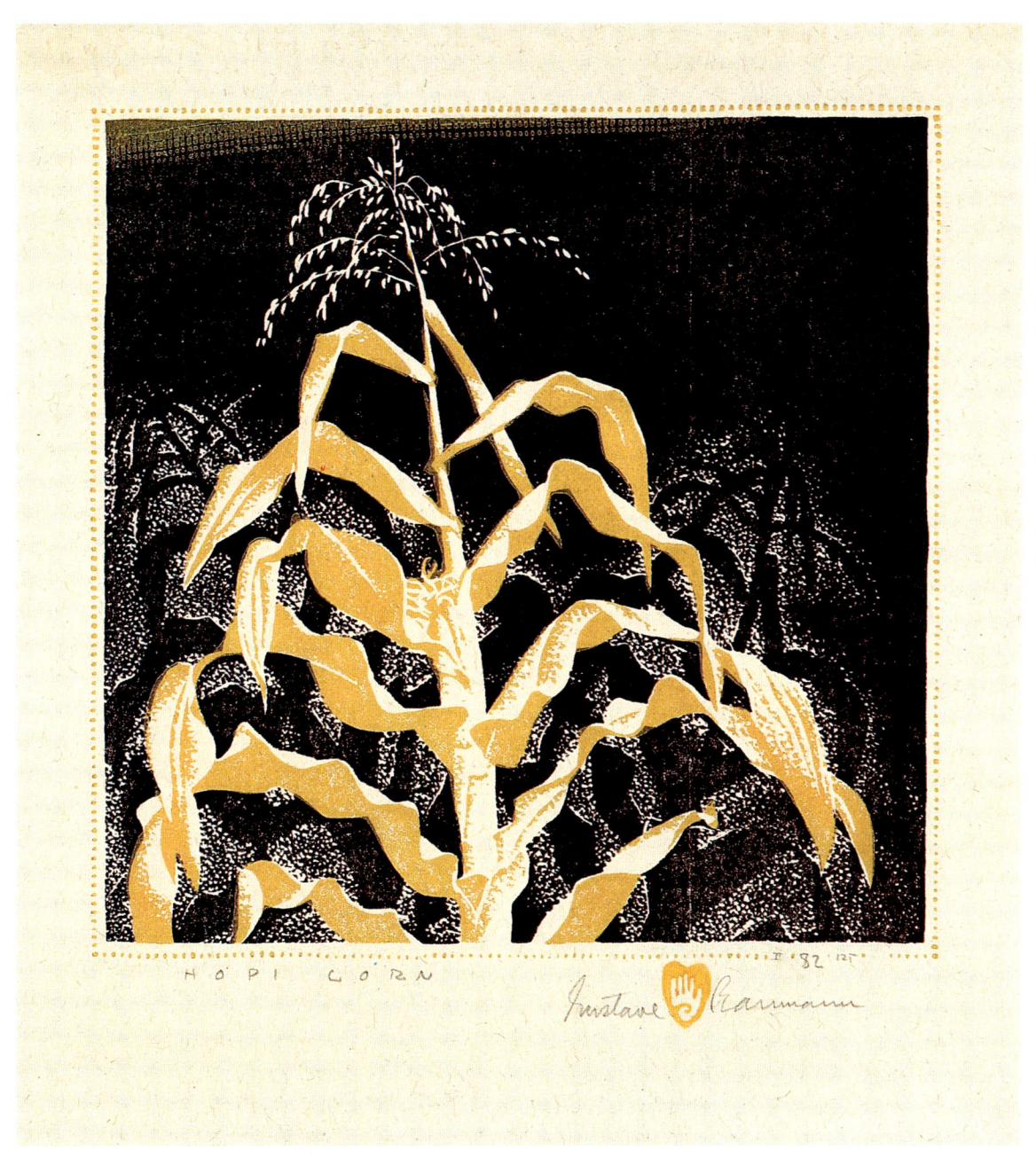

106. HOPI CORN, 1944

Color woodcut, 8⅛ × 8¼ in.

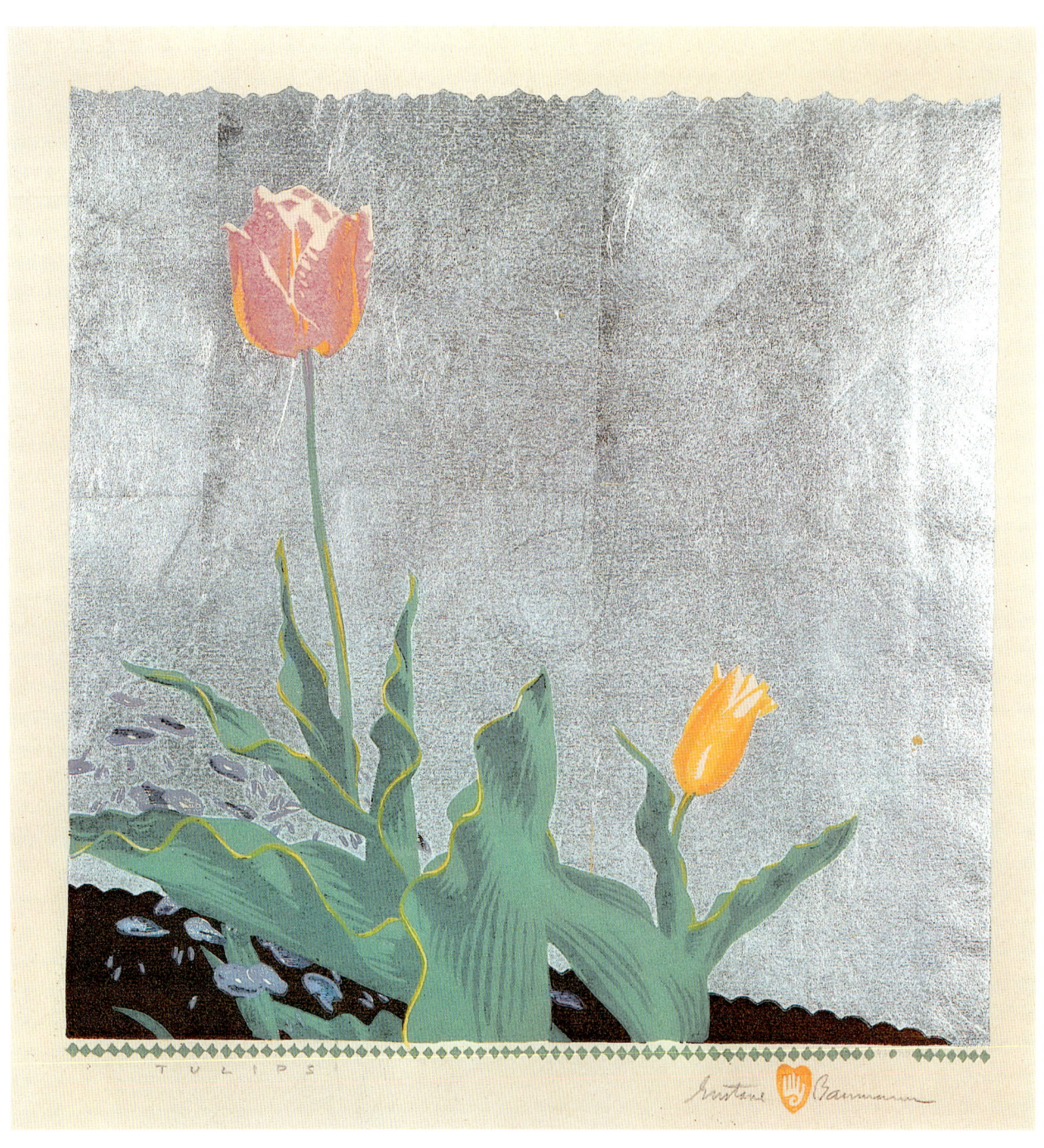

107. TULIPS, 1930

Color woodcut, 13 × 12¾ in.

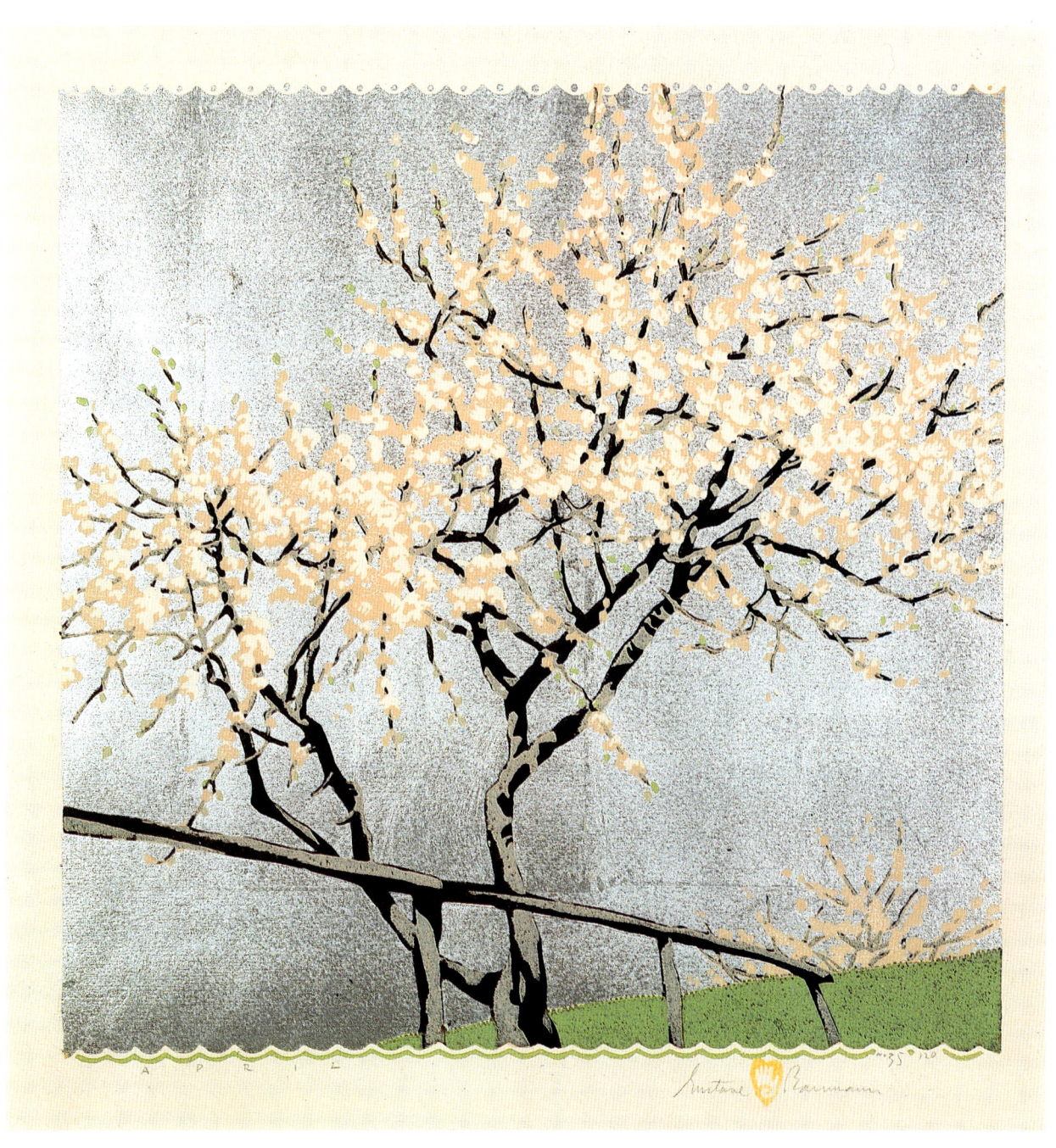

108. APRIL, *ca.* 1936

Color woodcut, 13×13 in.

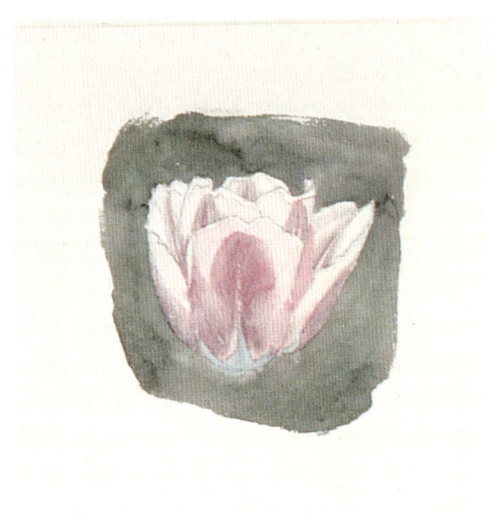

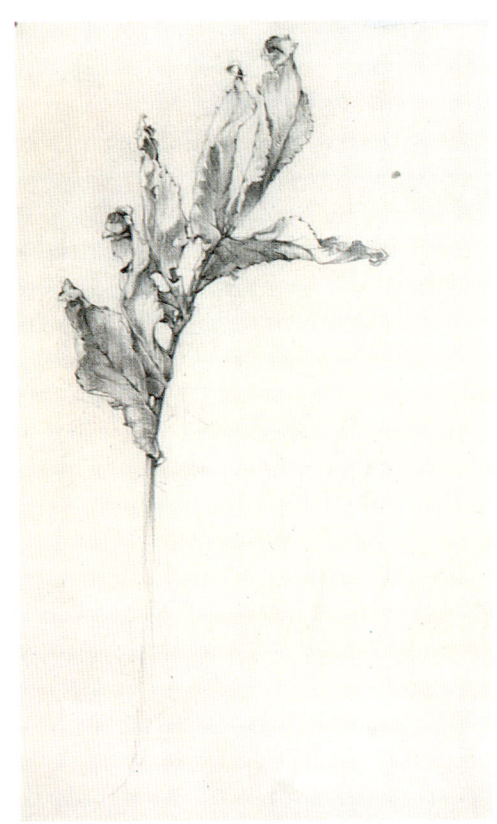

109. UNTITLED STUDIES, N.D.

Watercolor, 11×10 in.; pencil on paper, 17¼×11 in.

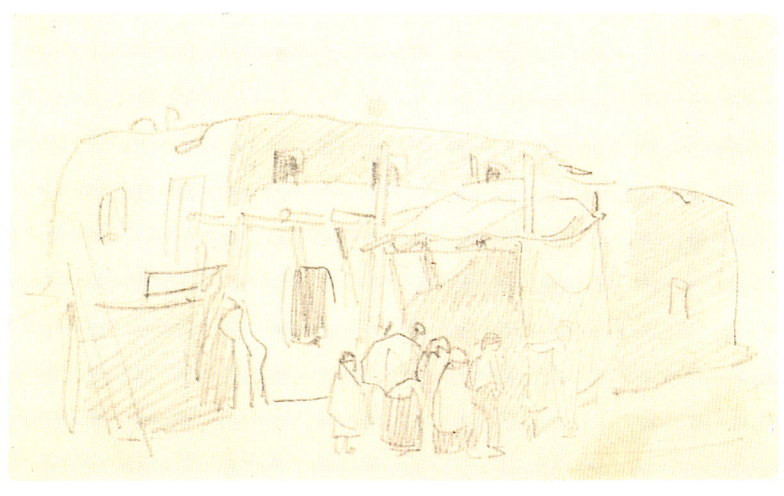

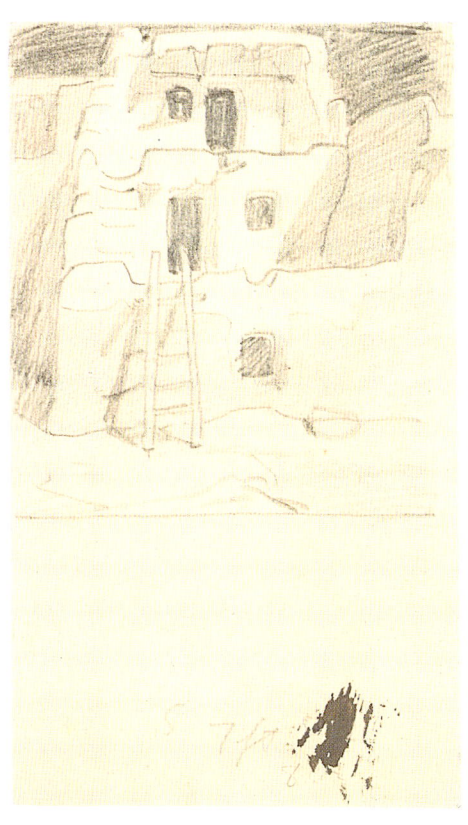

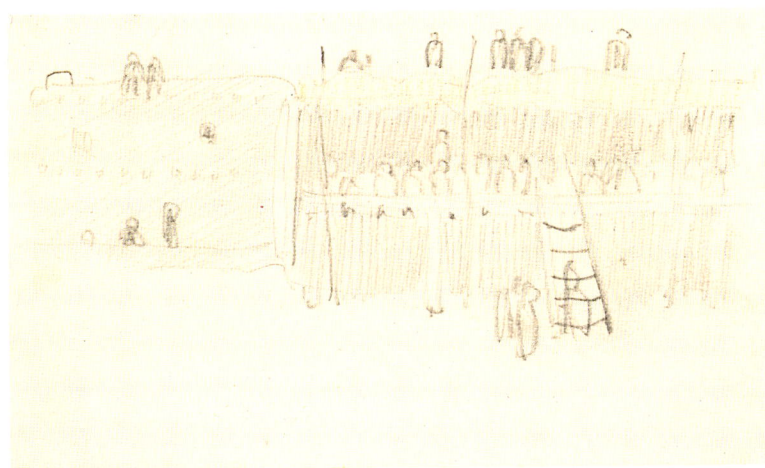

110. UNTITLED (PUEBLO SCENES), N.D.

Pencil, 14×20 in.

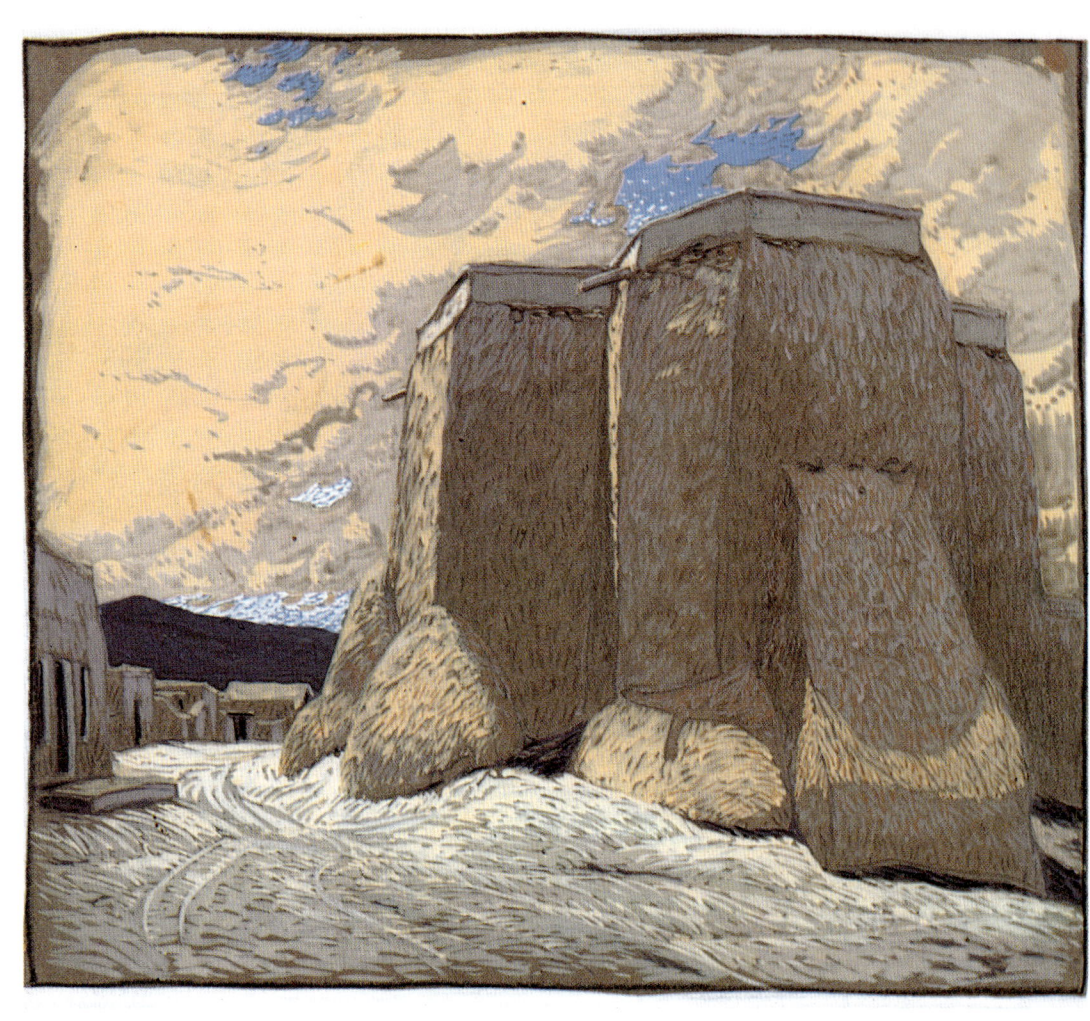

111. RANCHOS DE TAOS CHURCH, *ca.* 1918

Gouache, 10¼ × 11⅞ in.

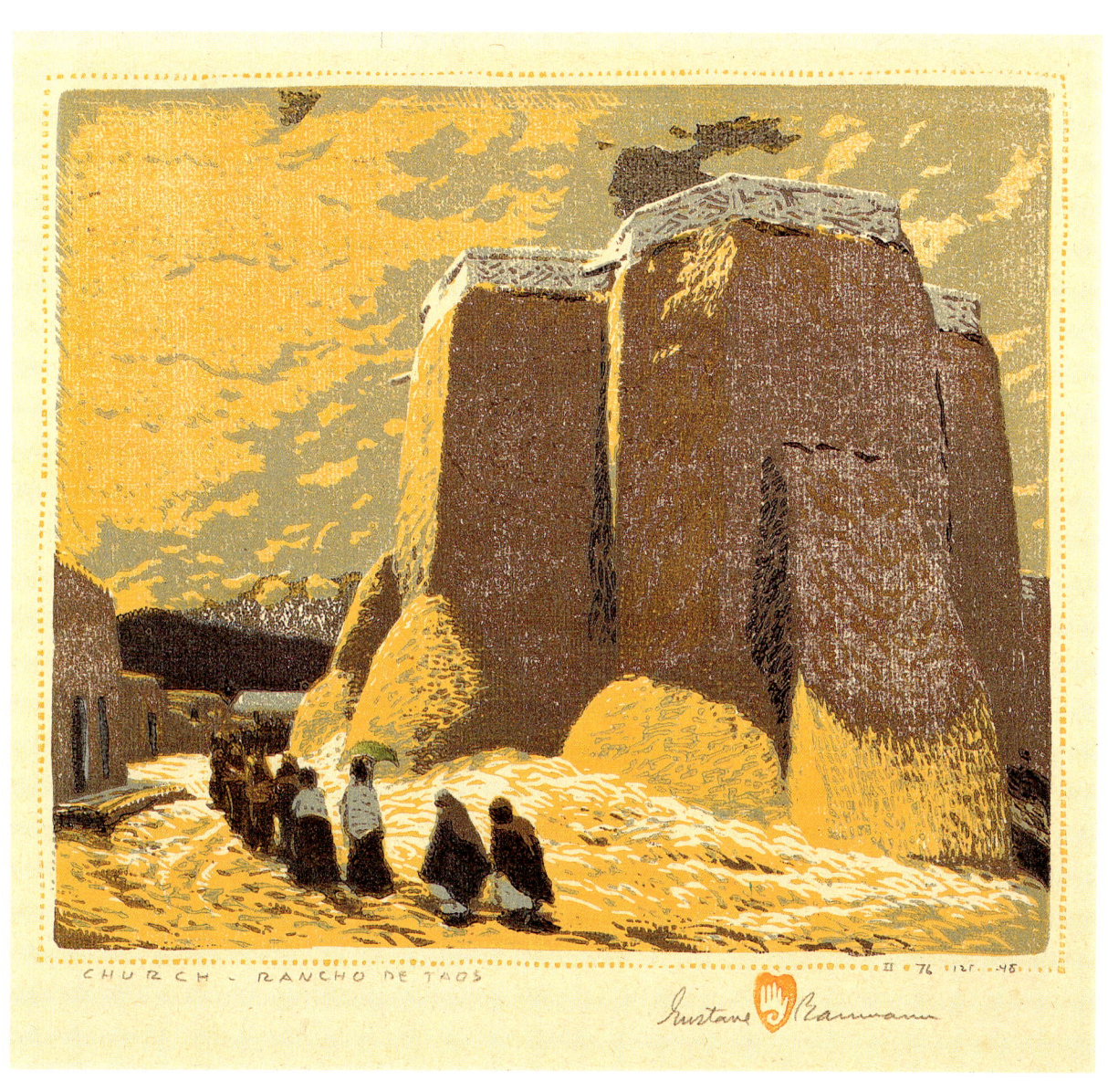

CHURCH – RANCHO DE TAOS

Gustave Baumann

112. CHURCH – RANCHOS DE TAOS, 1918

Color woodcut, 10½ × 11½ in.

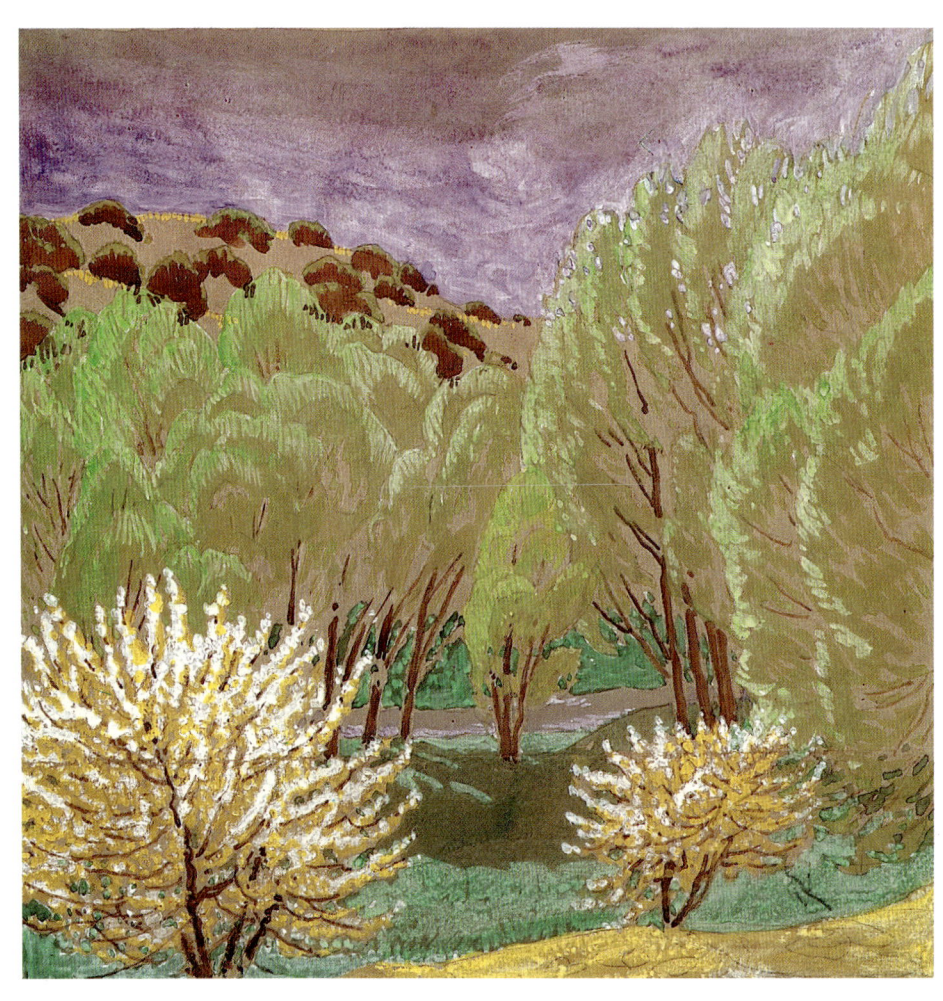

113. SPRING – TESUQUE VALLEY, N.D.

Gouache, 13½×13 in.

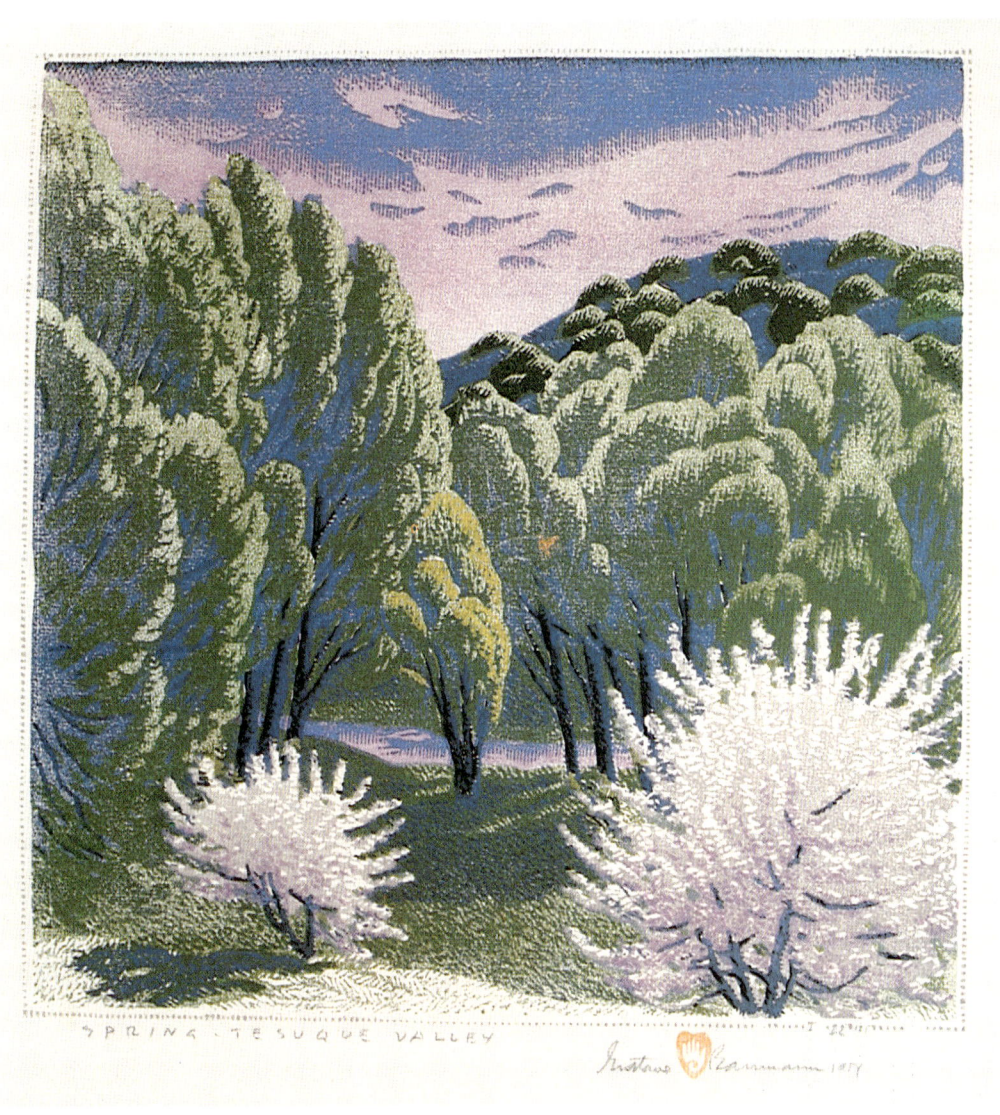

114. SPRING – TESUQUE VALLEY, 1918

Color woodcut, 13 × 12½ in.

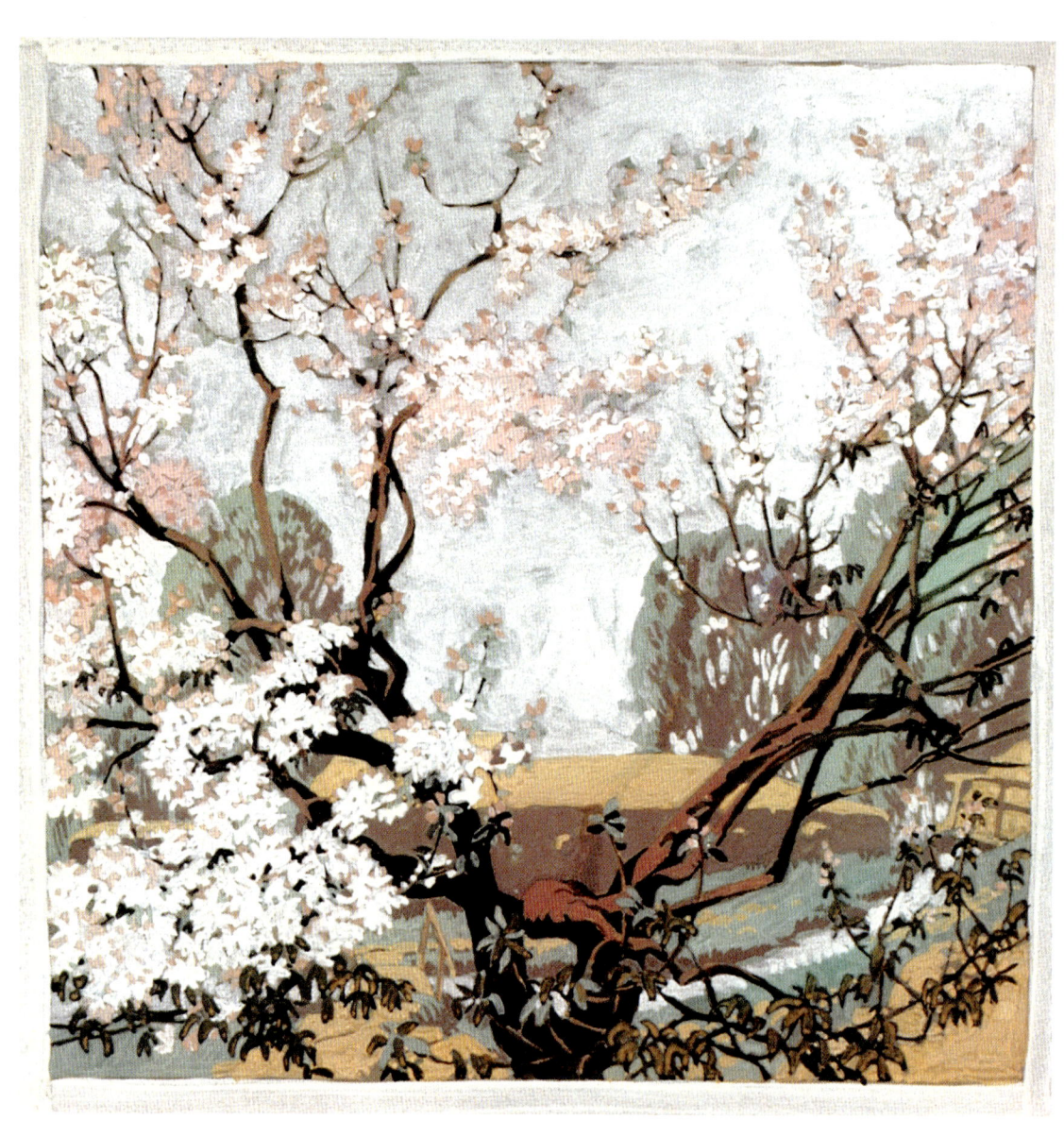

115. SILVER SKY, *ca.* 1916

Gouache, 13⅜ × 13⅜ in.

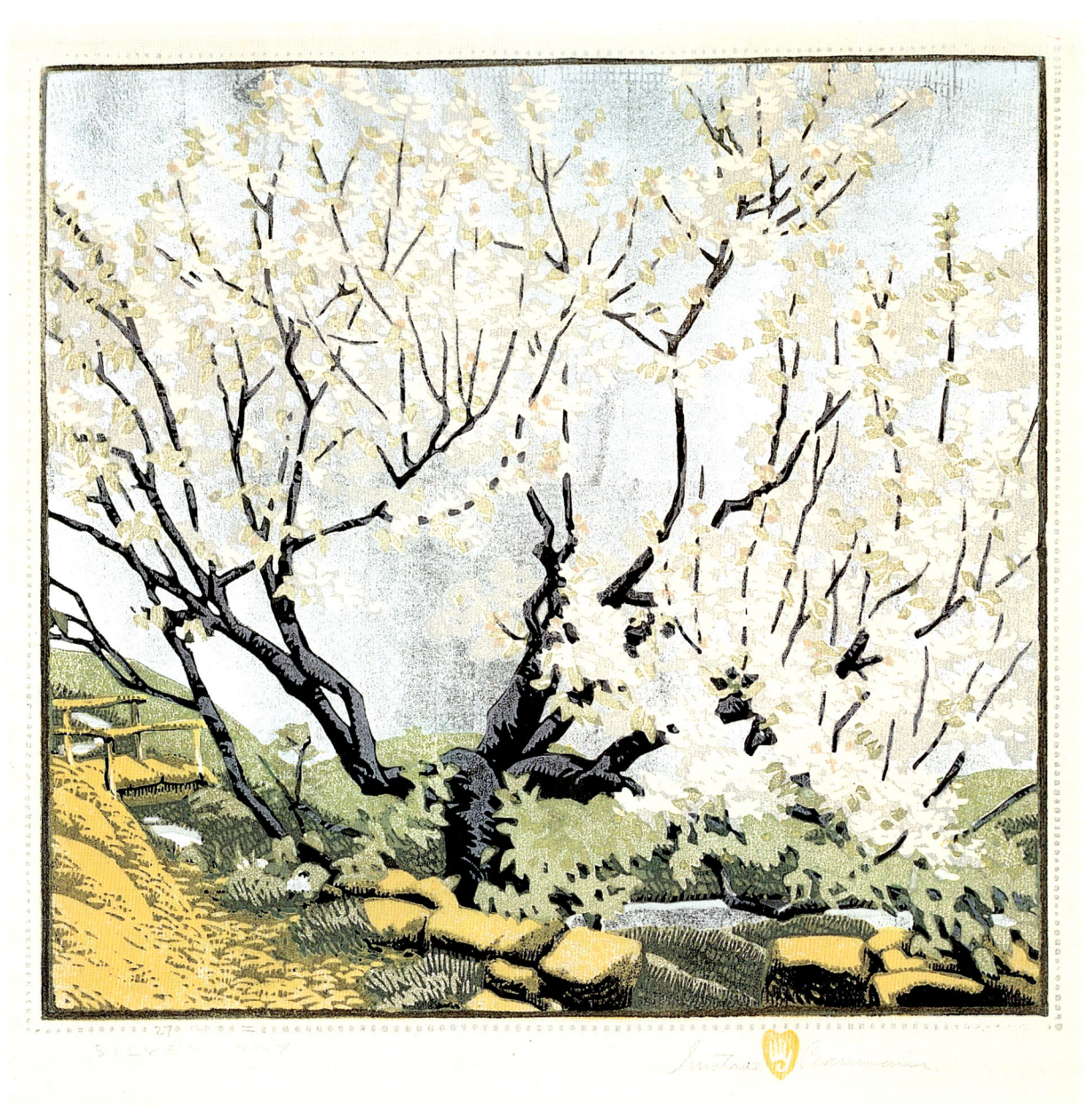

116. SILVER SKY, 1916

Color woodcut, 12×13 in.

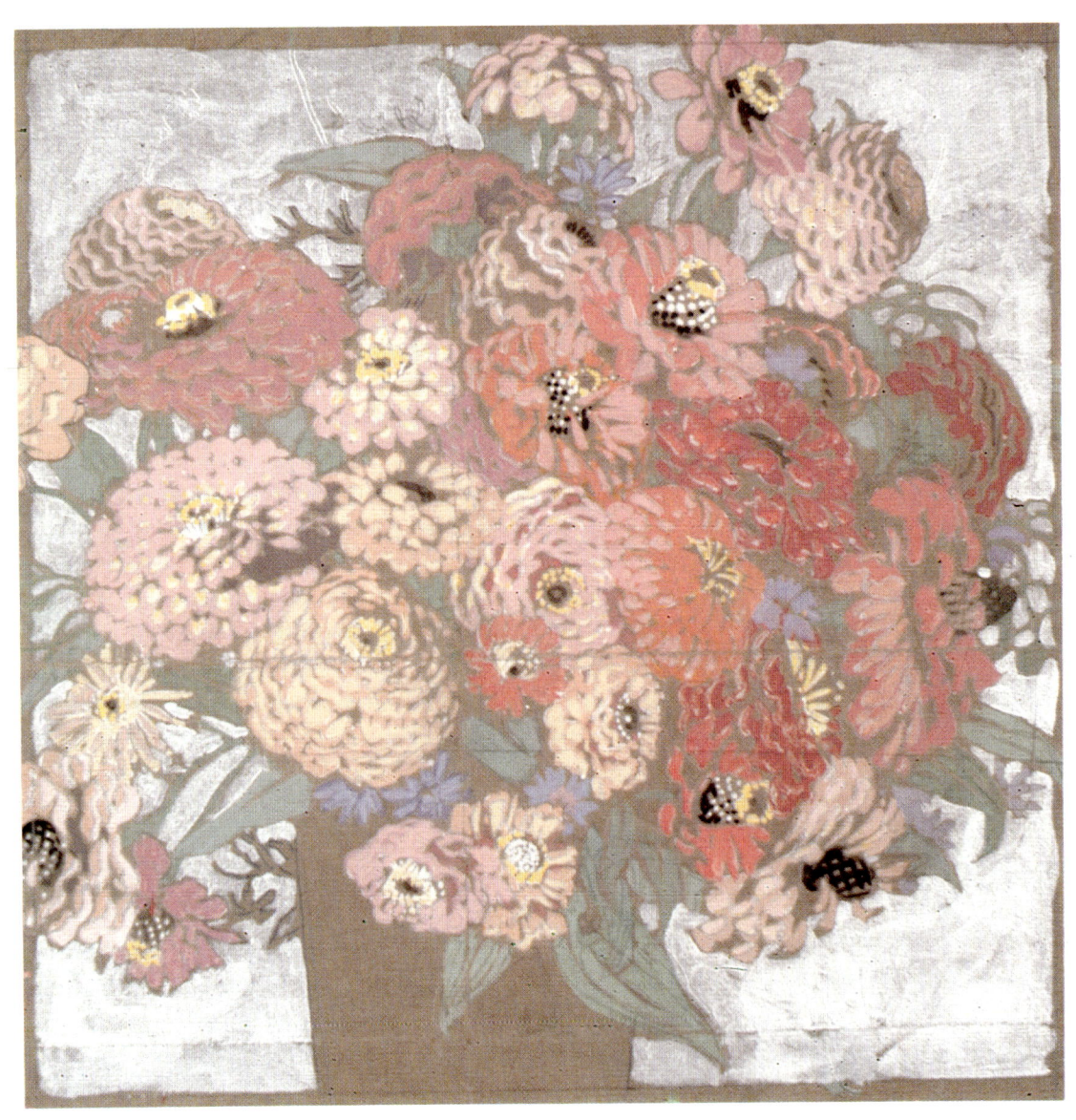

117. ZINNIAS, N.D.

Gouache, 12½ × 13½ in.

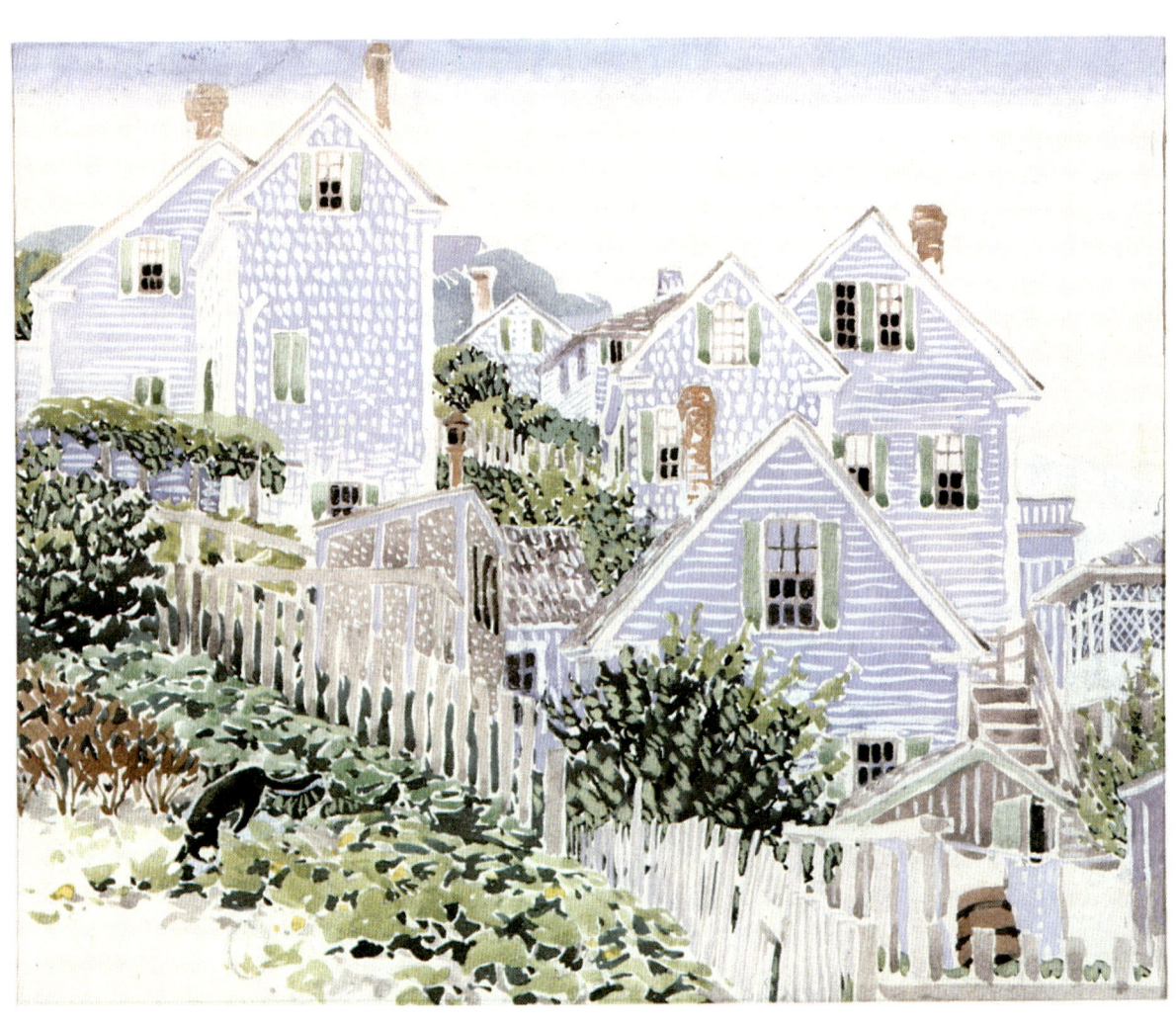

118. TOM A HUNTING, *ca.* 1917

Gouache, 11 × 13½ in.

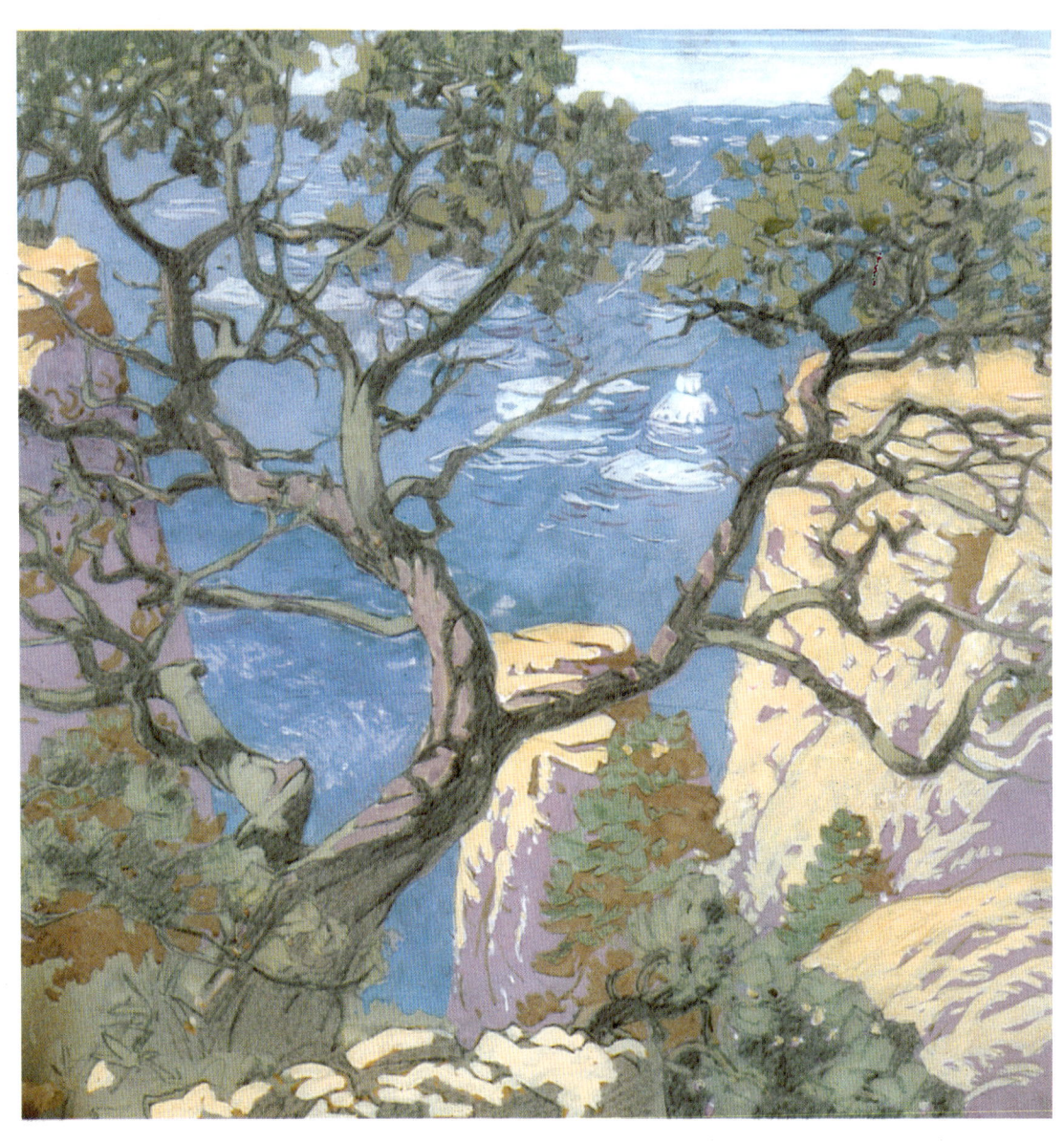

119. PIÑON – GRAND CAÑON, N.D.

Gouache, 14¾ × 14½ in.

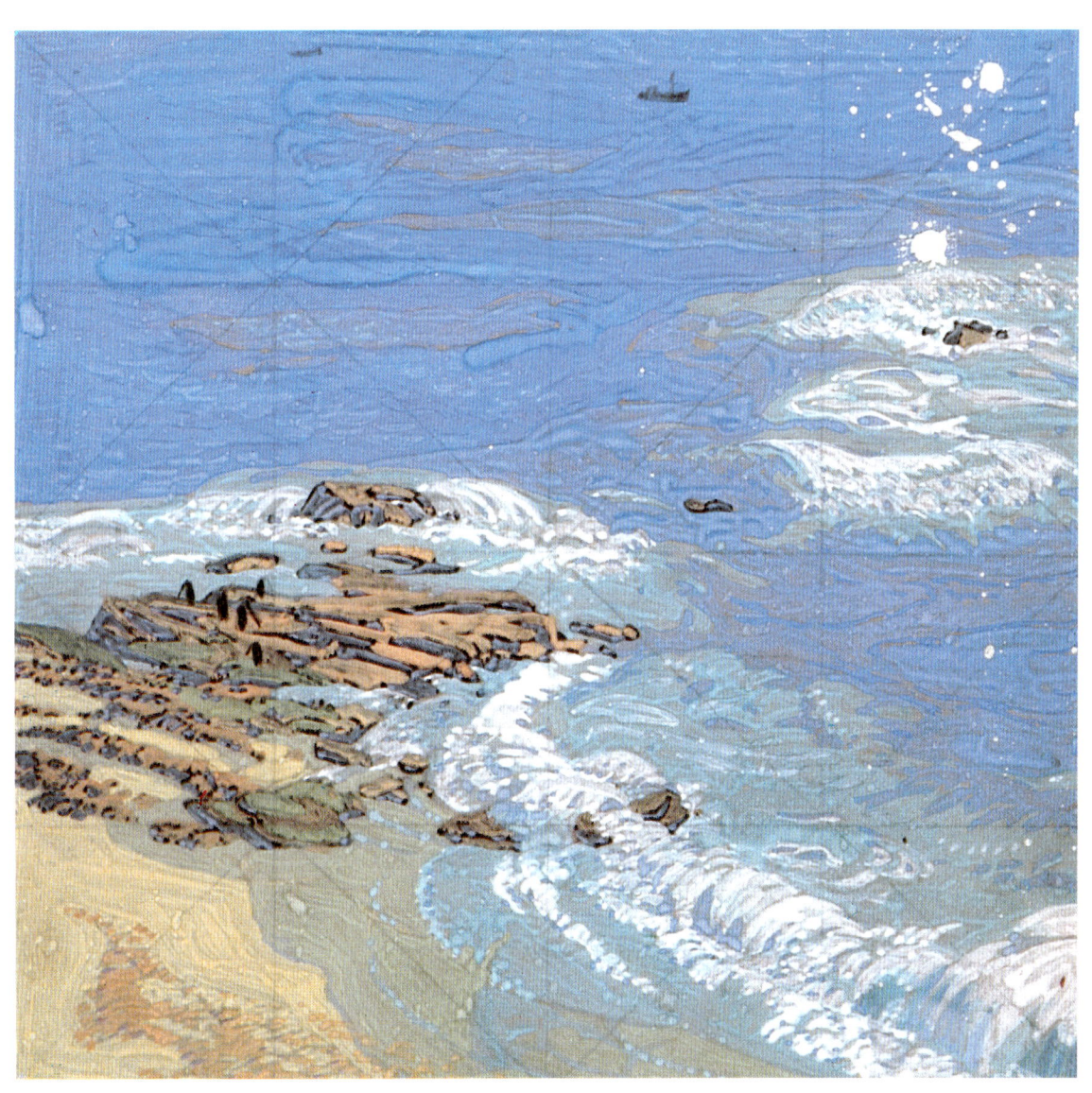

120. PELICAN ROOKERY, *ca. mid-*1920s

Gouache, 7 ½ × 8 in.

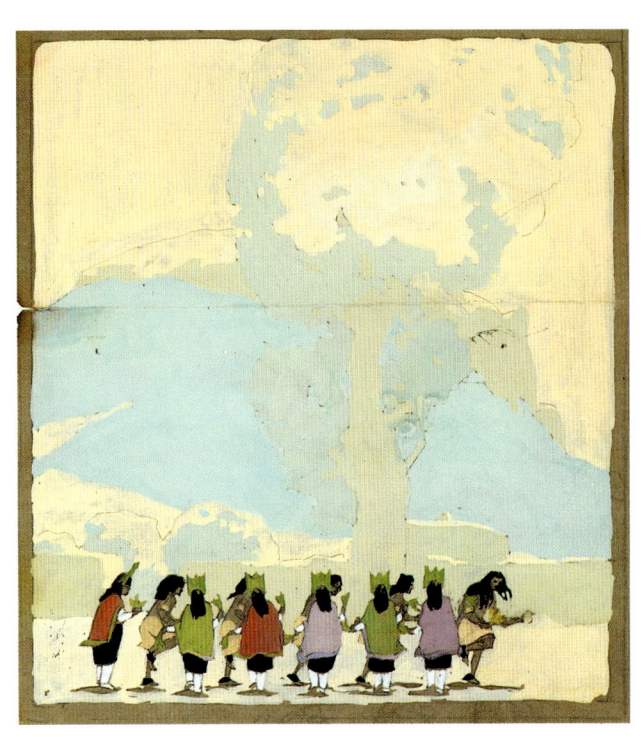

121. UNTITLED (CORN DANCE –
SANTA CLARA), *ca.* 1920

Gouache, 10½ × 19½ in.

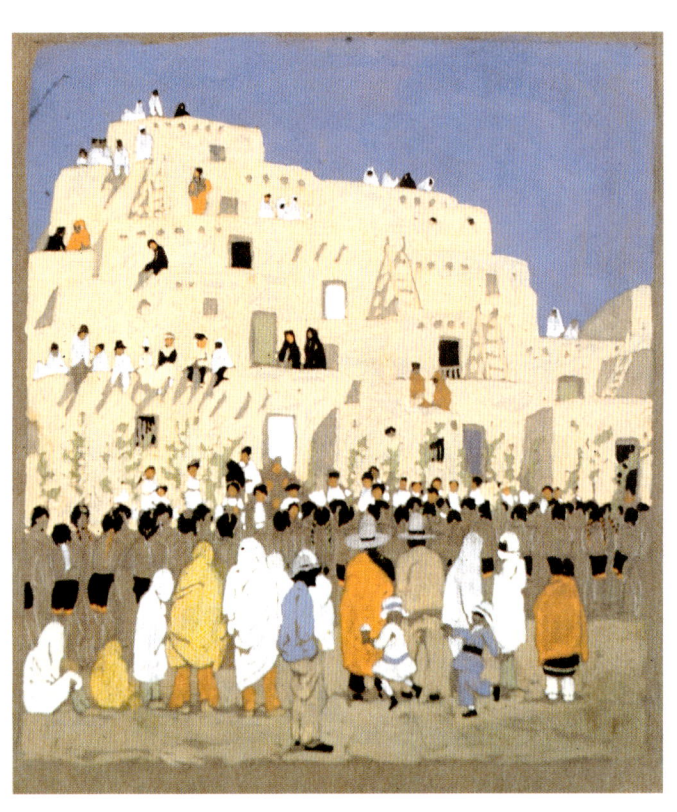

122. SAN GERONIMO – TAOS, *ca.* 1924

Gouache, 9⅜ × 6⅜ in.

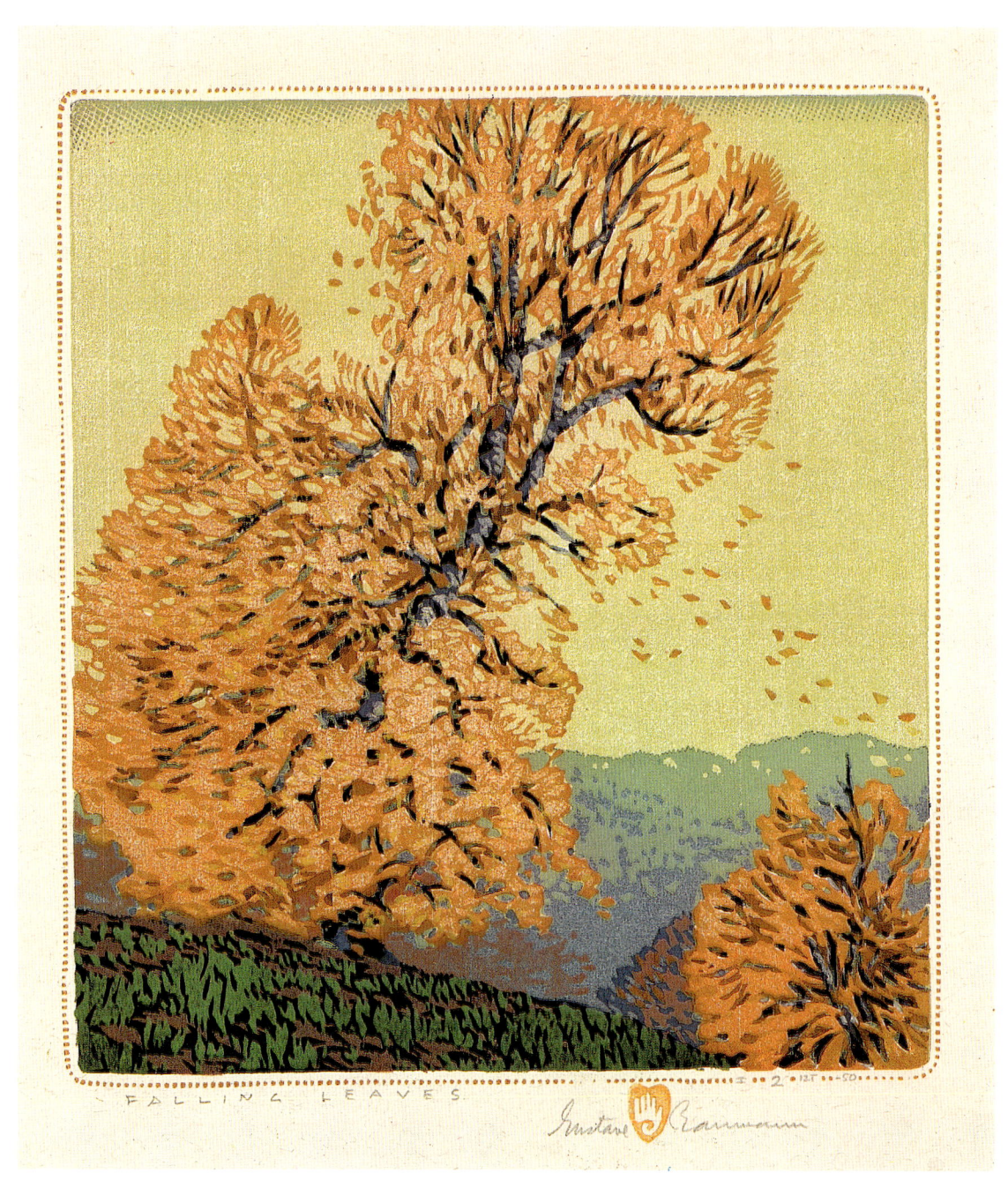

FALLING LEAVES

Gustave Baumann

123. FALLING LEAVES, *ca.* 1950

Color woodcut, 10½ × 9½ in.

NOTES

Hand of a Craftsman, Heart of an Artist

1. "'Gus' Baumann Talks about Brown County," *Brown County* [Indiana] *Democrat,* 10 December 1914.

2. Gustave Baumann to his sisters, Charlotte and Rose, 11 May 1970, Ann Baumann Papers, private collection, Santa Rosa, California.

3. E. W. Bredt, "Die Zukunft des Kunstgewerblers," *Deutsche Kunst und Dekoration* 20 (1907): 84.

4. Frances Johnson, *Indianapolis News,* 24 June 1911.

5. Ibid.

6. Erich Willrich, "Graphische Ausstellung des Deutschen Kunstler–Bundes im Deutschen Buchgewerbe–Museum Leipzig," *Deutsche Kunst und Dekoration* 20 (1907): 77–78.

7. An impression in The Art Institute of Chicago is inscribed "One of about 15 proofs, second printing, none faultless."

8. Sketch for *Old Munich* (Museum of Fine Arts, Museum of New Mexico, Santa Fe, 80.28.4) inscribed *Linol für Baumann/4 Platten Dazio.*

9. Baumann to his sisters, Ann Baumann Papers.

10. Edward Watts Russel, "Chicago," *American Art News* 15 (31 March 1917): 6.

11. Unidentified newspaper clipping, Palette & Chisel Club scrapbook, Newberry Library, Chicago.

12. Emma Lieber, *Richard Lieber by His Wife* (Indianapolis: privately printed, 1947), 71.

13. Adolph Shulz, "Brown County Talk," 17 October 1933, typescript, Stout Reference Library, Indianapolis Museum of Art.

14. Adolph Shulz, "The Story of Brown County," *Indiana Magazine of History* (December 1935): 285.

15. Gustave Baumann, "Of a County Called Brown," typescript, Ann Baumann Papers, private collection, Santa Rosa, California.

16. Harry L. Engle, "The Hills o' Brown," manuscript cited in *Brown County Art and Artists* (Nashville: Psi Iota Xi, 1971), n. 5.

17. Gustave Baumann, "Original Brown County Talk," delivered 19 January 1914 to the Woman's Department Club, typescript, Ann Baumann Papers, private collection, Santa Rosa, California.

18. Frances Johnson, *Indianapolis News,* 24 June 1911.

19. "Produces Color Prints of Brown County Hills," *Indianapolis News,* 16 November 1910.

20. "Brown County Pictures Designed on Wood," *Indianapolis News,* 17 December 1910.

21. Frances Johnson, *Indianapolis News,* 24 June 1911.

22. Mary Q. Burnet, *Art and Artists of Indiana* (New York: Century, 1921), 310.

23. Wilbur D. Nesbit, "Gustave Baumann," *Graphic Arts Magazine* (May 1914): 207.

24. Gustave Baumann, "Gustave Baumann Takes Backward Look at 80 Years," *Santa Fe New Mexican,* 2 April 1961.

25. Calla Hay, "Gustave Baumann," *El Palacio* 78 (1971): 28.

26. John Herron Art Institute, Indianapolis: "Seventh Annual Exhibition of Works by Indiana Artists," 1914, *Autumn Haze* (watercolor); and "Eighth Annual Exhibition of Works by Indiana Artists," 1915, *Fullness of the Year* (tempera);

The Art Institute of Chicago: "Eighteenth Annual Exhibition of Artists of Chicago and Vicinity," 1914, *Autumn Haze* (watercolor); "Nineteenth Annual Exhibition of Artists of Chicago and Vicinity," 1915, *The Patriarch* (tempera); and "Twentieth Annual Exhibition of Artists of Chicago and Vicinity," 1916, *Grannie's Garden* (watercolor).

27. Frances Johnson, *Indianapolis News*, 24 June 1911.

28. "Exhibition of Prints by Gustave Baumann," *Indianapolis News*, 14 February 1913.

29. Museum of Fine Arts, Museum of New Mexico, Santa Fe, 4495/23P.

30. Selma N. Steele, Theodore L. Steele, and Wilbur D. Peat, *The House of the Singing Winds* (Indianapolis: Indiana Historical Society, 1966), 139–140.

31. F. Weitenkampf, *American Graphic Art* (New York: Henry Holt and Company, 1912), 173–174.

32. "Panama-Pacific Information," *American Art News* 13 (17 October 1914): 2.

33. Of the twelve nonmedalists, only Carr, Gilmore, and McMillen were represented at the Panama-Pacific International Exposition. Only Carr showed more than one print.

34. Madeleine Barbin, "Des Américaines à Paris," *Nouvelles de l'estampe* 28 (July–August 1976): 18–19.

35. F. Weber, "Artists Flee Paris," *American Art News* 12 (19 September 1914): 6.

36. *New York Evening Post*, 31 October 1914.

37. Ada Gilmore Chaffee, "Cape End Early Cradled Gifted Group of Print Makers Who Added to Art," *The Provincetown Advocate*, 30 October 1952; typescript, B. J. O. Nordfeldt Papers, Archives of American Art, microfilm D 166.

38. *The Shore-going Sailor, The Hero, The Fisherman's Family, The Schooner, Monday Morning,* and *Putting to Sea*; compare with Fiona Donovan and Susan Brown, *The Woodblock Prints of B. J. O. Nordfeldt, A Catalogue Raisonné*, exhibition catalogue (Minneapolis: University of Art Museum, University of Minnesota, 1991), nos. 25, 35, 27, and 34. *The Shore-going Sailor* and *The Hero* are not catalogued under those titles.

39. "Too Many Oils Are Under Beds So Baumann Makes Woodcuts," *Santa Fe New Mexican*, undated; Clippings File, Museum of Fine Arts, Museum of New Mexico, Santa Fe.

40. "Exhibition of Wood Block Prints by Gustave Baumann," The Cleveland Museum of Art, July–August 1918, introduction.

41. H. Effa Webster, "Chicago," *American Art News* 14 (8 April 1916): 7.

42. H. Effa Webster, "Chicago," *American Art News* 14 (6 May 1916): 5.

43. C. C. C., "Art News from Summer Art Colonies – Provincetown," *American Art News* 15 (15 September 1917): 3.

44. *Indianapolis Star*, 30 December 1917.

45. Gustave Baumann, "Concerning a Small Untroubled World," *El Palacio* 78 (1971): 9–10.

46. Ibid., 10.

47. "Notes on Santa Fe Art and Artists," *Santa Fe New Mexican*, 6 July 1918.

48. Ernest L. Blumenschein, "Art News from Summer Art Colonies – Taos (New Mexico, U.S.A.)," *American Art News* 16 (14 September 1918): 3.

49. Gustave Baumann to William Coughlin, summer 1918; Clippings File, Stout Reference Library, Indianapolis Museum of Art.

50. Baumann, "Gustave Baumann Takes Backward Look at 80 Years."

51. "Gus Baumann Here," *Santa Fe New Mexican*, 12 October 1918.

52. "Baumann Woodblock Prints and Indian Pupils Display Art Events of the Past Week," *Santa Fe New Mexican*, 29 March 1919.

Gustave Baumann in the West

These notes make reference to impressions of Gustave Baumann's woodcuts in the collection of the Museum of Fine Arts, a unit of the Museum of New Mexico, Santa Fe. They are identified by their accession numbers, which are preceded by the prefix s f (for example, s f 973).

1. Juliet Currie, "Gustave Baumann, A Century of Delight," *El Palacio* 87 (1981): 25.

2. Gustave Baumann, *Autobiography*, unpublished manuscript, 34. The artist began this collection of reminiscences and musings in the 1940s and worked on it well into the 1960s. The author is grateful to the artist's daughter, Ann Baumann, for the opportunity to review the typescript of this unpublished essay.

3. *See* Haye W. Hansen, *Deutsche Holzschittmeister des 20. Jahrhunderts* (Toppenstedt: U. Berg, 1979), 25–29, 41–47, and 69–75. These German artists worked in styles that exploited the patterning effects created by the chips of wood or linoleum gouged from the printing surface. Their manners both of draftsmanship and wood carving were allied to craft but were also influenced by the *Jugendstil*. Generally, these artists favored landscape, rural, and nature subjects, which often focused on the peculiarities of a given region and the lives of its common folk.

4. *See* Una E. Johnson, *American Prints and Printmakers* (Garden City: Doubleday, 1980), 36–37. On the virtuoso American wood engravers of the nineteenth century, such as Timothy Cole and Henry Wolf, *see* George Edward Woodberry, *A History of Wood Engraving* (New York: Harpers Bros., 1883).

5. Baumann, *Autobiography*, 34.

6. Baumann spoke of hands as God's gift to every man. *See* Calla Hay, "Gustave Baumann," *El Palacio* 78 (1971): 35; herein reprinted.

7. In archival impressions of some prints (as, for example, *Tent Rock Trail*, s f 973), which the artist retained, the heart-and-hand stamp is imprinted several times in the lower margin, where the artist apparently experimented with the color and mixture of his orange ink before affixing the seal to several prints in an edition.

8. Baumann met Walter Ufer and Victor Higgins when they were fellow students at The Art Institute of Chicago. For an account of the tradition of American artists in New Mexico and the growth of the artists' colonies of Taos and Santa Fe, *see* Van Deren Coke, *Taos and Santa Fe, The Artist's Environment, 1882–1942* (Albuquerque: University of New Mexico Press, 1963). On Ufer, *see* Coke, *Taos and Santa Fe*, 22, 24–25, and 147; and "The Santa Fe–Taos Art Colony: Walter Ufer," *El Palacio* 3 (August 1916): 75–81.

9. Gustave Baumann, "Concerning a Small Untroubled World," *El Palacio* 78 (1971): 27.

10. *See* Janet Altic Flint, *Provincetown Printers: A Woodcut Tradition*, exhibition catalogue (Washington, D.C.: National Museum of American Art/Smithsonian Institution, 1983). The painter and printmaker B. J. O. Nordfeldt was an impor-

tant figure in the development of the single-block, white-line method of color-woodcut printmaking. Baumann knew Nordfeldt in Chicago during the second decade of the twentieth century. At the Panama-Pacific International Exposition in San Francisco in 1915, their color prints were awarded gold and silver medals, respectively. Their acquaintance continued in Santa Fe in 1918, and in the 1920s Nordfeldt was Baumann's neighbor there on Camino de las Animas. *See* Fiona Donovan and Susan Brown, *The Woodblock Prints of B. J. O. Nordfeldt, A Catalogue Raisonné*, exhibition catalogue (Minneapolis: University Art Museum, University of Minnesota, 1991).

11. Baumann, "Concerning a Small Untroubled World," 26.

12. Baumann, *Autobiography*, 31.

13. Ann Baumann and Gwilym G. Griffiths, "Packard's Artists: Gustave Baumann, Master of the Colored Woodcut," *The Packard Cormorant* 30 (Autumn 1983): 26.

14. On John Sloan, *see* James Kraft and Helen Farr Sloan, *John Sloan in Santa Fe*, exhibition catalogue (Washington, D.C.: Smithsonian Institution, 1981). On Julius Rolshoven, *see* Coke, *Taos and Santa Fe*, 34–35; and "The Santa Fe–Taos Art Colony: Julius Rolshoven," *El Palacio* 14 (July 1917): 70–79. A prominent portrait painter who had long lived in Florence, Rolshoven's move to New Mexico made a difficult change for his elegant wife Tina. She saw Baumann as an uncouth bachelor who needed training in the social graces, and she tried in vain to reform him. *See* Currie, "Gustave Baumann," 6–7.

15. Baumann, *Autobiography*, 53.

16. The woodcuts are *Tent Rock Trail*, SF973; *Day of the Deer Dance*, SF990; and *Ceremonial Cave*, SF972.

17. Baumann commented that this mural "is a composition of which any modern artist would be proud." See *El Palacio* 5 (1918): 299. The pictograph prints are *The Deer Dance*, SF978, and *The Deer Hunt* or *El Rito de los Frijoles*, a continuous image comprised of two long woodcuts (SF975 and SF976) designed to splice together vertically in the center.

18. *See* Raymond L. Wilson, *Index of American Print Exhibitions, 1882–1940* (Metuchen, N.J., and London: Scarecrow Press, 1988), 81; and *El Palacio* 8 (1920): 41.

19. The woodcuts are *Bright Angel Trail*, SF901; *Pines, Grand Canyon*, SF904; *Pinon, Grand Canyon*, SF902; and *Cedar, Grand Canyon*, SF905. A fifth print of this subject, *Grand Canyon*, SF903, seems to have been executed in 1927.

20. *See* Frederick C. Moffatt, *Arthur Wesley Dow (1857–1922)*, exhibition catalogue (Washington, D.C.: National Collection of Fine Arts/Smithsonian Institution, 1977), 117–121.

21. Wilson, *Index of American Print Exhibitions*, 21.

22. Los Angeles Museum of History, Science and Art, Exposition Park, *Exhibition of Wood Block Prints by Gustave Baumann*, exhibition catalogue (Los Angeles: Department of Fine and Applied Arts, 1–31 December 1919).

23. *Wood Block Prints by American Artists*, exhibition catalogue, with an introduction by Claude Burroughs (Detroit: Detroit Institute of Arts, 1919). This show included twenty-six of Baumann's woodcuts, far more than those of any other artist. The printmaker also loaned a set of blocks to the exhibition, along with a preparatory gouache drawing and seven progressive proofs. In this regard, this early exhibition anticipated a popular traveling show on Baumann's

technique organized in 1965. *See* Hay, "Gustave Baumann," 43.

24. Wilson, *Index of American Print Exhibitions*, 194. During the 1920s, the Print Makers Society of California held the largest and most important regular print exhibitions west of Chicago. This club was organized in 1914 by the brothers Benjamin C. and Howell C. Brown of Missouri, who had been attracted to the Los Angeles climate and who quickly became influential members of the Pasadena artists' colony. They worked with sisters Frances and May Gearhart, teachers who helped to organize and manage the Print Makers. Frances Gearhart's vivid, expansive woodcuts of distinctly Western views may well have influenced Baumann to seek out the enthralling landscapes of the desert and the Pacific Coast (*see* David Acton, *A Spectrum of Innovation, Color in American Printmaking, 1890–1960*, exhibition catalogue [New York: Worcester Art Museum, 1990], 78–79). After their first exhibition in the spring of 1915, the Print Makers began holding yearly shows at the Los Angeles Museum of History, Science and Art. In 1921, the Print Makers of Los Angeles became known as the Print Makers Society of California. Throughout the 1920s, their annual exhibitions progressively increased in size, particularly after they began accepting prints from Europe, Japan, and Australia. These shows continued on a smaller scale during the Great Depression.

25. Included in the 1924 *New Mexico Portfolio* were the color woodcuts *Cliff Dwellings*, SF885; *Sanctuario – Chimayo*, SF889; *My Garden*, SF892; *The Bishop's Apricot*, SF891; *Chile con Cabre*, SF890; *Night at the Fiesta – Taos*, SF893; *Talpa Chapel*, SF894; *Corn Dance – Santa Clara*, SF896; *Lost in the Desert*, SF895;

San Geronimo – Taos, SF886; *Beginning of the Fiesta*, SF887; and *San Domingo Pueblo*, SF888.

26. Baumann, "Concerning a Small Untroubled World," 19.

27. Included were five artists from Santa Fe (Frank Applegate, Jozef Bakos, Baumann, William Penhallow Henderson, and B. J. O. Nordfeldt) and three from Taos (Ernest Blumenschein, Walter Ufer, and Victor Higgins); *see* Coke, *Taos and Santa Fe*, 122. In 1922, Baumann was elected an associate member of the Taos Society of Artists; *see* Clinton Adams, *Printmaking in New Mexico* (Albuquerque: University of New Mexico Press, 1991), 142. The founding members of the Santa Fe Art Club were Baumann, Randall Davey, Raymond Jonson, B. J. O. Nordfeldt, and John Sloan.

28. *Summer Clouds* won the Storrow Prize as the best relief print in the Seventh International Print Makers Exhibition in Los Angeles in 1926; *see* Wilson, *Index of American Print Exhibitions*, 257.

29. *See* Corrine P. Sze, "The Gustave Baumann House," *Bulletin of the Historic Santa Fe Society* 19 (June 1991): 3–5.

30. Hay, "Gustave Baumann," 35; and Sze, "The Gustave Baumann House," 6.

31. At Santa Clara Pueblo, Jane Devereux Henderson learned songs by ear in the traditional manner, which she later would perform in public concerts while accompanying herself on a small drum. See *El Palacio* 28 (1930): 114.

32. The southern Arizona views are *Wild Horse Mesa*, SF906; *Cholla and Sahuaro* [sic], SF907; *Palo Verde and Ocotea* [sic], SF899; and *Superstition Mountains*, SF898. *Signs of the Eighties* or *Tombstone Epitaph*, SF897, represents not a

landscape but a montage of the buildings and shop signs of this legendary frontier town.

33. Baumann, *Autobiography*, 44. The artist's trip seems to have spanned much of the middle part of the state. Wild Horse Mesa is in north-central Arizona, overlying the border of Yavapai and Coconino counties. Baumann also made drawings near the town of Florence and in the Superstition Mountains near the village of Apache Junction.

34. The author speculates that the woodcuts resulting from this trip to California were *Singing Woods*, SF 914; *Windswept Eucalyptus*, SF 913; *Coast Range*, SF 912; *Pelican Rookery*, SF 911; *Redwood Muir Woods*, SF 916; *Sequoia Forest*, SF 915; *Point Lobos*, SF 910; *Point Lobos Rock Garden*, SF 919; *Monterey Cypress*, SF 909; and *Song of the Sea*, SF 917. *Pacific Shoreline*, SF 918, and *Torrey Pine* (not at Santa Fe) were executed later, near the end of the artist's life.

35. Although no checklist can be located, installation photographs enable us partially to reconstruct this exhibition of about fifty-eight color woodcuts. The show was organized by the museum director, George William Eggers, who had known Baumann in Chicago. In 1929, Eggers was preparing an exhibition of American paintings to be shown in Stockholm and arranged to include Baumann's *The Christmas Eve Dance at San Felipe*, along with Western paintings by such artists as Ernest Blumenschein, Walter Ufer, and B. J. O. Nordfeldt. The correspondence for this project indicates that the print show was planned and went on view in Worcester, Massachusetts, from 2 March through 30 May 1930. In one letter, dated 7 December 1929, in the Worcester Art Museum Archives, Baumann discussed his current work and some feelings of stagnation: "One of the new prints

turned out well, but I feel the need to look around in Europe. Heaven help us to keep our minds open and our fingers flexible."

36. On the influence of the American Arts and Crafts movement in the decorative arts and interior design, see the catalogues of two recent exhibitions: Wendy Kaplan, *"The Art That Is Life": The Arts & Crafts Movement in America, 1875–1920*, exhibition catalogue (Boston: Museum of Fine Arts, 1987); and Leslie Green Bowman, *American Arts & Crafts, Virtue in Design*, exhibition catalogue (Los Angeles: Los Angeles County Museum of Art, 1990).

37. Baumann, *Autobiography*, 38–41; Adams, *Printmaking in New Mexico*, 37–38, and see also 16–18.

38. Gustave Baumann, *Chips an' Shavings* (Santa Fe: Velarde Press, 1929).

39. *See* Edgar L. Hewitt, *The Excavations at El Rito de los Frijoles in 1909* (Washington, D.C.: Archaeological Institute of America, 1909).

40. Baumann, "Concerning a Small Untroubled World," 24.

41. Gustave Baumann, *Frijoles Canyon Pictographs, Recorded in Woodcuts and Hand Printed*, with a foreword by Alfred Vincent Kidder (Santa Fe: Writers' Editions, 1939), 14. Four hundred and eighty copies were printed, with typography by Willard Clark, bound and with handmade slipcase by Hazel Dreis. A new edition of *Frijoles Canyon Pictographs*, reprinted from the original blocks, was published by William and Victoria Dailey in Los Angeles in 1980.

42. The title *Wings of Prophesy* came from the observation of one of the artist's friends that the eagles' wings resemble the Stars and Stripes. Thus, Baumann romanticized that this pictograph seems to have foretold the history of this country long before the arrival of the Spaniards.

43. A recurrent theme in Baumann's prints, it also may be seen in the woodcut *Playroom Symposium* (ca. 1915, SF858), in which a group of dolls, made of yarn, carved wood, and stuffed fabric, gathers for music and conversation.

44. Baumann, *Autobiography*, 54.

45. These are illustrated by Hay, "Gustave Baumann," 42.

46. Baumann, *Autobiography*, 37.

47. *See* Acton, *A Spectrum of Innovation*, 14–20.

48. Baumann, *Autobiography*, 36; and Hay, "Gustave Baumann," 42–43.

49. These sheets most often bear the Gladbach, Van Gelder Zonen, or J. W. Zanders watermarks.

50. Usually, Baumann used a Roman numeral to indicate a printing campaign within an edition. An Arabic number represented the present impression, and a second number – usually 125 – was the anticipated number of the complete edition. Sometimes a date also appeared after the edition number to show when the present impression was pulled. The letters "R.C." before the edition number indicated that the blocks had been substantially recut since their previous printing. For discussions of numbering and inscription, *see* the exhibition catalogue *Gustave Baumann: An American Master Printmaker* (Santa Rosa, Calif.: Annex Galleries, 1985); and Acton, *A Spectrum of Innovation*, 92.

51. Using the same blocks as *Night Ceremony* (1948, SF949, 20.3×20.3 cm, image), *Fire Dance* was printed in tones of lavender with silver leaf. Baumann's other potsherd ornament print is *Winter Ceremony* (1948, not at Santa Fe), which is different in its design and in size (19.7×20.6 cm, image) and which is printed in tones of green with silver leaf. Using the same set of blocks and different colors, the artist created the variant entitled *Dancing Shards*.

52. Vincent Garoffolo, "The Woodblock Art of Gustave Baumann," *New Mexico Artists*, series 3 (Albuquerque: University of New Mexico Press, 1952), 39.

53. It is thought that *La Conquistadora* was carried to El Paso when the Spaniards were driven from Santa Fe and that it returned with de Vargas and his group of colonists in the Reconquest of 1693. According to popular legend, since 1712, the icon has been carried in the annual fiesta procession through the streets to the site where de Vargas and his soldiers entrenched when they recaptured the Governor's Palace at the Santa Fe Plaza from the Indians who had occupied it. In fact, it is probable that the processional celebration may date back only to the end of the eighteenth century. *See* E. Boyd, *Popular Arts of Spanish New Mexico* (Santa Fe: Museum of New Mexico Press, 1974), 330–331.

54. Baumann, *Autobiography*, 47–48. *La Conquistadora* is reproduced by Hay, "Gustave Baumann," 44.

55. The dedication was performed by the Right Reverend James M. Sontey in memory of the Right Reverend Frederick B. Howden, D.D., bishop of New Mexico and southwest Texas, 1914–40. *See* Hay, "Gustave Baumann," 44.

56. Garoffolo, "The Woodblock Art of Gustave Baumann," 40.

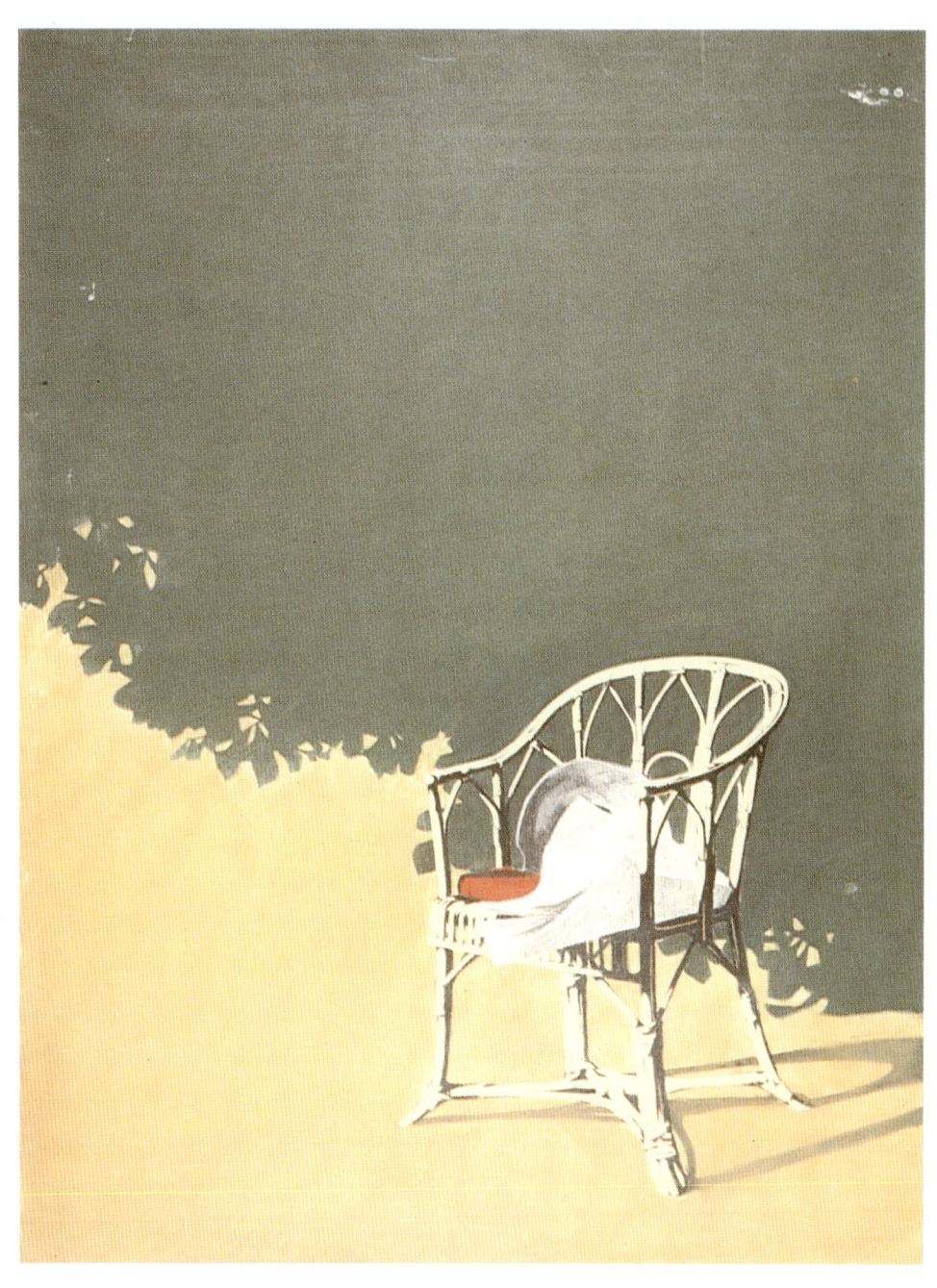

124. UNTITLED (CHAIR WITH NEWSPAPER), N.D.

Gouache, 36⅜ × 26¼ in.